RESEARCH HIGHLIGHTS IN SOCIAL WORK 26

Working with Offenders

Research Highlights in Social Work *series*

Planning and Costing Community Care
Chris Clark
ISBN 1 85302 267 5
Research Highlights in Social Work 27

Child Abuse and Child Abusers
Protection and Prevention
Edited by Lorraine Waterhouse
ISBN 1 85302 133 4
Research Highlights in Social Work 24

Performance Review and Quality in Social Care
Edited by Anne Connor and Stewart Black
ISBN 1 85302 017 6
Research Highlights in Social Work 20

Poverty, Deprivation and Social Work
Edited by Ralph Davidson and Angus Erskine
ISBN 1 85302 043 5
Research Highlights in Social Work 22

Social Work
Disabled People and Disabling Environments
Edited by Michael Oliver
ISBN 1 85302 178 X pb
ISBN 1 85302 042 7 hb
Research Highlights in Social Work 21

Privatisation
Edited by Richard Parry
ISBN 1 85302 015 X
Research Highlights in Social Work 18

RESEARCH HIGHLIGHTS IN SOCIAL WORK 26

Working with Offenders

Editor: Gill McIvor

Jessica Kingsley Publishers
London and Bristol, Pennsylvania

Contents

Editorial

Gill McIvor

This is the second volume in the *Research Highlights* series devoted specifically to social work with adult offenders. The need for a second volume was signalled by the extent and pace of change and development in the provision of services to offenders in the probation services and in Scottish social work departments over the 12 years since the publication of the earlier title in the series, *Social Work with Adult Offenders.*

The present book draws together developments in practice, locating them first in the context of changes in penal policy throughout the United Kingdom. In the introductory chapter David Smith examines the relationship between policy and practice in the probation service over recent years. He illustrates how policy has often been preceded by practice initiatives from within the probation service, despite policy U-turns by central government such as the assertion that 'prison works' and the threat to the professional base of probation training in England and Wales. Pointing to other positive developments since the introduction of the Criminal Justice Act of 1991 – such as the promotion of inter-agency co-operation and the increasing optimism regarding the potential for social work with offenders to achieve meaningful reductions in offending behaviour – he concludes that practice which is thoroughly evaluated and disseminated is more likely to influence policy in this area.

The following three chapters present an overview of practice developments in different parts of the United Kingdom. George Mair describes a range of initiatives introduced by the probation service and the Home Office in England and Wales and considers the implications of the 1991 and 1993 Criminal Justice Acts. He argues that the past ten years have represented a period of unprecedented change characterised by greater accountability in the probation service and increased central control. The

challenges facing the probation service will be to ensure that the traditional values and advantages of probation supervision are not forgotten
and to constrain and channel diversity of practice whilst making sure that
it is not eliminated.

Gill McIvor describes developments within social work departments
in Scotland. The most significant of these has been the introduction of full
central government funding of statutory social work services to the
criminal justice system and associated national objectives and standards
which have encouraged departments to develop specialist teams or identify designated workers for the delivery of services to offenders and their
families.

Scottish Office policy aimed at limiting the use of imprisonment was
at least in part a response to the high levels of imprisonment in that
country. Despite having a low crime rate, Northern Ireland has a high
prison population primarily as a consequence of long sentences imposed
for terrorist offences related to the civil conflict of the last 25 years. Breidge
Gadd describes how the Probation Board in Northern Ireland is characterised by the range and diversity of community supervision programmes
focused upon offending behaviour, by its singular sense of policy and
purpose in its customer-oriented delivery of services and by the links
between probation officers and local communities. She predicts that in the
future services will need to be increasingly flexible and responsive, with
probation officers serving as the co-ordinators, purchasers and managers
of provision rather than as the sole deliverers of services.

The next three chapters focus upon issues which have begun to receive
increasing attention from probation officers and social workers. Taking as
a starting point the recent reduction in England and Wales in the use of
probation orders with women offenders, Anne Worrall argues that court
reports on women are frequently gender-stereotyped. Women, it appears,
are more likely to be referred for reports and more likely than men to be
placed on probation, processes which in themselves may result in the
up-tariffing of female offenders. Women's explanations for their offending
are often disregarded and psychiatric labels are frequently ascribed, although relevant services often are not provided. Women generally view
their offending as a consequence of economic necessity or as a response
to severe emotional stress and will only change their lives if they are both
motivated to do so and have access to the structural pre-conditions of
social justice. She argues that a top priority for the probation service must
be reducing the number of women entering the prison system and notes

that, ironically, the probation service's concern about the treatment of women has increased almost in direct proportion to the declining numbers of women being supervised by the service.

The treatment of black and other ethnic minority offenders by the criminal justice system has likewise received increasing attention from the probation service though few services have made available black only groupwork provision. Duncan Lawrence illustrates how white probation officers' explanations of offending by black clients frequently differ from those put forward by the clients themselves, as do the perceived barriers to effecting change. He draws upon recent initiatives to demonstrate how relevant groupwork provision for black and other ethnic minority clients can be developed which reflects cultural diversity and which can facilitate diversion from the criminal justice process.

Bryan Williams and Anne Creamer describe the increased use of prediction tools in work with offenders as a means of identifying the likely risk of custody or of re-conviction. The latter, they argue, is particularly problematic, not least on account of the inaccuracy inherent in the use of aggregate measures to predict individual behaviour with the attendant risk of 'false positives' which may result in the imposition of unnecessarily intrusive sentencing options. They further argue that the use of prediction tools can reinforce discriminatory decision-making in relation to disadvantaged groups, and emphasise that such methods should be viewed as an aid to professional and clinical judgement rather than a substitute for it.

Specific areas of probation practice form the basis of Chapters 8 to 12. Mary Barker discusses the growth in probation service provision for sex offenders, which has been based primarily on a cognitive–behavioural model of intervention. Reviewing the range of approaches which have been employed in the treatment of sex offenders, she concludes that cognitive–behavioural methods are more consistently associated with positive outcomes, although the success of such programmes appears to vary according to a number of factors such as the type of offender, the length of the programme, its implementation and management and its content.

Intensive probation is another area of practice which has been characterised by significant growth in the last few years. George Mair describes and discusses the development of the intensive probation movement in England and in the United States. Drawing upon the Home Office evaluation of projects in eight English probation areas he concludes that, in terms of participants' views and experiences, intensive probation has been generally successful although different areas varied in their ability to target sufficient numbers of high tariff offenders, and had varying degrees of difficulty with implementation. He suggests, however, that the symbolic value of intensive probation is important insofar as the initiative has delivered a message to the probation service about the need to provide demanding programmes for the supervision of offenders in the community.

Now in its third decade in England and Wales, community service has proved to be a popular and enduring sentencing option. In Chapter Ten, Jean Hine and Neil Thomas examine the extent to which the measure has succeeded in meeting a number of diverse aims. They suggest that the evidence is mixed regarding the impact of National Standards on sentencers' confidence in the measure but argue that offenders and the community can benefit significantly through the completion by the former of worthwhile and valued unpaid work. They conclude by arguing that the emphasis in community service has shifted over the years since the order's introduction from the offender (signified by a concern with its rehabilitative potential) to the courts (and, therefore, a focus upon its retributive features) and, finally, to the community (with primary concern centering upon its reparative potential) as evidenced by the draft version of new National Standards for community service schemes.

Despite the proliferation of reparation and mediation programmes during the 1980s, with their emphasis upon the resolution of offences through a process of negotiation, this approach, which does not fit easily within a traditional adversarial system, has failed to gain wide support among criminal justice agencies. Describing the development of reparation and mediation in different parts of the world (including interesting developments in Australia and New Zealand which attempt to effect reconciliation between the offender, his or her family and the community and which potentially have more far-reaching implications for reform), Tony Marshall concludes that the majority of victims and offenders who take part in the process of direct mediation regard it as a constructive and satisfying experience. Most of the relevant research has, however, focused upon single schemes in the early stages of their development and there has been little rigorous evaluation of their impact upon re-offending. Many programmes suffer from sub-optimal caseloads as a consequence of the voluntary nature of the process, the number of parties upon which it is dependent and the reluctance of criminal justice agencies to make referrals. He cautions against the concentration on minor offences on essentially economic grounds at the expense of other types of offences for which the benefits to victims and offenders may be greater.

Brian Williams addresses key issues in the provision of probation and social work services in prisons. Against a backdrop of an increasing growth in groupwork programmes in prisons – most of which have been introduced by probation officers, with anger management as the most significant area of growth apart from the national sex offender treatment programme – uncertainty continues regarding the future of prison-based probation work in England, Wales and Northern Ireland. At the same time, shared work between prison officers and other professional groups has increased. As a consequence, one-to-one work with prisoners has been somewhat reactive in recent years and there is a risk that probation officers will be drawn increasingly into serving the needs of prisons rather than concentrating on direct work with prisoners. As such, throughcare is likely to have an increasingly important role to play, with greater official encouragement towards specialisation of field-based staff on the grounds that it produces more focused work.

Other significant developments over the past decade or so include a range of pre-trial services, and the development of a variety of programmes which are either offence specific (focusing, for example, upon car crime, violence and burglary) or which aim more generally to address offending behaviour. Despite a hardening of government policies towards offenders (and younger offenders in particular) the practice initiatives discussed in this volume, be they centrally or locally driven, have taken place against a backdrop of increased optimism concerning the potential for social workers and probation officers to offer programmes of intervention which can effect meaningful reductions in offending behaviour. This has been accompanied by a growing recognition of the need for initiatives to be subjected to systematic evaluation. In the concluding chapter of this volume, Peter Raynor argues for the development of evaluative research methodologies which focus on the process of intervention and which draw upon a range of outcome measures to assess the effectiveness of work with offenders undertaken within a framework – currently threatened by government policy – which is underpinned by social work values.

Chapter 1

Social Work and Penal Policy

David Smith

Introduction

The aims of this chapter are to describe and analyse the penal policy context of social work practice with offenders and to suggest, in general terms, how practice has been influenced by this context. Clearly all social work takes place within some context of policy, and cannot exist without it, at least in the public sector; but this is not to say that practice always reflects policy in a direct or unmediated way. Indeed, this chapter will suggest that the relationship between policy and practice is complex and sometimes conflict-ridden: it will show that at times developments in practice have had an influence on policy, to a greater extent than practitioners have been inclined to recognise, whilst at other times policy-makers have consciously tried to shape practice to their ends. It will be argued, too, that the term 'penal policy' is liable to be misleading if it is taken to imply rationality, coherence or consistency; whilst certain reasonably consistent trends can be identified over the period covered by this chapter – roughly, the years since 1980 – penal policy is inherently vulnerable, because of the high political profile which criminal justice issues have had during the same period, to sudden changes in the political climate (Downes and Morgan 1994).

Since this has also been a period of uninterrupted Conservative rule, the sudden climatic changes have tended to be from a moderately tough line to an even tougher one; they have also tended to occur in the autumn, during Conservative Party Conferences. This was the case, for example, with Leon Brittan's 1983 announcement of severe restrictions on parole eligibility for certain categories of long-term prisoners (Ashworth 1983, Cavadino and Dignan 1992), and with Michael Howard's announcement in 1993 – in the course of a speech one of whose key themes was that 'prison works' – of a range of new measures which became part of the 1993 Criminal Justice and Public Order Bill. (The implications for social work of this latest change will be considered towards the end of this chapter.) These dramatic changes of line can be understood as representing a breakdown of the normal process of policy formation. Policy as it is formally expressed in legislation, guidelines, national standards and so on is usually the result of a process of discussion and compromise, in which the political interests of ministers are balanced by the advice of civil servants as to what is feasible or sensible, and 'by consultation with professionals, practitioners, academics and representatives of informed opinion' (Faulkner 1993). When this process is abandoned or ignored, the result may be hastily conceived policies driven by immediate political pressures or considerations of electoral advantage; according to Faulkner, the civil servant most closely associated with criminal justice reform in the Home Office during the 1980s, the 1993 change of direction 'is probably the most sudden and the most radical which has ever taken place in this area of public policy'.

A chapter such as this one which aims to give an overview of policy in a particular field, must be shaped by more or less arguable decisions about its scope. In terms of geographical coverage, most of the discussion will refer to England and Wales, but a section on Scotland is included to show that differences in political and organisational traditions and structures can produce a different policy emphasis. In terms of time, various starting points would have been possible, such as the 1967 Criminal Justice Act, which introduced parole and with it the expectation of tighter forms of supervision in the community, and signalled the start of a series of Criminal Justice Acts concerned with reducing the prison population. Another possibility was the Act of 1972, which introduced Community Service Orders in England and Wales (Scotland followed a few years later), and thus made the probation service responsible for the administration of a community sentence whose aims were increasingly defined in punitive rather than in rehabilitative terms (with, again, important differences in Scotland (McIvor 1992)). The chosen starting point, however, is the more recent Act of 1980, the year of the White Paper *Young Offenders* (Home Office 1980). This, for many practitioners, represented the first modern endorsement of punishment as an end in itself for penal policy, but it also exemplified the key theme of 'bifurcation' – a sharp distinction between serious and less serious offenders – which Bottoms (1977) rightly predicted would form one of the threads of continuity in penal policy during the 1980s, and, as it has turned out, beyond. A final question about scope is about the scope of penal policy itself.

What is penal policy?

There is less agreement about just what penal policy is than might be expected, considering how readily the phrase rolls off the tongue. In recent years policy initiatives in a wide variety of fields – child care, education, housing, the youth service – have been justified in terms of their possible effects on crime rates, a process which has been described as the 'criminalisation' of the discourse of social policy (Blagg *et al.* 1988). It seems more reasonable, however, to restrict the term to policy affecting the formal criminal justice system, but even here there is no simple or universally accepted rule about what agencies and activities should be counted as part of the formal system, and many would argue that the term 'system' is a misnomer, implying a unity of purpose and a harmony of operation which are – perhaps inevitably – lacking in reality (Smith 1994). The Home Office (1992a) made a rare attempt in its Annual Report to state the purpose and aims of this 'system', in terms which are inevitably general but which do indicate some central themes and difficulties:

> 'The purpose of the criminal justice system is to sustain the rule of law and protect the public. The main aims are:
>
> > to prevent and reduce crime, especially violent crime, and to help victims;
> >
> > to ensure that those suspected, accused or convicted of crimes are dealt with fairly, justly and with the minimum of delay;
> >
> > to convict the guilty and acquit the innocent;
> >
> > to punish those found guilty in a suitable manner, and where possible, to discourage further offending;
> >
> > to achieve the foregoing as economically, efficiently and effectively as possible.
>
> For the system to achieve its objectives efficiently and effectively it is important that all the criminal justice services share a sense of common purpose and take account of their interactions with other services.' (p.9)

At one level it is difficult to dissent from such general propositions, although in the case of the third one it could be said that a preferable aim would be to refrain from arresting the innocent, or from prosecuting them once arrested. Nevertheless, the stated aims do raise questions, both about the success of penal policy in achieving them, and about what lies behind the emphases and nuances of their language. Much could be said about the system's success, or lack of it, in its pursuit of these aims: for example, the Home Office's own figures show that recorded crime has more than doubled over the past decade, and that expenditure on the criminal justice system rose relatively faster, during the same period, than that on health or education (Barclay 1993); that complaints about delays, although nothing new, are a commonplace among practitioners; and that a series of recent Court of Appeal judgements has suggested that the system is far too liable to convict the innocent.

A more relevant focus here, however, is on the ways in which these general aims express identifiable themes in penal policy since 1980, and on their implications for social work. Whilst all the aims raise issues for social work agencies, the most directly relevant are the first and the fourth, and the injunction about a sense of common purpose. The first aim explicitly singles out violent crime as the priority for crime reduction efforts, reflecting the 1991 Criminal Justice Act's special provisions for violent and sexual offenders, which allow for longer sentences in such cases than could be justified by the principle of proportionality between the seriousness of the offence and the sentence (Cavadino and Dignan (1992, p.108) describe this as a 'further twist in the bifurcatory spiral'). The fourth aim expresses both a commitment to punishment as an end in itself for sentencers, thus reiterating a consistent theme of the period under review, and doubt about the general feasibility of 'discouraging' further offending, whether through individual deterrence or rehabilitation (a term conspicuous by its absence). The wording is consistent with an acceptance of the 'nothing works' – or 'we might as well behave as if nothing works' – orthodoxy of the late 1970s and 1980s, suggesting that the Home Office remains unconvinced by recent argument and evidence that constructive work with offenders to reduce the likelihood of their offending is possible, and that we have an idea of what forms it will take (McIvor 1990, Raynor, Smith and Vanstone 1994).

The mention of 'suitable' punishment inevitably begs the question of what criteria are to be used to define suitability, and how they can be determined. For example, in the first five months following the implementation of the 1991 Criminal Justice Act in October 1992, the courts made less use of custody and more of fines and community penalties than in the preceding period. Thereafter, the intentions of the Act having been undermined by criticism from powerful quarters (the Home Secretary himself announced that important sections of the Act would be amended), the trend went, unsurprisingly, in the opposite direction – a less frequent use of fines and community penalties, and a more frequent use of custody (Home Office 1993). Over a period of months, therefore, one pattern of sentencing was replaced by another, very different one. How can we decide between them (as decide we must, since they cannot be equally 'suitable')? We can decide only on the basis of beliefs about appropriate levels of 'infliction of pain' (Christie 1993) which are derived from values and commitments extraneous to the 'justice model' itself. The irony is that an approach which originated in a radical critique of the excessive discretion and arbitrariness of the 'treatment model' should have lent itself so readily to incorporation into the punitive rhetoric of law and order; but the 'justice model's prescriptions were always stronger on the procedures we should follow than on the results we should try to achieve' (Hudson 1987).

The invocation of economy, efficiency and effectiveness, and of the need for a shared sense of purpose among all the criminal justice services, also reflects themes which have been reiterated in official policy since the early 1980s. Again, however, it is not clear how success in achieving these aims ought to be judged, or even to what extent they would be thought generally desirable. The 'three Es' are inherently liable to conflict with the aim of achieving justice, as was recognised long ago (Packer 1968), and below the most general level the interests and aims of the criminal justice services are more likely to be in conflict than to express a sense of common purpose. Inter-agency and inter-professional co-operation has necessary and inevitable limits within a criminal justice system which incorporates deliberate checks and balances to ensure that no one party has full control in a context in which conflict is inbuilt (Pearson *et al.* 1992). In day-to-day practice, the interests of the prosecution and of the defence are bound to be seen as in conflict, and gains in efficiency in one part of the system (for example, the reduction of the number of magistrates' courts open for business on Saturdays) may well entail losses in efficiency in another part (for example, prisoners held overnight having to be taken further to court). This is not to argue that the different agencies and professional groups which make up the 'system' should not try to behave considerately towards each other, but in practice, except where a well defined aim can be identified which *does* command broad support (an example is the cautioning of juveniles, discussed below) inter-agency co-operation is likely to be most feasible, and to achieve most, beyond the formal case processing system of police, prosecution, and courts, for example in local crime prevention projects (Foster *et al.* 1993, Raynor *et al.* 1994).

Thus far, then, we have seen that it is difficult to express the aims and purposes of penal policy in terms that are sufficiently specific to mean something and sufficiently general to be uncontentious. Some consistent themes have, however, been identified: those of bifurcation (making a sharp distinction between serious and less serious offences, which has increasingly been interpreted as between offences involving violence or sex and offences against property); of scepticism about the feasibility of using the formal sanctions of the criminal justice system as a means of reforming offenders, and hence a return to 'just deserts' as the basis for sentencing; and of the desirability of co-operation and consensus between the different parts of the system. These three themes will reappear as persistent motifs in the brief historical outline which follows.

Criminal justice policy since 1980

The White Paper *Young Offenders* (Home Office 1980) was widely received, by friends and foes, as the first attempt by the newly elected Conservative government to deliver its promises of a firmer line on law and order, and on young offenders in particular. The Conservatives had made crime a major issue in their 1979 election campaign, and the then current legislation on juvenile offenders, the 1969 Children and Young Persons Act, was one of their principal targets, despite the fact that its decriminalising intentions had never been implemented; partly in consequence of this, the number of juveniles in custody increased dramatically during the 1970s. Hence the rhetoric of the 'short sharp shock', of punishment rather than treatment, and of restricting the discretion of social workers and increasing that of sentencers (see, for example, Blagg and Smith 1989). However, although neither side saw this clearly at the time, the White Paper struck a balance, no doubt as a result of the kind of negotiation described above, between this anti-welfarist rhetoric and commitment to reducing the number of young people appearing in court and indeed in custody. It adopted a stronger version of labelling theory than even proponents of the 'Leave the kids alone' school would normally espouse, in arguing for cautioning rather than prosecution for juvenile offenders whenever possible (a line backed up by Home Office Circulars of 1985 and 1990); and even the new (and short-lived, as it turned out) provision for shorter but sharper detention centre sentences was accompanied by the hope that one result would be a reduction of the number of juveniles in custody (Cavadino and Dignan 1992).

The White Paper was followed by the Criminal Justice Act of 1982, which was greeted with general gloom by penological liberals. Whilst not going as far as repealing the 1969 Act, which had been one of the Conservatives' pre-election promises, it clearly tilted the balance in juvenile justice towards punishment and control. In addition to the shorter detention centre sentence the Act abolished the semi-determinate (because training-oriented) sentence of Borstal and substituted the determinate sentence of youth custody; and it introduced a range of new conditions which could be included in both juvenile supervision orders and probation orders, with the aim of increasing their credibility with courts and, arguably, the effect of shifting their emphasis from helping to controlling. But the Act also introduced for the first time criteria which had to be met before a custodial sentence could be imposed on offenders under the age of 21. These related to the seriousness of the offence, the protection of the public, and the offender's ability or willingness to respond to a non-custodial measure. Although these restrictions were introduced as an amendment in the House of Lords by a Conservative peer, Lady Faithfull, whose views on these matters were (and have remained) highly untypical (Downes and Morgan 1994), they fitted the emerging model of bifurcation very well. The principle which they introduced, of using legislation to make it more difficult for courts to impose custodial sentences (and doing so in a way which was compatible with a hard rhetorical line on sentencing) was to reappear in the Criminal Justice Acts of 1988 and 1991, the former strengthening the criteria and the latter extending the principle to all offenders, and making the sole criterion that of the seriousness of the offence, except in the case of violent or sexual offenders, for whom considerations of public protection were to remain relevant.

The significance of the 1982 Act for subsequent legislation was great because the figures on sentencing suggested, after some early pessimism (Burney 1985), that making it harder for courts to send young people to prison actually had the effect of reducing the number of custodial sentences on juveniles and, to a lesser extent, on young adults, over the decade following the Act (Barclay 1993). Whilst the extent to which the sentencing restrictions themselves brought this about is open to argument (Cavadino and Dignan 1992), there is no doubt that they were a contributory factor, and one which encouraged the government to pursue the same objective in the subsequent legislation. There were, however, other processes at work. One was the demographic change which reduced the number of juveniles in the total population by about 25 per cent during the 1980s (Pratt 1985), for which criminal justice policy can hardly take the credit. But there were also important changes within criminal justice which were widely believed, not least by the government, to have played a part in bringing about what was generally seen as a desirable outcome. One was the increased use of cautions, promoting diversion from the system itself rather than from custody; the other was the development of more intensive and focused forms of supervision in the community, coupled with the use of 'system management' to ensure that these were reserved for the intended target group, young offenders at risk of custody.

Both these developments are consistent with the theme of bifurcation; both required inter-agency co-operation; and both reflected the prevailing orthodoxy of the early 1980s, that since nothing worked it was better where possible to do next to nothing (cautioning), and in any case to do as little as possible (the 'principle' of minimum intervention). The role of social work agencies was defined (by themselves in many cases as well as by the government) as diversion from custody – changing the workings of the system – rather than as helping offenders themselves to change. The 1985 circular mentioned above encouraged both a greater overall use of cautions and greater standardisation between police force areas, and promoted inter-agency liaison and co-operation as a central element of good practice. Researchers have been sceptical about the specific effect of the circular: the use of cautions was rising before it was issued and continued to rise after it (Evans and Wilkinson 1990), although it was only from 1986 that there was a substantial increase in the cautioning of adults. To an extent, therefore, policy, as expressed by the circular, followed practice rather than determining it.

The same can certainly be said about developments in the supervision of offenders in the community. This was markedly the case with the provisions of the 1982 Act for new conditions to be included in probation orders. Schedule XI of the Act was a direct response to a Court of Appeal judgement in 1981 that the widespread practice of including conditions of day centre attendance in such orders was illegal. The practice had developed as a result of concern among probation managers about the apparent loss of credibility of probation as a measure suitable for relatively serious offenders (Raynor 1985). In the late 1970s the use of probation had declined in step with the increase in the use of community service. One response was to ask what it was about community service which was attractive, and to try to build the same features into probation. A more or less plausible answer was that community service had a clear punitive element, was well defined and readily understood, and carried with it guarantees that action would be taken in cases of breach; hence the solution was to make probation more like community service, or even more like prison (Jordan 1983). Thinking along these lines produced the strand in probation practice which Raynor (1985) called 'controlism', and, even when day centre programmes contained no overtly repressive aspects, encouragement from the probation service to the courts to enhance orders by the inclusion of more restrictive conditions. The Home Office had generally approved these developments, and therefore took the opportunity to use the 1982 Act to legalise them and reverse the position created by the 1981 Court of Appeal judgement. Although this provision of the Act aroused opposition in the probation service, and from the probation officers' trades union NAPO, it in fact merely legalised something which many officers had already shown themselves quite prepared to do.

Policy was to be further informed by practice during the mid-1980s, this time through developments in juvenile justice. It was here, and particularly in the voluntary sector projects which were directly funded by central government from 1983, that the combination of system management and offence-focused work with those most at risk of custody was most fully developed. Workers sought to use inter-agency panels and liaison bureaux to argue for diversion from prosecution, and, once offenders had been prosecuted, to extend the sentencing tariff by arguing for minimum intervention at the bottom end, and providing credible forms of community supervision at the top. The final report by the National Association for the Care and Resettlement of Offenders (NACRO 1991) on these projects suggested that they were generally successful in working with the intended target group; and the type of practice which they developed so commended itself to the Home Office that by 1988 it was encouraging the probation service to adopt a similar approach to work with adult offenders in the Green Paper *Punishment, Custody and the Community* (Home Office 1988a) and the associated 'Action Plan' for young adult offenders (Home Office 1988b). The Green Paper included a thinly veiled threat that if the probation service proved recalcitrant the government would find other, more tractable agencies to do what was required, and at the time it seemed that there would be no shortage of candidates from the voluntary sector. The probation service, in folklore the most tough-minded of social work agencies, thus found itself being told to curb its liberal conscience and follow the firm example of voluntary child care organisations (Blagg and Smith 1989).

The service should have seen it coming. The *Statement of National Objectives and Priorities* (Home Office 1984) had been explicit that the first priority for probation should be to establish and maintain facilities for community supervision which would command enough credibility with sentencers to encourage their use as alternatives to custody. In line with this, court reports were to be prepared more selectively, concentrating on defendants who might be at risk of custody, to give the courts an opportunity to consider the feasibility of alternatives. Other aspects of probation work – through-care and after-care, civil work, and wider work in the community – were to be given lower priorities, and their status was to be reflected in the resources allocated to them. SNOP, as it became known, was thus a clear statement of the Home Office's intent that the probation service's primary task should be to help reduce the prison population by providing persuasive 'alternatives'.

SNOP raised two kinds of anxiety for practitioners. First, it was feared that its emphasis on intensive work with high-risk offenders, and its downgrading of the more voluntarist, helping-oriented aspects of practice would continue the trend towards control and away from help. Second (and this was a more novel worry), it was rightly interpreted as a sign that the Home Office would in future wish to subject the probation service to closer central direction and scrutiny. The national statement was complemented by local statements which were meant to show how the broad national objectives were to be implemented in local services, setting new standards of accountability for probation officers and their managers.[1] There was a new circular on social inquiry reports (1986); the Green Paper (Home Office 1988a) and Action Plan (Home Office 1988b) of 1988, the year in which national standards for community service also appeared; White and Green Papers in 1990 (Home Office 1990a, 1990b) (and in the

---

1   For various perspectives on management in probation see Statham and Whitehead 1992.

same year a 'Peppermint Paper' (Home Office 1990c) on partnership with what was now called the 'independent sector', and a review of the service's management structure); a 'blue paper' in 1991 (Home Office 1991a) exploring possibilities for the amalgamation of probation services and the replacement of probation committees by smaller probation boards; in 1992 National Standards were published for eight distinct areas of probation practice (and by 1994 a revised version of them was awaited); the same year saw a 'Decision Document' (Home Office 1992c) on partnerships, a draft 'Statement of Purpose' (Home Office 1992d) which in the following year became a Three Year Plan (Home Office 1993b), and extensive training materials commissioned by the Home Office to prepare the service for the 1991 Act. The list could be extended, and certainly should include the scrutinies by the National Audit Office (1989) and the Audit Commission (1989).

Amid this flurry of activity from a Home Office which until the early 1980s had adopted a policy of more or less benign neglect towards the probation service, it is little wonder that many officers felt anxious about the erosion of their autonomy and the encroachment of more bureaucratic and directive styles of management (May 1991). Many were also understandably concerned about the implications of the Home Office's design for the service, which David Faulkner (1989) called '[its] transformation from a social work agency to a criminal justice agency with a social work base' (p.4). Faulkner also warned the service 'not to undermine its credibility with too much abstract argument about care and control' (p.4), and that it existed 'to perform a range of specific functions, for the courts, the public and offenders, in that order' (p.4). But, as in the past, the service itself had more influence on policy than may have been apparent to practitioners. It could point to a few victories, or, more modestly, cases of damage limitation. For example, the White and Green Papers of 1990 (Home Office 1990a, 1990b) were much clearer than the 1988 Green Paper (Home Office 1988a) that core statutory tasks were to remain the responsibility of the probation service, rather than being handed over to other agencies, and that the skills required of probation officers were largely those traditionally associated with social work. The National Standards (Home Office 1992b) too, bore the marks of probation influence, in the differences between the draft sent out for consultation and the final version, which allowed more room for discretion and was more realistic about the service's working environment and the extent of its dependence on other parts of the system for information and support.

The probation service and the 1991 Criminal Justice Act

The 1990 White Paper (Home Office 1990a) and the 1991 Act were undoubtedly couched in a language which the probation service was likely
to find alien and unsympathetic – a language of just deserts, of punishment in the community, of offence seriousness as the primary determinant
of appropriate penalties. The Act also introduced, in the combination
order, a new measure which had the potential both to displace less
intrusive sentences (either probation or community service alone) and to
present the service with problems of enforcement (although it should be
remembered that a similar measure already existed in Scotland). Probation officers might feel uneasy, too, about the explicitness of the Act's
bifurcatory division between offences against property (for which the
seriousness criterion was to be strictly adhered to) and violent or sexual
offences, for which considerations of public protection could justify sentences more severe or intrusive than just deserts demanded. And the Act's
new provisions for the early release of prisoners meant that a higher
proportion of officers' caseloads would in future consist of people who
had not consented to supervision, but were compelled to have it as part
of their prison sentence.

All this helps to explain the service's uneasy response to the new
legislation. Nevertheless, as was noted above, the Act produced a pattern
of sentencing in the first few months of its operation which presumably
was much what probation officers would wish for (Home Office 1993a),
and was certainly in line with the White Paper's assumptions that prison
was not likely to promote reform; and the service rather belatedly came
to acknowledge some virtues of the Act when it was amended less than a
year after its implementation. The Act's rhetoric of just deserts, which
seemed to exclude individualised sentences and therefore to deny the
probation service a role in influencing sentencers, in fact left room for
individualisation on the basis of mitigation or aggravation, and of an
offender's suitability, in terms of his or her problems, needs and aptitudes,
for different types of community penalty. Indeed the revised training
materials (NACRO 1993) which were produced to take account of the
amendments to the Act laid more stress on the need for pre-sentence
reports (PSRs) to address issues of suitability, and less on the analysis of
offence gravity, than the original version. As Raynor *et al.* (1994) argue,
the Act's sentencing framework allowed for PSR practice which was not
very different from what had been generally accepted for some time as
good practice in court reports, and encouraged the service to develop a

range of community resources tailored both to offenders' needs and to the seriousness of their offences.

Other developments, not directly connected with the Act, could also give the probation service some encouragement. The Home Office began, in 1989, to promote inter-agency co-operation at a strategic level, to complement initiatives on the ground, through a series of national and regional conferences (Smith 1994). The early regional conferences identified a need for local consultative forums which would bring together the criminal justice agencies and other relevant parties, such as local authorities, to develop coherent strategies for criminal justice and crime problems more generally. This suggestion was put to the Woolf inquiry into the riots at Strangeways and other prisons in the spring of 1990 (Home Office 1991b), and influenced the recommendations of its report, which included the establishment of a national consultative council and area criminal justice committees. The probation service was active at chief officer level in these developments, which were intended to improve communication between all parts of the system, and particularly to reduce the isolation of the prison service and to encourage sentencers to take a broader view of their responsibilities. Whilst the area committees which emerged in late 1992 were not as local as had originally been envisaged, the probation service (as the agency most dependent on co-operation from others in fulfilling its duties) could take some comfort from these signs that central government was taking seriously the need for a more coherent policy on criminal justice.

Developments in Scotland

The aim of this section is briefly to review developments in penal policy north of the border, not in the hope of giving a comprehensive account (for which see McIvor 1994) but in order to illustrate how a different political and organisational environment can produce different policy outcomes. The impetus for recent policy initiatives in this field came from a period of disturbance in Scottish prisons (so that there is a parallel with the origins of the Woolf proposals), which led the then Scottish Secretary, Malcolm Rifkind, to declare a commitment to reducing the use of custody (Rifkind 1989). This was to be achieved not, as in England and Wales, by increasing the range of non-custodial measures available to courts, but by improving the quality and credibility of those already available. The aim was to enable courts to feel that non-violent offenders (note the theme of bifurcation) could be sentenced to community-based measures instead of the short prison sentences which had contributed to Scotland's historically high prison population.

An important element in the strategy was community service. This had been introduced experimentally in 1977, and schemes were run and partly funded by local authority social work departments. By the late 1980s there was concern that provision for community service was insufficient to meet the demands of courts, and in 1989 the Scottish Office took over responsibility for 100 per cent funding, to coincide with the introduction of national standards and objectives. In contrast with the process which led to national standards in England and Wales, these were produced by a consultation group on which a wide range of interests was represented (McIvor 1994, p.432), and community service in Scotland has retained a more rehabilitative, offender-centred orientation than in England and Wales, where the national standards stressed the punitive character of the sentence rather than its positive potential (McIvor 1992).

Concern about the resourcing of community service was more than matched by concern about probation. The level of use of probation in Scotland increased during the 1980s but remained lower than in England and Wales, a difference generally attributed to the low priority given to adult offenders compared with the other client groups for which social work departments are responsible. The result was, according to a Sheriff cited by McIvor (1994), that probation became the 'sick man' of the system, being little recommended in social inquiry reports and commanding little credibility with the courts.[2] In April 1991, in an effort to cure the sickness, national standards for probation and other aspects of social work with offenders were introduced, along with full central funding (Social work Services Group 1991). As with the standards for community service, these differ from their counterparts south of the border in being less preoccupied with procedures for enforcement, and more hospitable to the aims of providing help and support, not necessarily within the framework of a court order.

Whilst it is not yet possible to judge the effect of these reforms, they have certainly allowed the re-emergence of work with adult offenders as a specialism within Scottish social work departments. More generally, the policy outlined by Rifkind (1989) appears to have been more steadily

---

2   See Raynor *et al.* 1994 for some discussion of this relationship.

maintained than the similar policy – of reducing the use of custody for offenders who do not constitute a physical danger to the public –espoused by the Home Office in the late 1980s and early 1990s. According to McIvor (1994, p.446) the law and order issue has generally been less prominent in political debates in Scotland than in England and Wales, and recent decreases in officially recorded crime mean that there is unlikely to be much political capital to be gained from trying to raise its profile. In speculation, one might add that a policy consensus may be easier to maintain in Scotland because of the advantages associated with smaller countries.[3] Policy makers, social work managers and practitioners and other criminal justice personnel are more likely to meet on a routine basis, and to exchange ideas based largely upon a common culture and education. What the Home Office made a special effort to achieve through its conference programme happens, to an extent, spontaneously in Scotland. The recent stability of Scottish criminal justice policy, combined with the funding initiatives of recent years, allows for an optimism among practitioners there which is less easily found in England and Wales.

Conclusion

What will be seen to work?

The policy context of social work with offenders in England and Wales became more confused and turbulent during 1993 and 1994. In a clear reversal of previous policy, the Home Secretary proclaimed that 'prison works', and showed little interest in whether anything else worked better. The 1991 Criminal Justice Act, which had been hailed by those responsible for it as establishing a coherent and durable framework for sentencing, was substantially amended to weaken its restrictions on custodial sentencing. New measures in the legislative pipeline include the establishment of secure training centres for 12–14-year-olds, despite universal opposition from informed opinion, and a removal of the requirement that courts should obtain a PSR before imposing a custodial sentence in all but the most exceptional cases. Probation service budgets were cut, leading to the closure of a number of bail hostels. The social work basis of probation practice was again placed under threat with the announcement of a review of pre-qualifying training whose brief was to explore what

---

3 See Christie, 1993, for discussion of these in the Netherlands and Norway.

other kinds of qualification might be appropriate. A service which less than five years before had been invited by the government to 'move centre stage' in the criminal justice system began to feel more like a disregarded extra, a spear-carrier at best.

Nevertheless, there were some grounds for optimism. If the policy U-turn criticised by Faulkner (1993) was unpredictable, the revival of a well-founded belief in the possibility of effective work with offenders was hardly less so. The orthodoxy of 'nothing works' was firmly entrenched during the 1980s not only in the Home Office but among probation officers themselves (Humphrey and Pease 1992). Much policy, much practice and much academic commentary were informed by this gloomy faith. But towards the end of the decade there were signs of change. Raynor (1988) and Roberts (1989) produced convincing research to suggest that something worked better than prison, and McIvor's (1990) review of research in the field suggested the same. It also provided powerful evidence that ever more intensive forms of supervision gave no guarantee of greater effectiveness: that the content and quality of programmes were more important than the quantity of intervention they involved.

At least one probation service, Mid-Glamorgan, responded whole-heartedly to these results by setting up a well resourced and well evaluated programme for high risk offenders – Straight Thinking on Probation or STOP. The continuing evaluation of this has produced, to date, some highly encouraging results (Raynor *et al*. 1994, Raynor and Vanstone 1994a and 1994b). These include reconviction data that favour community-based over custodial measures, and are especially positive for offenders who completed the STOP programme. They also show that it is feasible to implement a well structured and coherent programme in a way which is perceived as positive and productive both by probation officers (notoriously sceptical and suspicious of management-led innovation) and by offenders. And, as Raynor and Vanstone (1994b) argue, there are implications for the ethics of social work with offenders in the realistic possibility that we can say, at least, that some things work better than others.

There is, of course, no guarantee that the implications of these results will have a quick or direct (or any) influence on policy. But, as this chapter has shown, practice has influenced policy before, as in the case of juvenile justice during the 1980s, even if this has not always been clearly recognised or, if recognised, not welcomed. Practice which has been thoroughly evaluated, with full and relevant dissemination of the results, must stand a better chance of having an impact on policy than practice which remains obscure and unarticulated. Whatever one's scepticism about the rationality of the processes through which penal policy is formed, the empirically-grounded optimism of this recent research provides a more hopeful way forward for social work with offenders than the dead end of punitiveness for its own sake and an ever-increasing prison population.

References

Ashworth, A. (1983) 'Bifurcation and the public.' *Criminal Law Review*, 761–763.

Audit Commission (1989) *The Probation Service: Promoting Value for Money*. London: HMSO.

Barclay, G.C. (ed) (1993) *Digest 2: Information on the Criminal Justice System in England and Wales*. London: Home Office.

Blagg, H., Pearson, G., Sampson, A., Smith, D. and Stubbs, P. (1988) 'Inter-agency cooperation: rhetoric and reality.' In T. Hope, and M. Shaw (eds) *Communities and Crime Reduction*. London: HMSO.

Blagg, H. and Smith, D. (1989) *Crime, Penal Policy and Social Work*. Harlow: Longman.

Bottoms, A.E. (1977) 'Reflections on the renaissance of dangerousness.' *Howard Journal of Criminal Justice 16*, 70–96.

Burney, E. (1985) *Sentencing Young People: What Went Wrong with the Criminal Justice Act 1982*. Aldershot: Gower.

Cavadino, M. and Dignan, J. (1992) *The Penal System: An Introduction*. London: Sage.

Christie, N. (1993) *Crime Control as Industry: Towards Gulags, Western Style?* London: Routledge.

Downes, D. and Morgan, R. (1994) '"Hostages to fortune": the politics of law and order in post-war Britain.' In M. Maguire, R. Morgan and R. Reiner (eds) *The Oxford Handbook of Criminology*. Oxford: Clarendon Press.

Evans, R. and Wilkinson, C. (1990) 'Variations in police cautioning policy and practice in England and Wales.' *Howard Journal of Criminal Justice 29*, 155–176.

Faulkner, D.E.R. (1989) 'The future of the probation service: a view from government.' In R. Shaw. and K. Haines (eds) *The Criminal Justice System: A Central Role for the Probation Service*. Cambridge: Institute of Criminology.

Faulkner, D.E.R. (1993) 'All flaws and disorder.' *The Guardian*, 11 November.

Foster, J., Hope, T., Dowds, L. and Sutton, M. (1993) *Housing, Community and Crime: The Impact of the Priority Estates Project*. Home Office Research Study 131. London: HMSO.

Home Office (1980) *Young Offenders*. Cmnd 8045. London: HMSO.

Home Office (1984) *Probation Service in England and Wales: Statement of National Objectives and Priorities.* London: Home Office.

Home Office (1988a) *Punishment, Custody and the Community.* Cm 424. London: HMSO.

Home Office (1988b) *Tackling Offending: An Action Plan.* London: Home Office.

Home Office (1990a) *Crime, Justice and Protecting the Public.* Cm 965. London: HMSO.

Home Office (1990b) *Supervision and Punishment in the Community.* Cm 966. London: HMSO.

Home Office (1990c) *Partnership in Dealing with Offenders in the Community.* (The 'Peppermint paper'.) London: Home Office.

Home Office (1991a) *Organising Supervision and Punishment in the Community.* (The 'blue paper'.) London: Home Office.

Home Office (1991b) *Prison Disturbances April 1990.* Cm 1456. The Woolf Report. London: HMSO.

Home Office (1992a) *Annual Report 1991.* Cm 1909. London: HMSO.

Home Office (1992b) *National Standards for the Supervision of Offenders in the Community.* London: Home Office.

Home Office (1992c) *Partnership in Dealing with Offenders in the Community: A Decision Document.* London: Home Office.

Home Office (1992d) *The Probation Service: Draft Statement of Purpose.* London: Home Office.

Home Office (1993a) *Monitoring of the Criminal Justice Act 1991: Findings from a Special Data Collection Exercise.* Statistical Bulletin 25/93. London: Home Office.

Home Office (1993b) *Three Year Plan for the Probation Service 1993–1996.* London: Home Office.

Hudson, B. (1987) *Justice through Punishment: A Critique of the 'Justice Model' of Corrections.* London: Macmillan.

Humphrey, C. and Pease, K. (1992) 'Effectiveness measurement in the probation service: a view from the troops.' *Howard Journal of Criminal Justice 31,* 31–52.

Jordan, B. (1983) 'Criminal justice and probation in the 1980s.' *Probation Journal 30,* 83–88.

May, T. (1991) *Probation: Politics, Policy and Practice.* Milton Keynes: Open University Press.

McIvor, G. (1990) *Sanctions for Serious or Persistent Offenders: A Review of the Literature.* Stirling: Social Work Research Centre, University of Stirling.

McIvor, G. (1992) *Sentenced to Serve.* Aldershot: Avebury.

McIvor, G. (1994) 'Social work and criminal justice in Scotland: developments in policy and practice.' *British Journal of Social Work 24*, 430–448.

NACRO (1991) *Replacing Custody*. London: NACRO.

NACRO (1993) *The Criminal Justice Act 1991: Revised Training Materials for the Probation Service*. London: NACRO.

National Audit Office (1989) *Home Office Control and Management of the Probation Service in England and Wales*. London: HMSO.

Packer, H. (1968) *The Limits of the Criminal Sanction*. Stanford: Stanford University Press.

Pearson, G., Blagg, H., Smith, D., Sampson, A. and Stubbs, P. (1992) 'Crime, community and conflict: the multi-agency approach.' In D. Downes (ed) *Unravelling Criminal Justice*. Basingstoke: Macmillan.

Pratt, J. (1985) 'Delinquency as a scarce resource.' *Howard Journal of Criminal Justice 24*, 81–92.

Raynor, P. (1985) *Social Work, Justice and Control*. Oxford: Blackwell.

Raynor, P. (1988) *Probation as an Alternative to Custody*. Aldershot: Avebury.

Raynor, P., Smith, D. and Vanstone, M. (1994) *Effective Probation Practice*. Basingstoke: Macmillan.

Raynor, P. and Vanstone, M. (1994a) *STOP: Third Interim Evaluation Report*. Bridgend: Mid-Glamorgan Probation Service.

Raynor, P. and Vanstone, M. (1994b) 'Probation practice, effectiveness and the non-treatment paradigm.' *British Journal of Social Work 24*, 387–404.

Rifkind, M. (1989) 'Penal policy: the way ahead.' *Howard Journal of Criminal Justice 28*, 81–90.

Roberts, C.H. (1989) *First Evaluation Report, Young Offenders Project*. Worcester: Hereford and Worcester Probation Service.

Smith, D. (1994) *The Home Office Regional Criminal Justice Conferences May 1990 – March 1993*. Liverpool: Home Office Special Conferences Unit.

Social Work Services Group (1991) *National Objectives and Standards for Social Work Services in the Criminal Justice System*. Edinburgh: Scottish Office.

Statham, R. and Whitehead, P. (eds) (1992) *Managing the Probation Service: Issues for the 1990s*. Harlow: Longman.

Chapter 2

Developments in Probation in England and Wales 1984–1993

George Mair

Since 1984, when the Statement of National Objectives and Priorities – SNOP – (Home Office 1984) sent shock-waves through the probation service, probation officers in England and Wales have had to cope with an unprecedented number of new developments which have kept them in a state of almost permanent apprehension. In this chapter, I shall describe what I consider to be the most significant of these developments and draw some fairly simple conclusions about their importance. I have chosen 1984 somewhat arbitrarily as the starting date for this exercise: whilst there is no doubt that some of the developments to be mentioned were underway prior to this date, they reached their full flowering after 1984; and the symbolic nature of SNOP should not be underestimated.

First, however, to set the context for the developments to be outlined, it is necessary to say a little about the resources of the service (see Home Office 1993). In 1983–84 the annual expenditure on the service was £156 million, in 1991–92 (the last year for which figures are available) it was £348 million – an increase of 123 per cent. In 1984 there were 6061 whole-time equivalent probation officers in post; by 1992 this had risen to 7484 – an increase of 23 per cent. The number of ancillary workers and clerical and administrative staff also grew considerably during this period. The total number of persons being supervised by the service dropped from 148,660 to 139,555 (mainly accounted for by the near disappearance of matrimonial proceedings work), and average caseloads for criminal supervision fell: the average caseload per maingrade officer fell from 12.1 in 1985 to 8.7 in 1992 for probation orders, and from 27.5 to 20.8 for all criminal supervision; whilst the average number of reports completed per maingrade officer fell from 69 to 51 during the same period. Much of this apparent fall in workload in reality reflects changes in the seriousness of offenders dealt with by the service, better targeting of reports, changes in the numbers found guilty, etc., but there may also be a real decline which merits further study.

The developments to be discussed have been set out under three headings. First, professional developments which have occurred – at least initially – within the service itself; second, central government, managerial-style initiatives which the service has had to grapple with; and third, the Criminal Justice Acts of 1991 and 1993.

Professional developments

Day centres

Whilst the origins of day centres (renamed probation centres under the provisions of the 1991 Criminal Justice Act) could be traced quite far back in probation history, the centres came into being officially with the 1982 Criminal Justice Act. An offender can be ordered to attend at a day centre for up to 60 days as part of a probation order. The importance of the centres lies in their offering a different approach to probation supervision, and in aiming to divert relatively serious offenders from a custodial sentence. At day centres, groupwork is the dominant approach, whereas in traditional probation work one-to-one casework is the norm.

Despite a certain amount of opposition from some probation officers who saw them as overly controlling and argued in favour of voluntary attendance, day centres grew rapidly in number during the 1980s. There are probably between 70 and 80 of them (no central record is kept of their numbers) and in 1992 almost 3000 offenders received orders requiring them to attend centres; it is interesting to note that this is considerably fewer than those ordered to participate in specified activities or to report to a specified person, but this requirement has always excited less interest than day centres. Research has suggested that day centres are working quite well (Mair 1988a, Mair and Nee 1992, Vass 1990), and they have demonstrated that the probation service can devise imaginative programmes based on groupwork for serious offenders. This was of considerable importance for the new criminal justice strategies which began to be formulated in the late 1980s.

Risk prediction

Initially closely linked with the increasing significance of day centres has been the development of statistical prediction instruments – first to predict an offender's risk of custody or likely sentence and now to predict the risk of reconviction. Given the probation service's traditional adherence to social work values and its associated insistence upon the primacy of individual professional judgements, this shift towards statistical risk prediction is noteworthy.

The first moves to develop a risk of custody predictor came as a result of anxieties in one probation area about ensuring that their day centre was kept as an alternative to custodial sentence, thereby preventing tariff-slippage and net-widening. This predictor was rather crude but stimulated a great deal of interest amongst probation officers with the result that use of the predictor spread and other predictors were developed (see Mair 1990). With the advent of the 1991 Criminal Justice Act, risk of custody scales became outmoded and predicting risk of reconviction became much more significant. The Home Office Research and Planning Unit commissioned a leading statistician to devise a national risk of reconviction predictor (NRAS – the National Reconviction Assessment Scale) (Copas 1995), which predicts the probability of reconviction for a Standard List offence within two years. By using such a scale, probation officers can supplement their own judgement and help to ensure that different types of offender are matched to the most appropriate disposals; more resources can thus be devoted to those who need more care and control and fewer resources can be used on those who pose little risk of reconviction. The scale can also be used as an evaluative tool.

The issues which need to be addressed in using predictive scales (as opposed to the methodological issues involved in devising them) should not be underestimated. They must be introduced to probation officers carefully and openly and their limitations should be pointed out; they are not, for example, a substitute for professional judgement. Scales need to be revalidated regularly; and management objectives are necessary. NRAS is expected to be made available to the probation service in the near future, although further work will go on to refine it to take account of the time to reconviction and the seriousness of the reconviction offence.

Bail information schemes/PICA

During the 1980s two developments led to the introduction of bail information schemes on an experimental basis in eight areas: first, increasing prison overcrowding and the realisation that around 20 per cent of those in custody had yet to be found guilty and/or sentenced; and second, the introduction of an independent Crown Prosecution Service (CPS). The need for some action on the former, and a probation wish to forge links with the CPS neatly coincided; one method of liaising with the CPS was to provide information to prosecutors about defendants who might be remanded in custody (the only source of information for the CPS prior to probation involvement was the police). In a bail information scheme, a probation officer interviews briefly before their court appearance any defendants held in police cells for whom bail is being opposed by the police. The objective is to elicit from defendants themselves any 'positive' information which might help the case for bail rather than a remand in custody. Police information is negative as there is a presumption in favour of bail, and the information provided by the probation officer (who verifies it) may show that the defendant has a steady job, stable accommodation and good relationships with his or her family. This material is passed on to the prosecutor who then considers it along with the police arguments, and decides whether or not to oppose the granting of bail; the information is also available to the defence solicitor.

Whilst bail information schemes have not been without their critics in the beginning (there was apprehension among some probation officers that it was not part of their task to provide information about defendants prior to a finding of guilt), opposition has died away. In common-sense terms the provision of another source of information to aid bail decision-making can only be a good thing. The various research studies which have been carried out all suggest that bail information schemes do tend to lead to bail for defendants who would otherwise have been remanded in custody (Lloyd 1991b, Mair 1988b, Stone 1988). Since 1988 bail information schemes have been developed on a national basis and by mid-1993 there were 179 court-based bail information schemes and 31 prison-based schemes in England and Wales.

An extension of the schemes whereby probation officers provide the CPS with information which might help the decision to discontinue prosecution in the public interest (PICA – Public Interest Case Assessment) also has proved successful on a trial basis and such schemes are planned to expand (see Brown and Crisp 1992). A further development is bail support packages where probation officers would begin to work with those granted bail but deemed to be at risk of offending.

Other developments

Various other developments in probation work emerged during the years 1984 to 1993 which are also worth noting. Intensive probation, crime prevention, community probation work, involvement in assessment schemes for mentally disordered offenders, and in mediation, reparation and conciliation schemes are probably the most significant.

Intensive probation (IP) is not, of course, new – the IMPACT studies were an early form of such work (see Folkard *et al.* 1974, Folkard, Smith and Smith 1976) – but intensive now means something rather different than it did in the 1960s and early 1970s. Crudely, it then meant more social work counselling whereas now it means more surveillance and control. Following discussions with the Home Office, eight probation areas agreed to set up intensive probation schemes in April 1990; these schemes were expected to involve more frequent contact with offenders, strict breach policy and a target group of high-risk offenders. IP has been an important development insofar as it demonstrated the willingness of probation services to design and deliver systematic, demanding and rigorous pro-grammes for serious offenders (see Chapter 9 for a more detailed study of IP).

Probation officers have also been getting involved with community probation work. As might be expected, such an approach (and it is very much an approach, not a formal method of working) is based around methods and concepts which have been developed in the area of commu-nity work. In the mid-eighties a major research project investigated the amount and kind of community probation work which was being carried out, and assessed the policy and resource implications of this (Henderson and del Tufo 1991).

Growing unease about the number of mentally disordered offenders who are imprisoned or remanded in custody has led to the development of panel assessment schemes which aim to divert such offenders out of the criminal justice process (see Hedderman 1993). Probation officers have tended to play a key part as the co-ordinators of such schemes, and it is likely that such involvement will increase.

Finally, many probation officers are involved to some extent in crime prevention work (see Geraghty 1991), and also in the various mediation, reparation and conciliation schemes which have been appearing through-out the country.

These developments have originated from within probation services, although they have not been discouraged by the Home Office, and have in some cases been actively promoted. They are firmly located in day-to-day professional probation practice, but it is also true to say that they tend to encourage greater accountability as well as a more controlling approach to probation. The second set of developments is rather different.

Central government initiatives

SNOP

In April 1984, the Home Office published a *Statement of National Objectives and Priorities* (SNOP) for the probation service in England and Wales. This was a brief document of six pages, setting out in general terms the purpose of the service, listing the objectives it should be trying to attain, and suggesting an order of priorities which should be followed in allocating resources towards these objectives.

With the benefit of hindsight, it is easy to regard SNOP as an unassuming and uncontentious document. At the time of its publication, however, it was seen as something of a bombshell marking the end of the probation service as we knew it. The truth lies somewhere in between. In symbolic terms SNOP represents a watershed for the probation service, as it signalled a clear return by the Home Office to a more interventionist stance with regard to the service after more than a decade of *laissez-faire*. With SNOP the Home Office stated what it expected from the service and how it should go about its tasks. SNOP's influence can still be seen in the National Standards (see below) and in the *Three Year Plan for the Probation Service* (Home Office 1992a).

One immediate response to SNOP was that many services produced their own statements of local objectives and priorities (SLOP). A study of these local responses has pointed out that 'the most notable feature of the local statements of objectives and priorities is their great diversity' (Lloyd 1986). This is not surprising, as the probation service has tended to celebrate diversity and see it in positive terms, rather than consider its potential drawbacks. But in addition, SNOP itself was somewhat vague and open to interpretation – almost certainly deliberately. One consequence of the appearance of local statements was team statements (STOP); whether the process filtered down to individual statements is unclear.

PROBIS

Computerisation is a development which is often forgotten, but which is likely to have both profound and long-term consequences on probation work. For many probation officers computerisation is synonymous with PROBIS (Probation Information System), a system developed within the Home Office Research and Planning Unit for probation use. The Home Office receives statistical returns from the 55 probation services, and prior to computerisation these were completed manually; with the growth of computerisation, data can be transferred much more quickly and conveniently. But it is also important that data transfer be carried out in a standardised and compatible way, and thus from the Home Office point of view a single system was preferable. Individual services were encouraged to follow the PROBIS model and, despite some resistance from services to what was seen as Home Office interference, by 1988 most were using the PROBIS system.

Although there is no firm evidence on the matter, it seems likely that computerisation has had a deep-seated impact upon probation work and culture in general, and that it will continue to do so. PROBIS is now at the end of its shelf-life and new systems are being planned. These will play a key role in the development of a Resource Management Information System (RMIS) and a Case Management Classification System (see below); and with the computerisation of courts underway, there is considerable scope for systems to connect although there may be administrative and/or bureaucratic difficulties.

RMIS

RMIS began life as FMIS (the Financial Management Information System) which was part of the government's Financial Management Initiative. Since the Conservative government came to power in 1979 there has been a strong emphasis upon the efficient, effective and economic use of public funds, and a formal initiative to improve financial management in government departments was launched in 1982. In March 1986 a management consultancy firm was appointed to develop a financial management information system for the probation service (see Humphrey 1991). With the service at this time accounting for more than £200 million a year, there was increasing pressure on Chief Probation Officers (CPOs) to demonstrate good financial management. This work has carried on, although it has widened to cover resources generally and not simply financial information, and consultants are no longer in the lead (they were very expensive). The fact that a system is not yet in place shows just how difficult it is to develop a RMIS for the probation service; the system must be useful and acceptable to both probation and the Home Office. Further developments in this are underway: a Case Management Classification system is being piloted; and an Information Systems Unit within the probation policy division of the Home Office is looking at information needs from a more strategic perspective.

Performance indicators

Closely related to SNOP and RMIS is the area of performance indicators. If certain objectives are set for the probation service, then some indication of how these are being attained will be necessary. Without adequate tools to assess what probation staff are doing and how well they are doing it, resource allocation will be a hit-and-miss affair and a comprehensive resource management information system will be impossible. Performance indicators, then, are a major issue and a source of some unease amongst many probation officers.

The members of any organisation are likely to be anxious about the introduction of performance indicators. Probation unease was exacerbated by the fact that the indicators were developed by the Probation Inspectorate for use in their inspections of probation areas. In other words, probation officers were worried that they were going to be judged, and that therefore resources would be allocated, on the basis of quasi-scientific measures which had not been devised by them and would not be interpreted by them (confusion over performance indicators and measures of effectiveness was – and remains – common). The indicators were constructed around the objectives detailed in SNOP and this too fed service anxieties as local statements prepared in response to SNOP did not always have the same objectives.

A first set of performance indicators was published in April 1988 (Her Majesty's Inspectorate of Probation 1988) and was subsequently used by the Inspectorate. Since December 1992 a working group has been considering performance indicators further, this time partly in response to Treasury demands for 'high-level' indicators of probation service achievement, and a small group of Key Performance Indicators is being developed. Uncertainties and confusion over the precise status of a performance indicator remain, but they are certainly here to stay.

National standards

One of the major criticisms of probation work in general has been that it is inconsistent. Probation officers all too often seem to confuse such a criticism with an attack upon creativity and flexibility which, naturally, they see in a positive light. But bad practice and inequality of treatment for offenders can easily result from lack of consistency; in the 1980s, for example, in some areas a day centre order might require attendance for four hours, three days a week for 30 days, whilst in others it could mean eight hours a day, four days a week for 60 days (Mair 1988a). Sentencers could, as a result, lose confidence in the work of the service. The formulation of standards for aspects of probation work is one approach to getting round the problems of inconsistency and lack of credibility to sentencers. Whilst the fear of many probation staff has been that the imposition of standards would stifle creativity and flexibility, this is certainly not a necessary consequence and, indeed, standards could encourage innovative approaches to working.

The first set of National Standards – for community service orders – was introduced in April 1989. Essentially, they specified such matters as the length of time which should elapse between the making of an order by the court and the beginning of work by the offender, the number of unacceptable absences permissible before an offender is breached, the kind of work to be carried out, etc. Some basic monitoring of the Standards during their first 24 months of operation suggested that they were operating reasonably well (Lloyd 1991a), and on 1 October 1992 other National Standards – for pre-sentence reports, probation orders, supervision orders, combination orders, the management of hostels, supervision before and after release from custody, as well as revised standards for CSOs – were introduced (see Home Office 1992b). Unfortunately, no national monitoring system was organised for the National Standards, although a review is currently underway.

Partnership

Traditionally, the probation service has worked with offenders using – for the most part – only the skills of trained probation officers. It came as some surprise to find recently that about half of all probation officers were employed in specialist duties (Boswell, Davies and Wright 1993). The service has always made use of voluntary workers and ancillaries, but there has been a growing feeling that it may be more sensible to utilise the expertise and skills of other organisations and agencies instead of probation officers trying to do it all themselves.

Government policy in the past few years has been to try to build a more rational and coherent approach to the way in which probation services make use of the particular abilities of other organisations – both statutory and voluntary. In a decision paper *Partnership in Dealing with Offenders in the Community* (Home Office n.d.a), the government decided that the service should take the lead in developing local partnership arrangements with other organisations which might contribute to probation work. The key elements of this policy are that there should be joint agreement between each service and other agencies on best practice in dealing with offenders. Each probation area is expected to develop work with a range of independent organisations, and around 5 per cent of the revenue budget of each service should be allocated to partnership schemes. Thus, probation officers are being encouraged to use specialist drug treatment agencies, employment training organisations, adult education projects, etc. more regularly.

Cash limits and organisational changes

The kind of developments which were taking place in the probation service during the second half of the 1980s led to a reconsideration of how the service should be funded and organised. In the past, central government had an open-ended commitment to pay 80 per cent of probation expenditure (the remaining 20% being met by local government). Since 1992, however, the government contribution has been subject to cash limits which are calculated by a complex formula for each probation area (see Field and Hough 1993). It is hoped that the introduction of cash limits will act as an incentive to ensure effective use of expenditure; there are also plans to introduce a more structured resource planning process.

The role of probation committees is to be more clearly defined, with rules on the size of committees and membership; subsequently, Probation Boards are planned to replace committees. Services – particularly the smaller ones – are being encouraged to consider the possibilities of collaboration (Home Office n.d.b). Indeed, at one point the idea of a national probation service was mooted but this was dropped in the light of negative feedback from the various areas.

These government initiatives are all related to each other to a greater or lesser extent. They have tended to be seen by many probation officers as threatening, because they seem to point to a concerted move towards greater Home Office control over the service and therefore more accountability. In this way they complement the professional developments discussed earlier.

The Criminal Justice Acts 1991 and 1993

The 1991 Criminal Justice Act which came into operation on 1 October 1992 was hailed as one of the most important pieces of criminal justice legislation of the century, and some of its provisions are likely to have a profound impact upon the work of the probation service. The overall thrust of the Act was to encourage sentencers to make more use of community penalties within a just deserts sentencing framework.

The key provision of the Act which affects the probation service is the introduction of the combination order whereby an offender can be sentenced to a period of probation supervision (with or without added requirements) and community service for the same offence. This, of course, has been possible in Scotland for some time. It is hoped that the new order will encourage the courts to use the probation service for more serious offenders, and the National Standards have suggested that most combination orders should be made at the Crown Court. Early indications, however, point to the majority of combination orders being made in the magistrates' courts without a pre-sentence report suggesting such a course.

With the introduction of the Youth Court, probation services are having to set up formal working arrangements with social services departments for the first time. The Act also provides for greater use of pre-sentence reports (re-named from social inquiry reports), special requirements for drug- or alcohol-related offenders and sex offenders as part of a probation order, and changes in the parole system which will lead to the need for more supervision on release by probation officers. Extra resources would be necessary to carry these changes through, and expenditure on the probation service was planned to increase considerably in the years following the Act.

During 1993, however, government policy towards the service changed tack. The Criminal Justice Act 1993 modified the sentencing framework by allowing the court to look at all offences before it, not just the offence and one other associated with it as in the 1991 Act, and to take account of previous convictions; unit fines were also abolished. The long-term significance of the 1991 Act was, therefore, considerably diluted. Probation officers are having to modify yet again the way in which they work – particularly in assessing seriousness. A harsher penal climate generally means that probation is no longer seen as occupying centre stage, and cut-backs in expenditure are now planned.

Conclusion

Within ten years, then, there have been a considerable number of significant developments in the probation service in England and Wales. Can any general conclusions be drawn from these developments?

First, while it is important to emphasise that probation has not been an unchanging, monolithic entity since its inception at the beginning of the century, there can be little doubt that the past ten years or so have been a time of unprecedented change – and this process is by no means complete and may even just be beginning. Probation has been moving into new areas of work and trying out new methods of practice. One possible implication of such a situation is that the traditional virtues and advantages of probation supervision may be overlooked and forgotten.

Second, one key feature of the many developments discussed is that they tend to encourage greater consistency in probation work. Diversity of practice no doubt has its advantages, but the range of practices presented by different probation areas, teams and individual officers cannot all be equally efficient, effective or economic – and it could certainly lead to injustice. It will be a difficult task to constrain and channel diversity of practice but to ensure that it is not eliminated.

Third, and related to the previous point, these developments also point – directly or indirectly – to greater accountability throughout the probation service and increased control from the centre. It is this which seems to cause most unease amongst probation staff. But more accountability is an issue for all public services today, and one which cannot be shrugged off; and in practice the individual probation services continue to have a good deal of local autonomy.

There is no doubt that there are many problems and tensions both within and facing the probation service in England and Wales. In a sense this may be seen as a good thing – it is one sign of a healthy organisation. And indeed for the most part, the service has managed to carry on delivering good work during a decade of almost constant change. Further change is on the horizon and it is to be hoped that probation officers can continue to cope with any new developments and provide challenging and rigorous programmes for offenders in the community.

References

Boswell, G., Davies, M. and Wright, A. (1993) *Contemporary Probation Practice*. Aldershot: Avebury.

Brown, A. and Crisp, D. (1992) 'Diverting cases from prosecution in the public interest.' *Home Office RSD Research Bulletin 32*, 7–12.

Copas, J. (1995) 'On using crime statistics for prediction.' In M. Walker (ed) *Interpreting Crime Statistics*. Oxford: Clarendon Press.

Field, S. and Hough, M. (1993) *Cash-Limiting the Probation Service: a case study in resource allocation*. RPU Paper 77. London: Home Office.

Folkard, M.S., Fowles, A.J., McWilliams, B.C., McWilliams, W., Smith, D.D., Smith, D.E. and Walmsley, G.R. (1974) *IMPACT. Vol. I – The design of the probation experiment and an interim evaluation*. HORS 24. London: HMSO.

Folkard, M.S., Smith, D.E. and Smith, D.D. (1976) *IMPACT. Vol. II – The results of the experiment*. HORS 36. London: HMSO.

Geraghty, J. (1991) *Probation practice in crime prevention*. CPU Paper 24. London: Home Office.

Hedderman, C. (1993) *Panel assessment schemes for mentally disordered offenders*. RPU Paper 76. London: Home Office.

Henderson, P. and del Tufo, S. (1991) *Community Work and the Probation Service*. London: HMSO.

Her Majesty's Inspectorate of Probation (1988) *Performance Indicators for the Probation Service*. London: Home Office.

Home Office (1984) *Probation Service in England and Wales: Statement of National Objectives and Priorities*. London: Home Office.

Home Office (1992a) *Three Year Plan for the Probation Service 1993–1996*. London: Home Office.

Home Office (1992b) *National Standards for the Supervision of Offenders in the Community*. London: Home Office.

Home Office (1993) *Probation Statistics England and Wales 1992*. London: Home Office.

Home Office (n.d. a) *Partnership in Dealing with Offenders in the Community: a decision document*. London: Home Office.

Home Office (n.d. b) *Organising Supervision and Punishment in the Community: a decision document*. London: Home Office.

Humphrey, C. (1991) 'Calling on the experts: the financial management initiative (FMI), private sector consultants and the probation service.' *Howard Journal 30*, 1, 1–18.

Lloyd, C. (1986) *Response to SNOP*. Cambridge: Institute of Criminology.

Lloyd, C. (1991a) 'National Standards for Community Service Orders: the first two years of operation.' *Home Office RSD Research Bulletin 31,* 16–21.

Lloyd, C. (1991b) *Bail Information Schemes: Practice and Effect.* RPU Paper 69. London: Home Office.

Mair, G. (1988a) *Probation Day Centres.* HORS 100. London: HMSO.

Mair, G. (1988b) *Bail and Probation Work: the ILPS temporary bail action project.* RPU Paper 50. London: Home Office.

Mair, G. (ed) (1990) *Risk Prediction and Probation: papers from a Research and Planning Unit workshop.* RPU Paper 56. London: Home Office.

Mair, G. and Nee, C. (1992) 'Day centre reconviction rates.' *British Journal of Criminology 32,* 3, 329–339.

Stone, C. (1988) *Bail Information for the Crown Prosecution Service.* London: ACOP/Vera Institute of Justice.

Vass, A.A. (1990) *Alternatives to Prison: Punishment, Custody and the Community.* London: Sage.

Chapter 3

Recent Developments in Scotland

Gill McIvor

The face of social work services to the Scottish criminal justice system has changed dramatically over the last few years. These changes include both the breadth of services provided by social work departments and the organisational and financial framework within which these services are delivered. This chapter outlines some of the key developments which have occurred.

First, however, it is necessary to consider briefly the policy context which has served as a backdrop to these developments. The most significant landmark was an address to the Howard League (Scotland) in November 1988 by the then Secretary of State for Scotland (Rifkind 1989) in which he articulated the government's twin-track approach to penal policy. Against a background of unrest in Scottish penal establishments and a prison population among the highest in Europe, the Scottish Office was concerned that imprisonment should be reserved for the most serious offenders who might otherwise have received short prison sentences. Steps should likewise be taken to minimise the imposition of custodial sentences as a sanction for fine default, to reduce the use of custodial remands by the courts and to divert from the criminal justice process those offenders for whom alternatives to prosecution might more appropriately serve the public interest.

Whilst the broad principle of increasing the use of non-custodial measures for less serious offenders received parallel political support in England and Wales this position has now been eroded by demands for stiffer sentencing of certain groups of offenders and the introduction of tougher prison regimes. Despite the reversals of policy which have occurred south of the border, however, the Minister for Home Affairs in the Scottish Office confirmed, in the Kenneth Younger Memorial Lecture to the Howard League in November 1993, the government's continued commitment to the policy enunciated by the then Secretary of State in 1988 (Lord Fraser of Carmyllie 1993).

Developments in statutory services

A separate probation service ceased to exist in Scotland in 1969 when its functions were absorbed into the newly-created generic social work departments. Since then social work departments have assumed the responsibility for statutory services such as reports to the courts, probation supervision and through-care. When community service was introduced in Scotland – first on an experimental basis in 1977 and then nationally two years later – the local authority (regional and island) social work departments were given the task of operating the new community service schemes.

As in England and Wales, community service proved to be a popular sentencing option with the courts (Carnie 1990) and by the mid-1980s demand for places had begun, in some areas at least, to outstrip supply. Even though it had not been consistently imposed by the courts as a direct alternative to custody (McIvor 1990) community service was regarded as having the potential to impact significantly upon the use of imprisonment and detention in Scotland. This potential was, however, constrained by the financial arrangements in existence which required that local authorities contribute towards the funding of schemes and, as such, determine the ceiling of resources available for community service provision.

Following a national review and consultation process the Scottish Office assumed full responsibility for the funding of community service from 1 April 1989 and introduced from the same date national objectives and standards for community service schemes (Social Work Services Group 1989). The national standards clearly defined community service as first and foremost a punitive disposal – a fine on time – but stressed the importance of schemes making available work placements which maximised the benefit of the work both for the community and for the offender. Although the legislation did not preclude the use of community service as an alternative to other non-custodial disposals (mirroring the parallel legislation in England and Wales) the Scottish Office hoped, through the introduction of national standards, to promote the use of the community service order as a direct alternative to custody and thereby increase its diversionary potential.

Following the introduction of full central government funding for community service, consultation groups were convened by the Scottish Office to consider the extension of 100 per cent funding to other statutory social work services to the criminal justice system. National standards and objectives for probation, social enquiry reports and community-based through-care were introduced in April 1991 (SWSG 1991a), along with revised standards for community service, to coincide with the introduction of full central funding of these services. The legislative framework for the new funding arrangements was contained in the Law Reform (Miscellaneous Provisions) (Scotland) Act 1990 which, in addition, introduced amendments to the Community Service by Offenders (Scotland) Act 1978 requiring that the courts impose community service orders only if they would otherwise have sentenced the offender to a period of imprisonment or detention.

The objectives of social work practice in the criminal justice system were defined in the introduction to the national standards documentation. A primary objective was to increase the quality, quantity and targeting of social work disposals 'to enable a reduction in the incidence of custody, whether on remand, at sentence, or in default of a financial penalty, where it is used for lack of a suitable, available community based social work disposal' (SWSG 1991a, para. 12.1). Priority was accorded to the development of such disposals and other services for young adult offenders. A further key objective was 'to help offenders tackle their offending behaviour, assist them to live socially acceptable lives within the law and, whenever appropriate, further their social integration through the involvement and support of their families, friends and other resources in their community' (SWSG 1991a, para. 12.7). In October 1991 a research-based supplement to the national standards was published which outlined the principles and approaches most likely to achieve meaningful reductions in offending behaviour (McIvor and Roberts 1991).

Full central funding of community service had been introduced in part to prevent it becoming a victim of its own success. With probation, however, the impetus for 100 per cent funding was motivated by other concerns. The priority accorded to work with offenders had become eroded in the generic social work departments by the pressing requirements of child protection work and other statutory duties. This resulted in a gradual loss of confidence in probation supervision by the courts which was summed up by one sheriff (Lothian 1991) as follows:

'Orders, it seems, were not being allocated in such a way as to allow the offender to go from the hands of the court to those of the social work department; supervision was neither strict nor frequent enough; and finally no particular effort was being required by many offenders although unfairly perhaps someone who re-offended during a period of probation was likely to be treated as an even more lamentable case in that he was deemed to have spurned social work assistance which all too often had not been made properly available in the first case.'

National standards, in setting out the minimal requirements for the supervision of offenders subject to probation orders were, therefore, viewed as a crucial means of restoring the confidence of the courts in this particular disposal. The standards also highlight the importance of effective targeting of community-based social work disposals according to the risk of custody and the risk of re-offending in order to minimise the possibility of net-widening and to ensure that social work resources are directed at those most likely to benefit from them. More generally, predictive tools such as the Dunscore (Creamer, Ennis and Williams 1993) are becoming more widely used as an aid to professional judgement in targeting according to the risk of custody and in monitoring recommendations and sentencing at the local level.

Overall, the new arrangements have had a substantial impact upon the use of community-based social work disposals, with a virtual doubling of the number of community service orders over the last five years and a 50 per cent increase in the use of probation. But while the custodial figures decreased over much of the same period (although rising again significantly in 1992) it would appear that a substantial proportion of community-based social work disposals are still replacing other non-custodial sentences (McIvor and Tulle-Winton 1993).

Effective communication with the courts is necessary to maximise the use, in appropriate cases, of community-based social work disposals. An important medium is the social enquiry report, although prior to the introduction of national standards there were, apparently, wide variations across different areas in the credibility of these reports with the courts (Williams and Creamer 1989). In his interviews with sheriffs, Carnie (1990) likewise encountered criticisms of the quality of some reports which were described by one sheriff as 'frequently mis-spelt, frequently ungrammatical and invariably unrealistic' (p.27). As another sheriff commented, 'some reports I know looking at the signature have got to be good; some I rely on less confidently' (p.27).

The national standards for social enquiry reports require greater attention to be paid to information relevant to offending, to the disposal and to drawing conclusions based on the information presented which will require the social worker to review the likely impact of sentencing options open to the court. In proposing the imposition of a probation order the report author must outline what probation is intended to achieve, set out the main components of the action plan and indicate whether and why any additional requirements are considered necessary.

The re-organisation of social work services at the local level, which has come about as a consequence of the new financial arrangements, may also provide for more effective liaison with sentencers on both a formal and less formal basis. To facilitate strategic planning and resource allocation most social work departments (especially the larger authorities containing more densely populated urban areas) have re-organised their delivery of services to offenders along specialist lines, through the creation of designated teams or individuals devoted entirely or primarily to this area of work.

Whilst management structures differ across authorities each of the mainland departments have appointed staff to at least principal officer level with specific responsibilities for the management of criminal justice services. Nonetheless, services to offenders and their families remain firmly rooted within generic departments ensuring that they are, in the meantime at least, underpinned by shared social work principles and values.

The new funding arrangements have been accompanied by a framework of accountability which is evidenced, in particular, through the development of national core data systems and a programme of desktop and field inspections by the Social Work Services Inspectorate (SWSI), which replaced the Scottish Office social work advisory service in 1992. A national inspection which focused upon the arrangements being made by authorities to implement national standards concluded (SWSI 1993a) that:

'Overall, authorities have made rapid and commendable progress in the implementation of national standards for social work services in the criminal justice system. Authorities have improved their capacity to plan, re-organised their arrangements for delivering and managing services and established programmes and procedures for increasing the knowledge and competence of staff and for monitoring the quality of services.' (p.6)

Prison social work units had similarly been the subject of inspection earlier in 1992 (SWSI 1993b). Prison-based social work services have, since their introduction in 1973, been funded in full by the Scottish Prison Service which, in 1993, assumed agency status. As Williams indicates in a later chapter of this book, the priorities for prison social work were set out in 1989 by the Prison Service and the Social Work Services Group in a document entitled 'Continuity Through Co-operation'. Community-based through-care services were, however, brought under 100 per cent funding in April 1991 and national standards for these services (including voluntary assistance in the 12 months following release from a custodial sentence) were introduced. Field social workers are identified as having a role at three distinct stages: at court; during the currency of the sentence; and on release. Whilst it is envisaged that most direct work with prisoners will be undertaken by prison-based social workers, with field social workers normally undertaking long-term work with prisoners' families, 'this balance will shift in the final stages of the sentence, towards an increased level of contact between workers in the community and those prisoners who will be in receipt of statutory supervision or voluntary assistance on release' (SWSG 1991a, para. 5.10).

Community-based social workers will also be responsible for the supervision of prisoners subject to supervised release orders, a provision introduced by the Prisoners and Criminal Proceedings (Scotland) Act 1993 which enables the courts to impose a discretionary period of post-release supervision upon offenders sentenced to between one and four years who, under the new arrangements for discretionary release, would not be eligible for parole.

Other developments in social work with offenders

The introduction of national standards and full central government funding is, without doubt, the most significant development in social work services to offenders in recent years. There have also, however, been other important developments, albeit on a smaller scale, some of which have been brought under the umbrella of 100 per cent funding. A unifying theme of these initiatives has been their objective of diverting offenders at various points in the criminal justice process.

Social work diversion

The 1980s witnessed the introduction and growth in number of schemes aimed at diverting minor offenders from prosecution through the provision of appropriate social work services (Stedward and Millar 1989). Social work diversion schemes, which rely upon close co-operation between the social work department and the procurator fiscal, typically operate upon a model of waived prosecution in which the fiscal ceases, unless another offence is committed, to have involvement in the case once it has been accepted for diversion. Some schemes, however, have adopted a model of deferred prosecution whereby the fiscal reserves the right to proceed to prosecution subject to the outcome of social work intervention.

When diverting cases to the social work department the fiscal's primary concern is with the needs of the accused. As the evaluation of the first scheme which was introduced in 1982 in Ayr revealed, 'the major criterion for an accused person's inclusion in the scheme is...that "the person needs help and can get that without the necessity of a prosecution"' (Moody 1983, p.9). A subsequent study of the 12 diversion schemes which had been developed over the following years concluded likewise that 'diversion is viewed by procurators fiscal as an essentially humanitarian disposal... Fiscals were in agreement that diversion offered an appropriate disposal for "social problem-type cases"; a general term used to cover multifarious factors and circumstances of both the accused and the offence' (Stedward and Millar 1989).

Most cases identified initially by the procurator fiscal are then assessed by social workers to establish their suitability for social work assistance. In the schemes studied by Stedward and Millar (1989) 'a recognition of problems, coupled with a willingness on the part of the accused to co-operate with social work' (p.26) were the criteria most often identified by social workers as pointing to the appropriateness of diversion.

Social work diversion has tended to be used to deal with a wide range of predominantly minor victimless crimes and women and older people have tended to be over-represented in schemes in comparison with cases prosecuted. The duration of intervention varies from case to case and can range from one-off visits to contact lasting more than a year. Moody's (1983) study of the Ayr scheme indicated that marital difficulties, poor family relationships, depression and alcohol abuse were the factors most often identified as having precipitated the offence and serving as the primary focus of intervention. Social workers in Stedward and Millar's (1989) study viewed diversion work as essentially similar in character and in terms of the methods of intervention used to social work more generally.

The further expansion of social work diversion schemes has been constrained to a certain extent by the absence of full central government finance. It is likely, however, that diversion will be brought within the 100 per cent funding mechanism and that the number of schemes in existence will increase over the next few years.

Reparation and mediation

Funding difficulties were responsible for the demise of one of the two experimental pre-prosecution reparation and mediation schemes which were introduced by SACRO – a national voluntary organisation providing a range of services to offenders and their families through a network of regional schemes – in Glasgow and Edinburgh in the late 1980s. Operating on a model of deferred prosecution, mediators facilitated, in most instances through a process of 'shuttle negotiation', the reaching of agreements between victims and accused in cases assessed as suitable for reparation and mediation. The agreements involved direct financial compensation to the victim; the accused making an undertaking to 'behave'; the accused making a donation to charity; the accused making direct reparation to the victim (repairing damage); or the victim receiving an apology from the accused.

An independent evaluation of the schemes found that the majority of agreements reached between the parties were successfully completed. Moreover victims, accused, fiscals and mediators expressed considerable support for the use of reparation and mediation as a diversion from prosecution for minor offences (Warner 1992).

The scheme in Glasgow ceased to operate in 1991. Although a third pre-prosecution scheme has now been introduced by SACRO in Aberdeen, the potential for reparation and mediation in Scotland, whether prior to prosecution or at other points in the criminal justice process, has remained largely unexploited.

Bail information

Bail information schemes became firmly established throughout England and Wales during the 1980s (Cavadino and Gibson 1993, Williams 1993) and were introduced on an experimental basis in Scotland in 1991 (Warner 1993). As Mair indicates in Chapter 2 of this volume the primary objective of such schemes is to encourage, through the provision of verified factual information, the granting of bail to accused persons who would otherwise have been remanded in custody.

The Scottish bail services experiment was funded by the Scottish Office and introduced in two of the largest sheriff courts (Glasgow and Edinburgh). In addition to providing verified information the schemes also aimed to obtain accommodation for accused persons who were of no fixed abode or whose address was likely to be considered unsuitable (for instance men accused of domestic violence whom the courts would be unwilling to bail to their home address). The two schemes were established through partnerships between the relevant social work departments and SACRO. Whilst they operated under somewhat different arrangements, verifying the availability of a suitable address predominated in both schemes with public sector agencies (such as social work departments) most often serving as the source of verification (Warner 1993).

The Scottish schemes differed in one significant respect from similar schemes south of the border: instead of providing information to the prosecution in cases in which the police had indicated their opposition to the granting of bail, they concentrated upon cases in which bail was being opposed by the procurator fiscal and aimed instead to inform the bail decision made by the courts.

The experimental schemes were subjected to a detailed evaluation (Warner and McIvor 1994) which indicated, as have studies conducted in England and Wales (e.g. Godson and Mitchell 1991, Lloyd 1992, Stone 1988), that the availability of positive verified information had served, in a significant proportion of cases, to divert the accused from a custodial remand. More specifically, it was estimated that in around a fifth to a quarter of cases in which bail information reports were submitted, bail was granted to accused persons who would otherwise have faced a remand in custody (McIvor 1993).

In view of the encouraging results from the experiment and the finding that the costs of the schemes had been virtually offset by savings elsewhere in the criminal justice system (Netten 1993) bail information (and supervision) were brought within the 100 per funding mechanism with effect from April 1993. It is likely, therefore, that the number of such schemes in Scotland will increase over the next few years.

Supervised attendance orders

In his address to the Howard League (Scotland) in November 1993, the Minister for Social Work in the Scottish Office, Lord Fraser of Carmyllie, commenting on the fact that 5217 fine defaulters were received into custody in the first six months of that year, asserted that this was a waste of prison service resources and 'a policy objective must be to reduce receptions as close to zero as possible' (1993). Three years previously provision for the introduction of a unit fine system which would, arguably, have served to minimise default through inability as opposed to unwillingness to pay, had been included in a Law Reform Bill but failed to gain legislative expression in the subsequent Act. Another provision aimed at reducing the use of custody for those who defaulted on the payment of their fines did, however, survive the passage of the legislation through parliament.

The supervised attendance order, which can be imposed as an alternative to imprisonment for fine default, is a development unique to Scotland. Experimental schemes to administer and operate the new orders were introduced, under funding from the Scottish Office, in three regional authorities in 1992. One scheme – in Tayside – involves a partnership arrangement between the social work department and APEX (Scotland), a voluntary organisation which aims to increase the employability of offenders.

The supervised attendance order consists of between 10 and 60 hours of attendance supervised by the social work department, the aim of which is to 'provide constructive activity which is likely to include sessions on life skills as well as unpaid work, carried out wherever possible on a group basis' (SWSG 1991b, para. 6.3). Such orders are not intended to be 'geared to tackling offending behaviour' but constitute instead, like community service, a 'fine on the offender's free time' (SWSG 1991b, para 6.3).

In his Howard League address (Lord Fraser of Carmyllie 1993) the Minister for Social work expressed cautious optimism that supervised attendance orders would prove to be a useful option in tackling imprisonment for fine default. In Tayside, for example, the average monthly number of defaulters received into Perth prison had more than halved following the introduction of the scheme. The introduction of new schemes in three other local authorities was planned with further expansion possible subject to the outcome of an evaluation of the experimental schemes.

Intensive probation programmes

A variety of intensive groupwork programmes which operate as a requirement of probation have been introduced across Scotland in the last few years (see, for example, Creamer, Hartley and Williams (1992) for a discussion of the establishment of four such schemes). The voluntary sector, in the form of agencies such as SACRO, National Children's Homes (NCH) and Save the Children, have become increasingly active in providing programmes of this kind.

Intensive probation programmes are generally aimed at young male offenders (usually those between 16 and 25 years of age) who are assessed as being at risk of attracting a custodial sentence. Focusing to a large extent, although not exclusively, on offending behaviour, they tend to be characterised by their eclecticism, but draw to a significant degree on the work of McGuire and Priestley (1985) and, increasingly, on the cognitive–behavioural methods developed by Ross and his colleagues in Canada (Ross and Fabiano 1985, Ross, Fabiano and Ross 1986). Most intensive programmes are run with closed groups on a block basis although the alternative of modular programmes is now beginning to attract some interest.

More specialised programmes which focus upon specific types of offending behaviour – or the issues associated with it – have also emerged in recent years both in prisons (where they are often run with disciplinary and/or other staff) and in the community. These include sex offender treatment programmes, anger management programmes, programmes directed at the perpetrators of domestic violence (e.g. Morran and Wilson 1994), alcohol education programmes (e.g. Sinclair 1993) and, latterly, car crime projects.

Further impetus to the development of innovative projects was provided by the Social Work Services Inspectorate of the Scottish Office in 1993 through a two-day seminar which brought together small teams of practitioners and middle and senior managers from every local authority in Scotland, in some instances in partnership with voluntary agencies, to develop new programmes for offenders which addressed salient local issues or to give new direction to existing projects. This initiative resulted in the creation of 19 new projects covering a wide range of issues (including alcohol-related offending, sexual offending and violence) many of which had, by the time a follow-up seminar was convened 10 months later, become fully integrated into mainstream service provision.

Conclusion

Towards the future

The introduction of full central government funding and national standards has focused the energies of social work departments upon the provision of services to the criminal justice system which are subsumed under this new funding arrangement. Local authorities have been reluctant to contribute towards the funding of services to offenders which are not yet subject to 100 per cent funding, and the Scottish Office has been reluctant to bring some of these services into the 100 per cent funding mechanism. This is true, for example, of social work services in the context of a deferred sentence (which offers a means of providing assistance to offenders without the formality of a probation order) and of services to certain 16- and 17-year-old offenders who, if the necessary resources were available within the children's hearing system, could be dealt with more appropriately there than in the adult criminal justice system.

This said, social work services to young and adult offenders have certainly flourished in Scotland in the last few years. It is likely, too, that as social workers become more familiar with operating within the framework provided by national standards, the scope for increasingly imaginative practice will grow. It is to be hoped that this potential will not be wholly overshadowed and stifled by the reorganisation of local authorities in Scotland which is planned to take place in 1996. It is clear, however, that the smaller authorities which are envisaged will be unable to provide the full range of services currently available for offenders and their families. A more probable arrangement is that each authority will deliver certain core services, such as court reports and probation supervision, while entering into contractual agreements with other local authorities and voluntary agencies for the provision of more specialised services and training.

This scenario will be a not unfamiliar one for some of the smaller existing authorities, especially those covering predominantly rural areas, which have found out, through experience, the difficulty of extending the range of services that can be made available. Part of the problem lies in identifying a sufficient number of appropriate referrals to ensure that a particular initiative is viable and can be sustained. The attendant risk is of widening the net and 'up-tariffing' offenders in an attempt to achieve the numbers required. The alternative is to develop more flexible packages and methods of work (such as modular programmes which can be delivered on a group or individual basis) and to subject them to systematic evaluation to enhance the effectiveness of services and to maximise their potential to meet individual offenders' needs.

References

Carnie, J. (1990) *Sentencers' Perceptions of Community Service by Offenders.* Edinburgh: Scottish Office Central Research Unit.

Cavadino, P. and Gibson, B. (1993) *Bail: The Law, Best Practice and the Debate.* Winchester: Waterside Press.

Creamer, A., Hartley, L. and Williams, B. (1992) *The Probation Alternative: Case Studies in the Establishment of Alternative to Custody Schemes in Scotland.* Edinburgh: Scottish Office Central Research Unit.

Creamer, A., Ennis, E. and Williams, B. (1993) *The Dunscore: A Method for Predicting Risk of Custody within the Scottish Context and its Use in Social Enquiry Practice.* Dundee: University of Dundee, Department of Social Work.

Godson, D. and Mitchell, C. (1991) *Bail Information Schemes in English Magistrates' Courts.* London: Inner London Probation Service.

Lloyd, C. (1992) *Bail information schemes: practice and effect. Home Office Research and Planning Unit Paper 69.* London: HMSO.

Lord Fraser of Carmyllie (1993) *Young Offenders and the White Paper 'Scotland's Children'.* Kenneth Younger Memorial Lecture to the Howard League (Scotland), Edinburgh, November 1993.

Lothian, A. (1991) 'A prescription for the sick man of the system.' *The Glasgow Herald,* 9 January.

McGuire, J. and Priestley, P. (1985) *Offending Behaviour: Skills and Stratagems for Going Straight.* London: Batsford.

McIvor, G. (1990) 'Community service and custody in Scotland.' *The Howard Journal* 29, 101–113.

McIvor, G. (1993) *The Impact of Bail Services in Scotland.* Paper presented at the British Criminology Conference, Cardiff, July 1993.

McIvor, G. and Roberts, C.H. (1991) *Towards Effective Practice: Supplement to the National Objectives and Standards for Social Work Services in the Criminal Justice System.* Edinburgh: The Scottish Office.

McIvor, G. and Tulle-Winton, E. (1993) *The Use of Community Service by Scottish Courts.* Stirling: University of Stirling, Social Work Research Centre.

Moody, S. (1983) *Diversion from the Criminal Justice Process: Report on the Diversion Scheme at Ayr.* Edinburgh: Scottish Office Central Research Unit.

Morran, D. and Wilson, M. (1994) 'Confronting domestic violence: an innovative criminal justice response in Scotland.' In A. Duff, S. Marshall,

R.E. Dobash and R.P. Dobash (eds) *Penal Theory and Penal Practice: Tradition and Innovation in Criminal Justice*. Manchester: Manchester University Press.

Netten, A. (1993) *Bail Information and Accommodation: An Economic Perspective*. Paper presented at the British Criminology Conference, Cardiff, July 1993.

Rifkind, M. (1989) 'Penal policy: the way ahead.' *The Howard Journal 28*, 81–90.

Ross, R.R. and Fabiano, E.A. (1985) *Time to Think: A Cognitive Model of Delinquency Prevention and Rehabilitation*. Ottowa: Institute of Social Sciences and Arts.

Ross, R.R., Fabiano, E.A. and Ross, R.D. (1986) *Reasoning and Rehabilitation: A Handbook for Teaching Cognitive Skills*. Ottawa: Cognitive Centre.

Sinclair, J. (1993) *An Evaluative Study of SACRO's Alcohol Project for Probationers: Interim Progress Report* (unpublished). Edinburgh: SACRO.

Social Work Services Group (1989) *National Objectives and Standards for the Operation of Community Service by Offenders Schemes in Scotland*. Edinburgh: The Scottish Office.

Social Work Services Group (1991a) *National Objectives and Standards for Social Work Services in the Criminal Justice System*. Edinburgh: The Scottish Office.

Social Work Services Group (1991b) *Social Work Services in the Criminal Justice System: Summary of Objectives and Standards*. Edinburgh: The Scottish Office.

Social Work Services Inspectorate (1993a) *Social Work Services in the Criminal Justice System: Achieving National Standards*. Edinburgh: The Scottish Office.

Social Work Services Inspectorate (1993b) *National Inspection of Prison-based Social Work Units*. Edinburgh: The Scottish Office.

Stedward, G. and Millar, A. (1989) *Diversion from Prosecution Volume One: Diversion to Social Work*. Edinburgh: Scottish Office Central Research Unit.

Stone, C. (1988) *Bail Information for the Crown Prosecution Service*. London: Vera Institute of Justice/ACOP.

Warner, S. (1992) *Making Amends: Justice for Victims and Offenders*. Aldershot: Avebury.

Warner, S. (1993) *The Organisation and Effectiveness of Bail Services in Scotland*. Paper presented at the British Criminology Conference, Cardiff, July 1993.

Warner, S. and McIvor, G. (1994) *Pre-trial Bail Services in Scotland: An Evaluation of Two Experimental Bail Information and Accommodation Schemes*. Edinburgh: Scottish Office Central Research Unit.

Williams, B. (1993) *Bail Information Schemes in Prisons*. Paper presented at the British Criminology Conference, Cardiff, July 1993.

Williams, B. and Creamer, A. (1989) *Social Enquiry Within a Changing Sentencing Context*. Edinburgh: Scottish Office Central Research Unit.

Chapter 4

Probation in Northern Ireland

Breidge Gadd

The provision of a probation service in Northern Ireland prior to and immediately after World War I followed steps broadly similar to the rest of the British Isles, albeit on a scale proportional to the size, rural nature and crime rate in the country at that time. Although no formal history of the service has been produced, written and verbal evidence suggests that local magistrates' courts employed religiously-minded, committed altruists who worked with suitable young criminals – usually those with a drink problem who also showed remorse – in helping those people to become sober citizens, to espouse Christian beliefs, to stay out of trouble and to find a job. This situation, locally based at petty sessions level, began to change in the mid-1950s when the first probation officer was appointed by the then Ministry of Home Affairs. The following 15 years saw a slow development of the service with staff employed as civil servants as part of the Ministry of Home Affairs but deployed and operating within a specialist department which was geographically spread throughout Northern Ireland. Most staff were grouped in Belfast where most crime was committed. In the recruitment of staff less emphasis was placed upon an academic qualification than on finding suitably mature persons whose life experiences gave them the necessary values, wisdom, commitment and skills to help criminals reform. In the late 1960s, an increase in crime coupled with slight overcrowding in the one male prison in Belfast led the Civil Service to address its attention to the future development of the probation service.

A policy decision was taken to recruit in the future, where possible, either fully qualified social workers or trainees – both graduate and non-graduate – who would be seconded on a reduced salary to professional training. This decision was no doubt influenced by developments in England and Wales (Seebohm Report 1968) and in Scotland (Kilbranden 1964). Eventually in 1975 the Government appointed its own Northern Ireland Committee charged with making recommendations on future legislation for children and young persons and on making recommendations regarding the future administration of the Probation Service. The report of the Children and Young Persons Review Group was published in 1979 and subsequently became known as the Black Report (1979). Most of the recommendations concerning future legislation have not yet become law although many relating to children have already been inculcated into good practice by social workers, probation officers and youth workers. Almost 20 years on these recommendations stand the test of time and have influenced probation practice with adults as well as with children. Contrary to the trend at that time in the rest of the UK, the Government accepted the recommendations of the Black report that juvenile offenders should continue to remain the responsibility of the probation service and that the principle of just deserts and proportionality should inform the sentencing process. The report did not suggest that young people's welfare needs should be ignored but rather that they should be identified at an early stage and dealt with outside the judicial, criminal process by school based multi-disciplinary teams trained to provide qualitative support services in the community, geared to supporting the family unit.

Recommendations specifically concerning the future of the Probation Service were accepted and implemented in legislation in 1982 – The Probation Board (Northern Ireland) Order 1982 – and in that year the first Probation Board for Northern Ireland came into operation. Its key features were:

(1) The Board was given a clear mandate, defined in legislation, to determine the policy and monitor the effectiveness of the probation service.

(2) The Board would consist of not more than 18 persons drawn from a cross-section of the community with background skills relevant to a probation service. Sentencers, apart from juvenile court lay magistrates, were not to be appointed to the Board.

(3) Board members, Chair and Deputy Chair were to be appointed by the Secretary of State and the Chair paid a remuneration.

(4) The Chief Probation Officer was to be the Accounting Officer.

(5) The Board was given the power to fund individuals or groups providing a service for the Board – either in the supervision of the offender or the prevention of crime.

(6) 100 per cent funding was provided from the Northern Ireland Office.

(7) One province wide service was created.

(8) Civil work (i.e. matrimonial court or divorce court welfare) was excluded.

Thus in 1982 the scene was set for the development of a probation service anchored firmly within the criminal justice system but with the authority for the running of the service clearly in the hands of the community with the 100 per cent central funding giving Government the financial power to influence policy and to control if necessary. A further key element in the legislative mandate was the ability to purchase services from organisations or individuals to enable the supervision of the offender or to fund more broadly-based crime prevention schemes provided by individuals, voluntary organisations or community groups.

The development of a community-based Board for probation was clearly the right way forward for the particular circumstances in Northern Ireland but it also held attractions as a model for other public services. Indeed the current proposals in England and Wales for the future administration of probation services suggest a very similar structure to that of the Northern Ireland Board.

There is no doubt that the civil conflict in Northern Ireland during the past 25 years has influenced the nature of the current probation service – both in terms of what it does and how it approaches the task. In addition, its distinct legislative basis has always created differences between the service in Northern Ireland and the rest of the UK. Mention has already been made of juvenile offenders for whom the Probation Service still retains responsibility. Furthermore in the area of civil work responsibility for a social work service to courts and the clients in matrimonial work was transferred from probation to Health and Social Service Boards by mutual agreement in the late 1970s after the Matrimonial Causes (N. Ireland) Order 1978 and the Domestic Proceedings N.I. Order 1980 were introduced. As a consequence the Probation Board of Northern Ireland (PBNI) has no role in the Divorce Court welfare.

The Probation Service in Northern Ireland also differed from that of the rest of the UK in that it had never supervised released parolees. A low crime rate prior to 1970 meant there was no great need for either a Parole

Board or release from prison on parole. Some young offenders and those serving three or more years imprisonment were subject to supervised after-care licences.

However, rapid development of the civil unrest in the 1970s, resulting in prison sentences imposed on paramilitary offenders who considered that their crimes were politically motivated and who refused to be subject to community surveillance, resulted in all statutory supervised after-care, with the exception of non-terrorist murderers, being suspended to be replaced in 1983 by the introduction of 50 per cent unsupervised remission[1] for all sentenced prisoners except those sentenced to life imprisonment. In these latter cases the Life Sentence Review Board[2] recommends release on licence to the Secretary of State with non terrorist 'lifers' receiving the usual supervised licence.

There are other differences in Criminal Justice legislation in Northern Ireland which impact on the work of the Probation Service. The provision for Social Enquiry Reports prior to custody for young offenders introduced in the Treatment of Offender Order (England and Wales) 1983 does not apply, although provision for 'Day Centres' and specified activities as part of a Probation Order was introduced in the Northern Ireland Treatment of Offender 1989 Order. The 1993 Criminal Justice Act England and Wales does not yet, however, apply to Northern Ireland.

In spite of legislative differences in broad terms the work of the Probation Service in the Magistrates, Crown and Appeal Courts in Northern Ireland mirrors that in England and Wales, with the same rapid shift up-tariff to include the supervision of more serious offenders, which has occurred particularly since the legislative introduction of Day Centres in the Northern Ireland Treatment of Offender 1989 Order (similar to the 1983 Treatment of Offenders Order (England and Wales)).

Thus, in summary, the Northern Ireland Probation Board completes social enquiry reports on juveniles pleading or found guilty, on adults appearing in the magistrates court – if remanded for a Social Enquiry

---

1   The 1990 Prevention of Terrorism Order changed the 50 per cent remission rule for sentences for serious terrorist offences to a requirement that two-thirds of sentences are served for such offences. Community supervision on release is still not an option.

2   The Life Sentence Review Board is an internal Civil Service administrative committee plus a forensic psychiatrist and the Chief Probation Officer which makes recommendations to the Secretary of State regarding release of all Life Sentence prisoners.

Report (SER) – and on defendants pleading guilty on a pre-trial basis in the Crown Courts. Offenders receive community service and probation orders, with both offenders and orders similar in most respects to the rest of the UK. However all work with prisoners, released prisoners and their families is provided on a voluntary basis to this category of client. The exception is the non-terrorist released life sentence prisoner who is normally subject to a supervised licence.

Aside from the impact of legislative differences and of the past 25 years of civil conflict – if one can dismiss both so lightly – how is Northern Ireland different and how does the probation service in its methods work differently from the rest of the UK?

First, a very important point to bear in mind is that Northern Ireland has a low crime rate, even including the crime directly related to the civil conflict. Further, there is little evidence that the crime rate is increasing. Northern Ireland Office (NIO) statistics indicate that in 1992 the crime rate per 100,000 inhabitants in Northern Ireland was 4145[3] compared to the England and Wales average of 10,535[4] and as against Northumbria's 14,185 (roughly similar in size to Northern Ireland) (Home Office 1993).

The latest 'attitudes to crime' survey carried out by the Government (Northern Ireland Office 1994) confirms this low crime figure and shows a low level of fear among the population regarding crime, with the usual exceptions of increasing fear of attack felt by women and elderly people. It is worth noting that the detection rate in Northern Ireland for crime has, in spite of the 'troubles', remained higher than the rest of the UK: 34 per cent in 1992 (Northern Ireland Office 1993) as opposed to an England and Wales average of 25 per cent (Home Office 1993). Also, perhaps surprisingly, 74 per cent of the population think that the Royal Ulster Constabulary (RUC) do either a very good or a fairly good job. Although there is a difference in the attitudes of the Catholic and Protestant population it is not substantial: 77 per cent of Protestants thought the police did a very/fairly good job compared to 69 per cent of Catholics (Northern Ireland Office 1994).

---

3   Excludes offences of 'other criminal damage' of the value of £200 and under [a commentary on N.I. Crime Statistics 1992: Northern Ireland Office].
4   Excludes offences of 'other criminal damage' of value £20 and under [Criminal Statistics England and Wales 1992: Home Office].

When we come to look at the prison population, the figures are not quite so low, with Northern Ireland near the top in rates of imprisonment. Recent figures from the Council of Europe (1992) indicated a detention rate of 110 per 100,000 inhabitants for Northern Ireland, which thus finishes joint top with Hungary. The Netherlands figure, one of the lowest, is 44, with Scotland at 92, England and Wales at 90, and the Republic of Ireland at 63. Northern Ireland's figures reflect the comparatively large number of people imprisoned for terrorist related offences: approximately 400 prisoners are serving a life sentence out of a total sentenced population of 1600.

Concentrating on offences committed and excepting terrorist-related offences the similarities between Northern Ireland and the rest of the UK are greater than the differences. Theft and burglary now account for 74 per cent of all crime in Northern Ireland and for 78 per cent of all crime in England and Wales. Both regions continue to show an increase in offences against the person – these now account for 7 per cent of all crime in Northern Ireland and for 4 per cent of all crime in England and Wales. The broader category of violent crime, including offences against the person, sexual offences and robbery now account for 10 per cent of all crime in Northern Ireland compared to 5 per cent of all crime in England and Wales (Home Office 1993, Northern Ireland Office 1993). This should not be taken to mean that violent crime is more prevalent in Northern Ireland – just that it makes up more of a much smaller crime picture. In fact rates of violent crime are lower in Northern Ireland than in England and Wales, a finding backed up by victimisation surveys which find that Northern Ireland has lower rates of victimisation than most other countries (Van Dijk and Mayhew 1993). Finally, car theft, often associated in popular conception with joyriding, is in fact less prevalent in Northern Ireland than it is in England and Wales at 11.5 thefts per 1000 population in England and Wales, compared to 5.9 per 1000 in Northern Ireland (Home Office 1993, Northern Ireland Office 1993).

Sentencing patterns also are more similar than different, with a higher use of suspended sentences by the Magistrate Courts in Northern Ireland and a slightly smaller use of community supervision orders. There is some evidence that Crown and Appeal Courts in Northern Ireland make more use of community supervision orders for non-terrorist offences than their counterparts in England and Wales.

Many reasons have been presented for Northern Ireland's low crime rate. One hypothesis presented is that the existence of paramilitary community organisations who severely punish anti-social behaviour makes people afraid to commit crime. Yet most crime is committed in the areas where the paramilitary organisation is strongest. Perhaps, then, ordinary criminals in Northern Ireland find their 'outlet' for crime through terrorist-type offences? There is little evidence to validate this explanation either. The vast majority of the republican prisoners did not have criminal records before sentence and while the loyalist prisoners have a higher percentage of previous offences, it is still relatively low. The notion that paramilitary crime has 'soaked up' all criminal tendencies is unconvincing.

Although little has been done to research empirically Northern Ireland's interesting blip in the inexorable rise in crime reported in all Western European countries, one's sense is that the low crime rate has its origins in the essentially rural nature of the province, the lack of serious urbanisation, the continual existence of tightly linked communities characterised by strong traditional values, church-going people and strong extended family links and a very small 'hard' drug problem. Thus most young people live at home where parental influence is strong, moral values strict and where, compared to some parts of the UK, homelessness and drug abuse are at a minimum. This somewhat idyllic picture would be a convincing model for all beleaguered Home Secretaries were it not for Northern Ireland's capacity for killing, either through terrorism or, indeed, on the roads. Northern Ireland has among the highest rate of road deaths per 100,000 of population in the UK. RUC statistics show that there were 8.9 road deaths per 100,000 inhabitants in 1993 – a rate which exceeds that of most counties in England and Wales.

Within this framework, then, how does the Northern Ireland Probation Service work? Visitors to the service, both with and without a probation background, invariably remark on three key factors:

(1) the close working links between probation officers and their local communities;

(2) the wide range and diverse nature of community supervision programmes;

(3) the singular sense of policy and purpose with a 'customer' orientation in the delivery of services.

It is not suggested that these characteristics are unique in any way to Northern Ireland or to probation services. However within the Northern Ireland context the salience of these factors is fairly easy to explain.

Close working links with the community

One of PBNI's strategic statements asserts that 'PBNI seeks to work in partnership with the community in addressing the causes and dealing with the consequences of crime'. Last year, from a revenue budget of £10 million, almost £2 million was spent in direct grant aid either to voluntary organisations or community groups. This money purchases all PBNI's hostel and workshop provision from the voluntary sector as well as supporting small community groups in local crime prevention schemes where local people, in conjunction with local probation officers, set out to tackle a particular local problem of crime. In West Belfast, for example, local parents, jointly with PBNI, manage a project aimed at reducing joyriding amongst persistent offenders. A staff team comprising two probation officers and six to eight local youth/community workers work at times when joyriding is most severe, often through the night and at weekends to provide exciting alternatives to car theft and dangerous driving. This scheme, which was piloted three years ago, costs £170,000 per annum and is already showing a marked reduction in joyriding among those who have participated in the scheme.

This partnership with the community has developed for several reasons. Moving at the client's pace and within the limits of the client's definition of the problem – a key principle of good social work practice – was considered by probation managers to be likewise essential to good probation practice. In addition Probation Board members, coming from the community, instinctively know that such an approach makes good sense and are enthusiastic about the allocation of money to community based groups. Legislation since 1982 enables such practice. Finally in a country ghettoised by civil conflict, without local government power at council or province level, it becomes of critical importance that a probation service is accepted at local community level. In a situation where whole sections of society question legitimate governmental authority, as has happened in both Catholic and Protestant areas in Northern Ireland over the past 25 years, Statutory bodies, in order to survive, must be clear about their role and purpose, must understand the limits of their own authority and must be able to articulate their *raison d'être* and negotiate their position accordingly. Thus from the start of the conflict probation officers (led by the National Association of Probation Officers of Northern Ireland) initially undertook painful professional soul-searching regarding the probation service's role with the terrorist-related offence and offender. The professional conclusion, not initially popular with government nor with the courts, was that the Probation Service had no statutory role in the supervision or formal assessment of those convicted of politically moti- vated crimes. Instead our area of expertise was located in the supervision of the ordinary criminal. While not espousing a statutory role, the proba- tion service did see itself as being able to offer help on a voluntary basis to anyone appearing before the courts, in prison, on release, or to families of prisoners. This position, originally determined by staff in the early 1970s and readily endorsed by the Board a decade later, enables the staff of PBNI to be viewed throughout Northern Ireland as 'professionally neutral'. As such they are accepted in all areas and are one of the few services within the criminal justice system able to move freely without police protection. Nevertheless there are still some in both republican and loyalist movements who view the probation service as agents of British control – although relatively harmless and useless ones.

The wide range and diverse nature of community supervision programmes
When the Board was first appointed, its chair, a businessman, insisted on a clear aim for the organisation followed quickly by a corporate plan. Such an approach meshed well with senior Probation Staff who in the late 1970s had embarked on an organisational development programme focusing on management by objectives. The aim 'to help prevent reoffending' was adopted, and staff at all levels were encouraged to think, plan and act laterally in providing opportunities to offenders which helped them stop offending. This process commenced at a time when the criminal justice world was beginning to shake itself free from the 'nothing works' scenario which for so many years had been wrongly assumed from Martinson's (1974) research.

Over the past decade PBNI has put in place a range of programmes designed to offer the offender the opportunity to tackle his or her offend- ing behaviour. These vary in intensity from the local community-based schemes run by community groups funded by PBNI, to an intensive residential 19-day programme for juveniles and adults in two separate centres based on a cognitive–behavioural approach. One of the most successful developments has been the introduction of the Duke of Edin- burgh's Award Scheme for offenders. This scheme's unique combination of new skill learning, voluntary effort and outdoor pursuits seems to be particularly relevant to PBNI's client group, and it is refreshing to observe the success of an approach which concentrates on building positive skills whilst minimising the problem areas in an individual's life – unless these problems inhibit progress – when the individual is highly motivated to effect change in him- or herself. In addition, the importance to this group of the achievement of an award – be it bronze, silver or gold – cannot be over-estimated. The development of such a range of opportunities could not possibly have occurred without a commensurate range of staff skills. PBNI, in its purchase of service from the voluntary and community sector, has already established the practice of a mixed skill staff group including youth workers, advice workers, outdoor pursuits experts etc. In addition PBNI employs its own range of highly skilled specialists, such as forensic psychologists, and is currently engaged in the purchase of forensic psychiatric services.

The singular sense of policy and purpose with a customer orientation
The clear legislative siting of Probation firmly within the criminal justice system, the development of an aim 'to help reduce re-offending', and the Board requirement to establish and define core business, to develop business plans and to measure effectiveness, has given PBNI a focus and sense of purpose which, if managed well, enhances morale and enables staff to view change as a positive opportunity. During the past few years our management approach has widened to include a marketing strategy approach, with interesting changes in focus as a result. Defining who our customer is was not an easy process but it did provide clarification about the purpose of activities. For example, using this process for courts enabled us to see the Judge or Magistrate, the defence and the prosecution as customers of the service – not the offender, who in this terminology becomes the consumer. Thus it became important to PBNI to market its range of community-based supervision programmes to courts. This has led to an increase of resources allocated to the production of user-friendly information regarding our 'products' – such as a video and a regularly updated Information Directory which sets out the full range of community supervision programmes available to the court. This is regarded as essential background information for courts and we believe that its introduction has led to increased confidence in our service by courts.

Using this approach also led us to see the prisoner, the released prisoner, and the families of prisoners – none of whom had any statutory requirement to use our services – as customers of the service whose views about the kind of service they wanted were critical to policy development. This in turn has led to interesting developments in this area of work such as a team known as 'Prison Link' which specialises in the development of a service to families of prisoners. This service is characterised by a strong emphasis on self-help groups and a range of practical services such as babysitting, a families newspaper, transport facilities, holidays and away breaks for families, parents, partners etc. All services are provided in partnership with the voluntary organisations, employing where possible released prisoners or prisoners' families in the delivery of service.

Consulting the potential customer has also led to greater emphasis on creating employment opportunities for released prisoners. PBNI has a staff team dedicated to employment issues, and with the voluntary sector manages a job training agency, funded by the Training and Employment Agency which specialises in job training and placement provision for ex-offenders. Indeed, given the clear evidence from research that proper employment is the most effective way of reducing recidivism, it is likely that in future more attention will be given by PBNI to the development of job creation schemes, including the possibility of European Union funding for such ventures.

Developing a Probation Service in this manner in Northern Ireland has presented challenges and difficulties for an organisation whose core background professional training is that of social work. Forming partnerships with those who do not necessarily share the same value base or principles is not easy for any professional group which considers itself uniquely skilled. Sharing power – for that is what partnership is essentially about – does not even come easy to a profession whose key role is declared as empowering people, particularly when the empowered people demand a service defined by their needs – such as weekend provision – rather than when it suits the professionals. We have learned that working with the community means being more accountable to the community, listening and responding in the development of services attuned to community needs. It requires openness and great patience and skill.

With regard to community supervision we have encountered, and still struggle with, many professional difficulties. Probation practice, certainly in Northern Ireland if not in the rest of the UK, has clearly outpaced theory, leaving the academic text books somewhat behind. For example, even recently qualified social workers are poorly trained in using research methods in their work. Such an approach is no longer an add-on extra but a core element in good practice. This applies not only to defining one's own work in such a way as to enable ongoing measurement of what works but also using external research as an essential element before commencing a new piece of work. Maintaining the integrity of a programme – an essential component in evaluating what works – is itself a new experience for probation officers who have been trained to develop an eclectic approach.

While it has become of critical importance for the practitioner to approach his or her work in a manner which enables the measuring of effectiveness, so also is it important that the Agency creates a culture which makes research essential and easy. PBNI has had very limited success in this area. It has only been within the last year that we have gained access to criminal records in order to measure the effectiveness of community programmes compared to prison sentences and other disposals. Providing staff with useable research data and up-to-date library facilities has only recently become a top priority in the allocation of resources.

Allocating offenders to programmes on the basis of seriousness of offence, with a consequent deprivation of liberty, whilst demanded by government and courts and whilst logical and reasonable in theory, is very difficult to put into practice. The most highly-motivated offender is not necessarily the most serious or persistent, and very often the most serious offender is the one who performs the legal minimum requirements of the order. Instilling motivation and maintaining it, as any probation worker will testify, is a complex and at times potentially soul-destroying task. PBNI is currently grappling with the development of a paradigm which grades programmes on the basis of factors such as intensity and duration and then matches offender and seriousness of offence to programme. This approach, difficult because of the complexities of offender motivation as outlined above, is also difficult because of the individualised nature of court sentencing practices. It does however make sense to us, particularly using a just desert model, that the most intrusive and most expensive supervision programmes are reserved for the most serious offenders.

All of the above is a long way from the original notion of 'advise, assist and befriend' where the probation order was made instead of a sentence (still in fact the legal position in Northern Ireland). However the nature of the client group has changed significantly and probation services throughout the United Kingdom are working with more serious and more potentially dangerous offenders than ever before. Indeed not only is the client group more difficult, but the expectation of society and government that one of the key responsibilities for a Probation Service is to protect the public (Home Office 1990) is a cause for concern, having gradually become a key function of probation services without the consideration and debate necessary to define exactly what is meant by this requirement. This notion that a Probation Service can be the guardian of public safety raises dangerous expectations in itself, particularly when one bears in mind the unforgiving media attention which can be brought to bear on any public body which is viewed to have made a mistake.

This concern has led us in Northern Ireland to realise that more attention urgently needs to be given to:

(1) defining what we mean by the dangerous offender (not the same as serious at all);

(2) developing objective user-friendly assessment models;

(3) training staff to use them and;

(4) developing service policies regarding what type of offender probation services can effectively supervise in the community and – just as important – who they *can not*.

Such work requires a multi-disciplinary approach and endorses the essential nature of underpinning ongoing research. In addition, the issue of identifying those we cannot work with is an issue for public and positive debate which should be encouraged, if not led, by Government.

Conclusion

Looking to the future and what it holds for the Probation Board of Northern Ireland

Although Northern Ireland has a different crime profile and perhaps different crime problems from the rest of the UK, the main challenges facing the Probation Board for Northern Ireland are very similar to those facing Probation Services in Britain and in the rest of Europe. The worldwide recession and the consequent hardening of attitudes in society towards the offender, the growth in intolerance, the growth in the demand for revenge and the lessening of compassion as a popular virtue have made the job of the probation officer harder. Public attitudes, as portrayed through the media, identify a public determined on punishing those who appear to offend against it, even if this is both expensive and at the expense of rehabilitation. Within this hostile climate probation services in future will need to devote more attention and resources to public relations and to the development of communication strategies which inform the public and also engage the commitment of the public to the work to which the Probation Service aspires.

The Probation Board undertook extensive consultations with a range of relevant statutory bodies, community groups and individuals (including prisoners) before publishing its latest Corporate Plan. We see the publication of business plans and annual reports as a key feature in accountability – not only to the government but also to the community.

This process of explaining and negotiating role and function will be a key feature in the future for the effectiveness of the service in Northern Ireland. So too will be a willingness to change and a staff team which is flexible in its work patterns and committed to developing programmes of supervision which research shows are effective in reducing recidivism. Such work will undoubtedly be delivered by a multi-skilled staff team providing services seven days per week with the probation officer continuing to be the interface with the court, and the assessor of individuals and their needs, but becoming the co-ordinator, 'purchaser' and manager of provision rather than the sole deliverer of services.

We will also have to take some difficult decisions about those offenders whom we cannot supervise effectively in the community – not so that they can be denied help but so that the courts, the Government and the community is enabled to make an honest appraisal of risk and so that the Probation Service can be judged fairly on its effectiveness in the community.

Such challenges are exciting and raise many questions about the nature and quality of education and training for probation, the nature and quality of management and, ultimately, society's expectations of a Probation Service. Indeed even as this chapter is being written the peace process in Northern Ireland is moving at a swift pace. These changes will pose a whole new set of issues for Probation in Northern Ireland. I hope we are ready to meet that challenge.

References

Black Report (1979) *Report of the Children and Young Persons Review Group, December 1979.* Belfast: HMSO.

Council of Europe (1992) *Prison Information Bulletin No. 16.* Strasbourg: Council of Europe.

Home Office (1990) *Crime, Justice and Protecting the Public.* Cm 965. London: HMSO.

Home Office (1993) *Criminal Statistics England and Wales 1992.* London: HMSO.

Kilbranden Report (1964) *Children and Young Persons (Scotland)*. Edinburgh: HMSO.

Martinson, R. (1974) 'What works: Questions and answers about prison reform.' *The Public Interest 23*, 22–54.

Northern Ireland Office (1993) *Northern Ireland Crime Statistics 1992*. Belfast: Northern Ireland Office.

Northern Ireland Office Policy Planning and Research Unit (1994) *Community Attitudes Survey*. Belfast: Northern Ireland Office.

Seebohm Report (1968) *Report of the Committee on Local Authority and Allied Personal Social Services*. London: HMSO.

Van Dijk, J. and Mayhew, P. (1993) *Criminal Victimisation in the Industrial World: Key Findings of the 1989 and 1992 International Crime Surveys*. The Hague: Ministry of Justice Department of Crime Prevention.

Chapter 5

Gender, Criminal Justice and Probation

Anne Worrall

'Gender appears to be the single most crucial variable associated with criminality.' (Heidensohn 1987, p.22)

Until perhaps five years ago, the use of the word 'gender' in relation to probation practice with offenders would have meant only one thing – work with female offenders. The 1980s was undoubtedly the decade which rendered female offenders visible and witnessed an exponential rise in interest in 'women and crime'. In addition to major publications, numerous modest research studies were carried out by (predominantly female) criminology and social work students, some of which have seen the light of day as publications but many more of which, sadly, have not.

However, with the dramatic decline in the numbers of women placed on probation during the decade (from nearly 12,000 in 1982 to fewer than 8000 in 1992, compared with an increase in men placed on probation from 25,000 in 1982 to 34,000 in 1992) (Home Office 1993a), it has become increasingly difficult to justify a specialised focus on *women*. Consequently, 'gender' has come to refer to a particular approach to *all* offending (and therefore predominantly *male* offending) which highlights the part played in such behaviour by gender socialisation and role expectations. As yet, however, very little research has been undertaken into the significance of the social construction of 'masculinity' for probation practice with male offenders, except in work with sex offenders, which is the subject of another chapter in this volume.

Acknowledging its limited interpretation of the term 'gender', therefore, this chapter aims to provide:

(1) an overview of the development of research directly related to probation practice with women offenders and

(2) a selective review of other research concerned with criminal women, which is nevertheless relevant to probation practice.

The chapter excludes discussion of women as victims of male-perpetrated crime and discussion of women as workers in the probation service, except where this is relevant to working with female offenders.

Probation Service interest in women offenders

In an article bemoaning the declining use of the probation order, Robinson (1978) presented, without comment, figures which demonstrated that, whilst probation orders on men had declined in ten years from 23,000 to 20,000, those on women had increased from 6500 to 9000. The figures were followed by the observation that 'defendants of all *ages* are affected by the *fall* in proportionate use of probation' (1978, p.42, emphasis added). This apparent reluctance to allow facts to get in the way of a good argument reflected the Probation Service's traditional tendency to render its women clients invisible.

The first article on sexual discrimination and the law to appear in the *Probation Journal* suggested that, contrary to popular mythology, women offenders were dealt with more severely than men and that 'when previous record is taken into consideration, females are more likely to be imprisoned than males' (Mawby 1977, p.42). Four years later, a second article on the processing of women offenders through the courts, based on a study of sentencing in a magistrates' court over a period of six months, came to the conclusion that 'women are more likely than men to be processed according to an assessment of their personal circumstances, rather than their offence' (Worrall 1981, p.90). Both articles were criticised for their statistical naiveté (Walker 1981, Farrington and Morris 1983) but the underlying arguments – that different and not wholly rational criteria are applied when sentencing men and women and that probation officers may unwittingly contribute to discriminatory sentencing through social enquiry reports – appeared to strike chords with many practitioners. However, it was a further three years before a third article highlighted the under-utilisation by courts of community service for women (Dominelli 1984) and no further articles on women appeared in the *Probation Journal* until 1989. It would be unfair to argue that three articles in 12 years reflected the overall level of interest in women offenders throughout the

Probation Service but it does indicate a slowness to enter a debate which was becoming increasingly sophisticated within the academic discipline of criminology. (For a summary of research on the differential treatment of males and females in the criminal justice system during this period, see Gelsthorpe 1987). It was not, in fact, until the publication of the Home Office Inspectorate Thematic Report on Probation Service Provision for Female Offenders (HM Inspectorate of Probation 1991) and the (in)famous Section 95 of the Criminal Justice Act 1991 that the Service officially accepted the need to develop particular policies in this area.

Social inquiry reports and women offenders

In the early 1980s, the main concern among those practitioners who were prepared to cast a critical eye over their practice was that too many women were being placed on probation at too early a stage of their criminal careers. Although women offenders represented between 15 and 17 per cent of all known offenders, they accounted for about one third of all probation orders. With increasing awareness of the dangers of net-widening (thanks largely to the insights of writers in the field of juvenile justice) an optimistic view emerged that reducing the numbers of women on probation would result in a reduction in the numbers of women being sent to prison. (This optimism proved quite unjustified, as will be discussed later.) The social inquiry report was identified as a key document in the social construction of female offenders as suitable candidates for supervision. Worrall (1981) and Eaton (1985, 1986) drew attention to the dangers of seeking to locate such women within the ideology of the nuclear family and of portraying (or failing to portray) them as good wives, mothers or daughters. By comparing reports on men and women, and the differential use of home visits by probation officers preparing reports Eaton (1986) also highlighted the significance of differing gender role expectations in reports. Such expectations go beyond a description of a conventional division of labour in the home to the belief that women have a responsibility for the emotional well-being of everyone in the domestic sphere. Even when they themselves are law-abiding, they are expected to take some responsibility for – or at least shed light on – the offending behaviour of male partners. The reverse is rarely the case.

In a statistical comparison of court disposals of male and female defendants, Mair and Brockington (1988) concluded that women tend to be referred for social inquiry reports more readily than men (when offence and previous record are matched) and are more likely to be recommended for (and to receive) probation orders. Mair and Brockington observe that there is some evidence that referral for reports is in itself likely to move a defendant 'up-tariff' and that this should be a matter of concern for a service seeking to target reports on specific groups seen to be at risk of custody.

Deciding when a female offender is 'at risk' of custody, however, has been a vexed issue. Jackson and Smith (1987) found that many women are in prison for an accumulation of minor offences, having been considered unsuitable for community service as a result of domestic responsibilities. Similarly, Dunkley (1992) found a lack of consensus amongst probation officers about the appropriateness of referring women to Day (now Probation) Centres. Consciousness of sentencing discrimination may lead one officer to recommend centre attendance to forestall a custodial sentence, whilst another officer may view such a recommendation as collusion with that same discrimination.

Representing women in social inquiry reports as 'programmable' – as motivated towards and able to benefit from the resources of the Probation Service – requires their construction within the discourses of domesticity, sexuality and pathology (Worrall 1990). It is an exercise fraught with dilemmas:

> 'The trap for probation officers who might want to construct female lawbreakers within alternative discourses is that, in an area where such stereotypes dominate, they run the risk of seriously disadvantaging their client. Hence many officers justify their continued writing of gender-stereotyped reports on the grounds that they are working tactically in their clients' best interest.' (p.116)

Stephen (1993) confirms the view that female offenders are 'muted' (Worrall 1990). Whilst their own accounts of their offending differ little from those given by men (and are predominantly based on external social factors), they are more likely to find their accounts disregarded by probation officers, who apparently still tend to prefer seeing women's crime as the result of 'underlying emotional problems'. Female offenders are still not being listened to.

Very little research exists which is specifically concerned with the portrayal of black women in social inquiry or pre-sentence reports. Denney (1992) suggests that probation officers tend to write assessments of white women offenders which are more detailed and sympathetic than those of black women. There is a tendency to assume that at the root of black women's offending lies a problem of identity resulting from not belonging to the dominant culture. Whilst white women may be portrayed as neurotic and irrational, black women are portrayed as unpredictable and 'suffering from a peculiarly "feminine" form of "silliness"'(Denney 1992, p.109). Chiqwada (1989) argues that racism in social inquiry reports is more overt:

> 'Black women may be seen as over-protective, over-religious or over-punitive, and labelled as "bad" mothers. Expressions of emotion, whether anger or affection, may be misinterpreted. Similarly, value judgements concerning issues such as sexual or family relationships, work status, parental responsibility based on a Eurocentric view of society, are then used to justify prison sentences.' (p.104)

Psychiatry and women offenders

As long ago as 1974, concern was being expressed about the inappropriate treatment of women offenders who appeared to be mentally disordered (Woodside 1974). Probation orders with conditions of psychiatric treatment, it was argued, ought to be a useful method but 'more often than not it doesn't work' (Woodside 1974, p.342). Difficulties of liaison, shortages of staff and competing claims on scarce resources have meant that, over the years, women offenders identified as 'mad' have suffered the worst of both worlds. They have to endure a psychiatric label without the benefit of the treatment implied by its imposition. And if they re-offend, the court will say they have had their chance and abused it – when in fact they have had nothing.

Allen argues that:

> 'female defendants are consistently more likely than males to be referred for psychiatric examination, to be assessed as suitable subjects for psychiatric treatment, and ultimately to be dealt with by psychiatric means.' (1987a, p.2)

There may be two explanations for this. First, women who commit violent crime are 'rendered harmless' through manoeuvres which neutralise their guilt, responsibility and dangerousness, whilst violent men, who may appear more obviously 'mad' and dangerous, are constructed as behaving intentionally and rationally (although wickedly) and therefore as being unsuitable for psychiatric treatment (but 'suitable' for prison) (Allen

1987b). Second, all women offenders are susceptible to a psychiatric gaze which tends to attribute their criminal activity to mild and ill-defined mental disorder which might be amenable to low-key medical intervention.

Worrall (1990) found that, whilst psychiatrists appear very willing to diagnose psychiatric conditions in women offenders, they were far less willing to treat them. When it comes to treatment, they seem to redefine 'sickness' as 'social neediness'. Commonly, psychiatrists see women perhaps every three months and leave the routine work to probation officers who often feel ill-equipped in these circumstances. Although Allen (1987a) has argued that medicalisation may be better than imprisonment, as an adjunct to probation it seems to have little to commend it. This view is endorsed by the recent HM Inspectorate of Probation report (1993) which suggests that (in relation to both male and female offenders) 'there appears little current agreement about the type of patient for whom such orders are appropriate' (p.38) and counsels a cautious approach to any suggestion that their use should be increased.

Individual and groupwork with women offenders

Worrall (1989) found that probation officers recognised the structural and personal oppression experienced by women offenders but they also recognised that the women themselves often colluded with stereotypical descriptions of themselves as good wives and mothers or as emotionally unstable. In addition, many women on probation were felt by officers to be either over-demanding and dependent or evasive and manipulative. Work with women typically consisted of crisis intervention followed by weeks of failing to keep appointments. Groupwork was often an uphill struggle. The playing off of probation officers, social workers and health visitors against each other was a common complaint. Women clients were seen as difficult to manage!

But what of the women themselves? How did they view their situations? Most of them did not see themselves as 'real criminals'. They committed their crimes out of economic necessity or as a response to intolerable emotional stress. Key themes emerged – loneliness, fear (including fear of the power of experts and officials), low self-esteem, bewilderment, anger – frequently suppressed into depression – and a sense of not being listened to, heard or understood. Perhaps frustratingly, they were not radical in their views – they did not want to break out of their traditional roles. But they did want the worst effects of those roles to be alleviated. The help they appeared to appreciate most was friendship, material help and the opportunity to make some real choices for themselves – however trivial these might seem to others.

Perhaps the most striking thing to emerge was that the notion of 'contract' (as in popular use in probation) seemed meaningless to them. They could not, or were not prepared to, organise their lives to suit the experts – however well-intentioned – and if forced to do so, would find all sorts of subtle ways of resisting such control. Although women offenders are subject to a matrix of controlling and oppressive mechanisms, they do not respond totally passively. They do find ways of eluding control and of challenging professionals and, far from being frustrated by this, probation officers should be looking for ways to harness and capitalise on this potential creativity (Worrall 1990).

Eaton (1993) interviewed women ex-prisoners who had somehow managed to turn their lives around. The factors which enabled them to do this may offer insights to probation officers working not only with women ex-prisoners but with all women offenders – and perhaps all offenders. Women offenders will only change their lives if and when they have access to the structural pre-conditions of social justice – housing, employment and health facilities. Without these things they have no chance of reconstituting their own lives and those of their 'families', however they choose to define that term.

But structural factors alone are insufficient. The women Eaton interviewed had all made a conscious decision to re-direct their lives – they wanted things to be different. In Probation jargon, they were motivated to change. But such motivation was not something which just happened. In order to make that decision, they had to feel confident that change was possible. And to feel confident, they had to achieve both self-recognition and recognition by others. They had to feel that they were people of worth who had something to contribute.

The key to recognition was reciprocal relationships. For many women offenders, their only experience of relationships is oppressive and exploitative. Whether in personal or official dealings their expectations have been of hierarchical relationships in which they are told what they should do and how they should behave in order to please other people. Anything which contributes to the breaking down of those expectations and the development of mutuality in relationships will help to motivate women towards change. Probation officers who listen and encourage and avoid judging are more likely to motivate women to re-direct their lives than are those who insist on hierarchy and the strict application of National Standards.

There is a great deal of imaginative work being undertaken by probation officers with women offenders, characterised by democracy and empowerment and focusing on the experiences that unite rather than divide women. Carlen (1990) found that over half of the Probation Service areas which she surveyed were making, or planning to make, separate provision for women offenders. Specific justifications for running women-only groups included:

- concern about the numbers of women going into custody;

- recognition that women who have been victims of child abuse and domestic violence need a space where they can recover their confidence away from men;

- recognition that the material and psychological conditions conducive to women's offending are different from those conducive to men's offending and that routes to the avoidance of re-offending will therefore also be different;

- promotion of solidarity among isolated women.

Buchanan, Collet and McMillan (1991) in Merseyside found that women viewed the Day Training Centre as a 'haven where they are regarded as individuals of worth and potential' (p.60). In contrast to the drab exploitation of their daily existences, the Centre provided opportunities for personal growth and personal choice (and this despite the authors' uneasiness that the women's offences were insufficiently serious to warrant the recommendation in the first place).

In an attempt to accommodate the reality of the requirements of 'punishment in the community', Jones *et al.* (1991) devised the 'Miskin Model' of groupwork with women offenders, which combines formal activities to address offending behaviour with informal activities designed to empower women and promote personal growth. Such an approach seems to have secured the commitment and enthusiasms of middle management, so crucial to the success of such experimental ventures.

Mistry (1989) describes and evaluates the benefits of a 'feminist model' which enabled women to negotiate with probation officers about the structure and content of groups. She is also the only writer to address the implications of groupwork for black female offenders (half of the women in the group were black) and for black workers. As a black worker herself,

Mistry discusses the challenges of co-working with a white colleague and concludes that:

> 'having a feminist perspective is not enough. As workers we had to be open and responsive to our own history and the needs of the group.' (1989, p.154)

Women and community service

Sentencers have always had ambivalent feelings about ordering women to do community service. Overall, about five per cent of female offenders receive community service orders, compared with nine per cent of male offenders (Home Office 1992). The difference, however, is even more significant in the 17–20-year-old age range, where 14 per cent of men receive orders, compared with six per cent of women. As Hine (1993) points out, the most pertinent question to ask of these figures may not relate to the low level of sentencing women but to the high level of sentencing men. Community service, it could be argued, is permeated with the ideology that it is a 'young man's punishment'.

Hine (1993) also identifies greater inconsistency in the use of community service for women than for men. Using elements of the Cambridgeshire Offender Gravity Rating, Hine found that, whilst two-thirds of the men on community service in her study were convicted of 'mid-range' offences and had 'mid-range' criminal histories, this applied to only half of the women. Hine concludes:

> 'there is less consensus for female offenders on community service, which suggests that factors other than offence and previous criminal history played a greater part in their sentencing than it did for male offenders.' (p.69)

This concern is reflected in Barker's (1993) investigation of the attitudes and experiences of women serving community service orders. For one third of the 48 women she interviewed, this sentence represented their first contact with the criminal justice system. For most of the women interviewed, community service had been an enjoyable and worthwhile experience, despite difficulties in organising child care. Criticism is levelled at probation officers who, in the majority of cases, did not argue well for community service in pre-sentence reports (and this study, it must be remembered, was concerned with women who had received such orders). Barker is optimistic about the future of community service for women, arguing that, as numbers increase following the 1991 Criminal Justice Act, some of the problems identified will resolve themselves. Her study, however, significantly omits interviews with women who are experiencing difficulty in completing orders or who have been subject to breach proceedings. Armstrong (1990) paints a more pessimistic picture of women's completion rates and lays greater emphasis on the sexual harassment some women experience, especially when placed in predominantly male work groups.

Women in prison

Throughout the 1980s research on women's imprisonment highlighted how particularly difficult women find it to 'do time' (Carlen 1983, Mandaraka-Sheppard 1986, Genders and Player 1987, O'Dwyer, Wilson and Carlen 1987, Catan 1992, Woodrow 1992). This tends to be explained in terms of women prisoners' particularly disturbed backgrounds and/or the particularly destructive impact of confinement on women. That women in prison are disproportionately dependent on medication and prone to self-harm is well known. Until recently, however, it was assumed (except by campaigning groups) that women did not actually take their own lives in prison as frequently as men. Liebling's (1994) research on suicide in prison challenges that myth. Female suicide in prison has been masked by misclassification (that is, as 'open', 'misadventure' or 'lack of care' verdicts). Given that the suicide rate in the community is more than twice as high for men as for women, the recent realisation that the female suicide rate in prison is now very similar to that for men must be a cause for concern. Liebling (1994) argues that it may also be inappropriate to assume that responding to suicide risk is the preserve of psychiatry:

> 'Access to social service agencies, legal aid, probation officers or other sources of advice and practical assistance may be a more effective and humane response to distress than referral to a psychiatrist or isolation in a prison hospital.' (p.7)

In women's prisons, probation officers are struggling in a hostile environment to work alongside some equally committed prison officers to help women offenders come to terms with and survive their experiences both inside and outside prison. Individual and groupwork in women's prisons now routinely acknowledges that many women in prison are survivors of sexual abuse. Prison probation officers have also taken the initiative in equipping themselves to undertake assertiveness training with women, which is often the key to helping women negotiate fair and non-oppressive relationships (Worrall 1993).

Sadly, little of this work has been researched or published. One exception is work undertaken at HM Prison Styal with female sexual abusers (Barnett, Corder and Jehu 1989). In an account of a groupwork programme with six such women, the writers conclude tentatively that they found several indications of therapeutic improvement in the women including enhanced understanding of the reasons for their own offending and its adverse effects on their victims, acceptance of responsibility and greater assertiveness in coping with situations likely to lead to offending.

An area in which probation officers have shown little interest is that of offences against prison discipline, which are proportionately about 50 per cent more frequent in women's prisons than in men's prisons (Home Office 1993b). Denton (1992), a senior probation officer in a women's prison, compared policies and practices in three women's prisons. Whilst he found significant differences between the prisons, he was, nevertheless, drawn to the conclusion that 'female misbehaviour is not tolerated to the same degree as men's [and] women's prisons expect higher standards of domestication and femininity from their inmates' (1992, p.37).

There has been virtually no published research specifically concerned with the imprisonment of black women. Hood and Cordovil's (1992) important study of race and sentencing in Crown Courts concludes that, overall, there is no evidence that black women are being sentenced more harshly than either white women or black men. He argues that the over-representation of black women in prison is significantly affected by a relatively small number of drug couriers serving long prison sentences. If these were to be discounted, the proportion of black women in the prison population would be about 13 per cent, not the much publicised 25–30 per cent.

Abernethy and Hammond (1992), however, argue that the Probation Service has a role in working with drug couriers (not all of whom, of course, are black, but about one third of whom are women). They report on a project undertaken by Middlesex Area Probation Service (which is particularly affected because of its proximity to Heathrow Airport). The aim of the project was to test the feasibility of preparing reports to a good standard on people who are not resident in the UK and to identify what services could or should be offered by probation to those people while awaiting trial. They have been encouraged by their ability to produce full and informative reports and to provide help and support for drug couriers through liaison with statutory and voluntary agencies.

Conclusion

Policy implications

It is perhaps ironic that the Probation Service's concern about the treatment of female offenders has increased almost in direct proportion to the declining numbers of women being dealt with by the Service. Nevertheless, it is apparent that successful gatekeeping at one end of what used to be called the 'tariff' has not succeeded in reducing the numbers of women being sent to prison. Consequently, it has to be conceded that the 'minimal intervention' approach of juvenile justice is not directly transferable to work with female offenders. This may simply be because, whilst many juveniles 'grow out of' crime, most women commit crime in response to more deeply-rooted and enduring socio-economic conditions. Less simply, it may be because 'part of the problem is that it is unclear what the "better treatment of women" actually means' (Harris 1992, p.98). Increased gender consciousness is a necessary pre-condition to, but does not guarantee, a reduction in discrimination. As Cohen (1983) argues, one ideology can be used to support quite different policies and one policy can be supported for very different ideological reasons. It is not possible to 'read off' from a critique of current reality a series of reforming solutions.

It does, however, seem reasonable to argue that the top priority for the Probation Service in relation to women offenders is to find ways of keeping more of them out of prison, *even if that means offering alternatives rather earlier in a woman's criminal career than may appear to be ideologically sound.* Nothing can be less sound ideologically than jeopardising a woman's freedom by rigid commitment to a dogma of minimal intervention at all costs. On the other hand, 'setting women up to fail' by placing unrealistic multiple demands on them in the name of 'punishment in the community' also has little to commend it.

Are we perhaps approaching the problem from the wrong angle? Does gender consciousness also mean learning lessons from the positive aspects of women's experiences? Should we perhaps be asking why women's rates of offending, despite various moral panics, remain no more than a fraction of men's? Should we be examining why so many women offenders feel so positively about all-women probation and community service provision? Given the relatively low level of women's offending, can the Probation Service afford to be more adventurous in its arguments in pre-sentence reports, openly using research to demonstrate the damaging effects of imprisonment and the constructive impact of alternatives?

Finally, should there now be a research agenda which investigates the significance of the social construction of masculinity for male offending behaviour (and not just sex offending)? There is evidence that such analyses are beginning to inform probation practice (Cordery and White-head 1992, McCaughey 1992) as are critiques of heterosexism (McCaughey and Buckley 1993) but this writer is unaware of any publish-ed research in either area. Heidensohn has suggested that 'the answer to football hooligans might not be identity cards, barbed wire enclosures or life sentences, but rather the feminisation of socialisation' (1987, p.26). Is it possible that current demands for 'toughness' in sentencing and proba-tion practice are serving to reproduce the masculine 'hardness' which epitomises so much of the offending behaviour the Probation Service is being exhorted to address?

References

Abernethy, R. and Hammond, N. (1992) *Drug Couriers: a Role for the Probation Service*. London: Middlesex Area Probation Service.

Allen, H. (1987a) *Justice Unbalanced: Gender, Psychiatry and Judicial Decisions*. Milton Keynes: Open University Press.

Allen, H. (1987b) 'Rendering them harmless: the professional portrayal of women charged with serious violent crimes.' In P. Carlen and A. Worrall (eds) *Gender, Crime and Justice*. Milton Keynes: Open University Press.

Armstrong, S. (1990) *Alternatives to Custody? Day Centre and Community Service Provision for Women*. Occasional Paper 4, University of Keele Centre for Criminology.

Barker, M. (1993) *Community Service and Women Offenders*. London: Association of Chief Officers of Probation.

Barnett, S., Corder, F. and Jehu, D. (1989) 'Group treatment for women sexual offenders against children.' *Practice 3*, 2, 148–159.

Buchanan, J., Collett, S. and McMullan, P. (1991) 'Challenging practice or challenging women? Female offenders and illicit drug use.' *Probation Journal 38*, 2, 56–62.

Carlen, P. (1983) *Women's Imprisonment*. London: Routledge and Kegan Paul.

Carlen, P. (1990) *Alternatives to Women's Imprisonment*. Buckingham: Open University Press.

Catan, L. (1992) 'Infants with mothers in prison.' In R. Shaw (ed.) *Prisoners' Children: What Are the Issues?* London: Routledge.

Cohen, S. (1983) 'Social control talk: telling stories about correctional change.' In D. Garland and P. Young (eds) *The Power to Punish.* London: Heinemann.

Chiqwada, R. (1989) 'The criminalisation and imprisonment of black women.' *Probation Journal 36*, 3, 100–105.

Cordery, J. and Whitehead, A. (1992) 'Boys don't cry: empathy, warmth, collusion and crime.' In P. Senior and D. Woodhill (eds) *Gender, Crime and Probation Practice.* Sheffield: PAVIC Publications.

Denney, D. (1992) *Racism and Anti-Racism in Probation.* London: Routledge.

Denton, M. (1992) *Reports are Still Coming In: An analysis of offending against discipline in three women's prisons.* Occasional Paper 5, University of Keele Centre for Criminology.

Dominelli, L. (1984) 'Differential justice: domestic labour, community service and female offenders.' *Probation Journal 31*, 3, 100–103.

Dunkley, C. (1992) *Group Work with Women in Probation Day Centres: An Exploration of Contemporary Practice.* University of Manchester: Department of Social Policy and Social Work.

Eaton, M. (1985) 'Documenting the defendant: placing women in social inquiry reports.' In J.Brophy and C. Smart (eds) *Women in Law.* London: Routledge and Kegan Paul.

Eaton, M. (1986) *Justice for Women?* Milton Keynes: Open University Press.

Eaton, M. (1993) *Women After Prison.* Buckingham: Open University Press.

Farrington, D. and Morris, A. (1983) 'Sex, sentencing and reconviction.' *British Journal of Criminology 23*, 3, 229–248.

Gelsthorpe, L. (1987) 'The differential treatment of males and females in the criminal justice system.' In G. Horobin (ed) *Sex, Gender and Care Work.* Research Highlights in Social Work 15. London: Jessica Kingsley Publishers.

Genders, E. and Player, E. (1987) 'Women in prison: the treatment, the control and the experience.' In P. Carlen and A. Worrall (eds) *Gender, Crime and Justice.* Milton Keynes: Open University Press.

Harris, R. (1992) *Crime, Criminal Justice and the Probation Service.* London: Routledge.

Heidensohn, F. (1987) 'Women and crime: questions for criminology.' In P. Carlen and A. Worrall (eds) *Gender, Crime and Justice.* Milton Keynes: Open University Press.

H.M. Inspectorate of Probation (1991) *Report on Women Offenders and Probation Service Provision.* London: Home Office.

H.M. Inspectorate of Probation (1993) *Probation Orders with Requirements for Psychiatric Treatment*. London: Home Office.

Hine, J. (1993) 'Access for women: flexible and friendly?' In D. Whitfield and D. Scott (eds) *Paying Back: Twenty Years of Community Service*. Winchester: Waterside Press.

Home Office (1992) *Gender and the Criminal Justice System*. London: HMSO.

Home Office (1993a) *Probation Statistics England and Wales 1992*. London: Home Office.

Home Office (1993b) *Statistics of Offences Against Prison Discipline and Punishments, England and Wales 1992*. London: HMSO.

Hood, R. and Cordovil, G. (1992) *Race and Sentencing: A Study in the Crown Court*. Oxford: Clarendon Press.

Jackson, H. and Smith, L. (1987) *Female Offenders: An Analysis of Social Inquiry Reports*. Home Office Research Bulletin 23. London: HMSO.

Jones, M., Mordecai, M., Rutter, F. and Thomas, L. (1991) 'The Miskin Model of groupwork with women offenders.' *Groupwork 4*, 3, 215–230.

Liebling, A. (1994) 'Suicide amongst women prisoners.' *The Howard Journal of Criminal Justice 33*, 1, 1–9.

Mair, G. and Brockington, N. (1988) 'Female offenders and the Probation Service.' *The Howard Journal of Criminal Justice 27*, 2, 117–126.

Mandaraka-Sheppard, A. (1986) *The Dynamics of Aggression in Women's Prisons in England*. London: Gower.

Mawby, R.I. (1977) 'Sexual discrimination and the law.' *Probation Journal 24*, 2, 38–43.

McCaughey, C. (1992) 'Making masculinity explicit in work with male offenders.' In P. Senior and D. Woodhill (eds) *Gender, Crime and Probation Practice*. Sheffield: PAVIC Publications.

McCaughey, C. and Buckley, K. (1993) *Sexuality, Youth Work and Probation Practice*. Sheffield: PAVIC Publications.

Mistry, T. (1989) 'Establishing a feminist model of groupwork in the Probation Service.' *Groupwork 2*, 145–158.

O'Dwyer, J., Wilson, J. and Carlen, P. (1987) 'Women's imprisonment in England, Wales and Scotland: recurring issues.' In P. Carlen and A. Worrall (eds) *Gender, Crime and Justice*. Milton Keynes: Open University Press.

Robinson, R.H. (1978) 'The probation order – its decline?' *Probation Journal 25*, 2, 42–45.

Stephen, J. (1993) *The Misrepresentation of Women Offenders*. Social work Monograph 118. Norwich: University of East Anglia.

Walker, N. (1981) 'Feminists' extravaganzas.' *The Criminal Law Review*, 379–386.

Woodrow, J. (1992) 'Mothers inside, children outside.' In R. Shaw, (ed) *Prisoners' Children: What are the Issues?* London: Routledge.

Woodside, M. (1974) 'Women offenders and psychiatric reports.' *Social Work Today 5*, 11, 341–342.

Worrall, A. (1981) 'Out of place: female offenders in court.' *Probation Journal 28*, 3, 90–93.

Worrall, A. (1989) 'Working with female offenders: beyond "alternatives to custody"?' *British Journal of Social Work 19*, 77–93.

Worrall, A. (1990) *Offending Women: Female Lawbreakers and the Criminal Justice System.* London: Routledge.

Worrall, A. (1993) 'The contribution to practice of gender perspectives in criminology.' In P. Senior and B. Williams (eds) *Values, Gender and Offending.* Sheffield: PAVIC Publications.

Chapter 6

Race, Culture and the Probation Service
Groupwork Programme Design

Duncan Lawrence

For many years, concern has been voiced by the probation service regarding the lack of quality rehabilitation programmes and options for black and other ethnic minority clients. A specific concern has centred around the disproportionate number of black people entering or re-entering the criminal justice system at various points in the criminal justice process via arrest, remand, conviction and sentencing (e.g. Hood 1992, Hudson 1989, Moxon 1988). Groupwork has been widely accepted as one possible option for use by the probation service in attempting to reduce this number.

The introduction of various policy and practice initiatives has clearly helped to make the criminal justice system as an institution more fair and just. The probation service has successfully developed and run high-tariff groupwork programmes for several years. However the development of practice initiatives focused upon the needs of black and other ethnic minority probation clients, and aimed at diverting them from the criminal justice process, has not met the same level of success.

In a survey of groupwork provision in the probation services of England and Wales, which included responses from 43 of the 56 services, conducted in 1989 only three of the 1463 groups registered in the survey were black-membership only groups (Caddick 1993). Whilst acknowledging that 'mixed' groups of black and white offenders (which constituted 61% of all groups identified in the survey) could in some circumstances be valuable, Caddick nevertheless reached the conclusion that:

'It is impossible to accept that groupwork which gives such scant attention to race as a cultural factor is seriously addressing the real experiences and consequent needs of black offenders and, in light of the considerable over-representation of black offenders in the criminal justice system, this finding is painfully ironic...the existence or non-existence of such groups conveys something important about the service's attention to anti-discriminatory practice and about its approach to offenders generally.' (Caddick 1993, p.28)

A number of reasons can be identified for the limited growth of groupwork practice with black and other ethnic minority clients over the past two decades, some of which apply to the development of groupwork programmes more generally. These include the pessimism engendered by the attack on the effectiveness of 'rehabilitative' programmes during the 1970s; cash limited resources; lack of black staff; lack of black management; lack of real institutional commitment; and lack of professionally trained groupwork specialists. The development of high quality, integrated groupwork provision and guidance materials was never a priority that materialised into institutional actions and outcomes.

This chapter will highlight some of the recent research and practice developments in the areas of race, culture and the probation service, with a primary emphasis upon people from African–Caribbean heritage. By focusing in particular upon five recent research and development projects, it will consider how certain lessons learned from them might be applied in the development of quality groupwork practice with black and other ethnic minority probation service clients and might assist the probation service in meeting its often stated aim of providing fair and appropriate service opportunities to black and other ethnic minority clients.

Recent research and development projects

The majority of the material discussed in the present chapter is drawn from three research and development projects: the Black Offenders Project (Lawrence, Pearson and Aina 1992); the INSIGHT Young Offender Pilot (Lawrence 1994); and the Laketown Project (Denney 1992). Reference will also be made to the Inner London Probation Service Black Groups Initiative (ILPS 1993) – a study of Black Empowerment Groups – and Painter's (1993) household crime survey in two Midlands council estates which involved 307 young people aged between 12 and 17.

In the Black Offenders Project, which was commissioned by Safer Cities, interviews were conducted with a sample of 30 black offenders, 15 probation service staff (black and white) and 15 representatives from local voluntary associations and other community groups in Islington, London. The interviews were aimed at gathering their views and perceptions about the probation service. The INSIGHT Project was a three-year educational research and development project. It was based on a ten-week life and social skills curriculum and targeted primarily at probation clients aged 17–26 in the south east London areas. The project aimed to prepare students to undertake a further or higher education programme, or other training, upon completion of the course. The Laketown Project involved analysis of social inquiry reports prepared for 25 black and 25 white offenders by 13 white probation officers and interviews with the same officers which focused upon their probation work. The primary purpose of the research was to compare and contrast probation officers' explanations of offending behaviour by black and white offenders.

Perspectives on offending by black people

Probation service groupwork programmes for black offenders are usually built around two premises: first, that black offenders are a product of racism; and second, that they therefore need groups focused upon empowerment and related issues to reduce their numbers in the criminal justice system.

If groups that are targeted upon black and other ethnic minority probation clients are to be both responsible and effective it is essential that these underlying premises are subject to careful examination. Do they represent an accurate assessment and explanation of black offending, and how might change be effected?

In the Black Offender Project probationers, probation officers and representatives of community groups were asked to indicate what they believed to be the reasons for black offending. The responses – which have been rounded to the nearest five per cent – are summarised in Table 6.1.

Whilst some areas of general agreement emerged, it is also clear that the different groups of respondents placed differing emphasis upon particular explanatory categories. Probationers, for example, were most likely to identify financial issues or unemployment as a reason for offending by black people. Community group representatives placed greater emphasis than did the other groups of respondents upon education and training and upon discrimination and frustration, whilst probation staff were more likely to attribute black offending to individual or family circumstances.

Table 6.1 Reasons for crime

	Community Groups	Probation Staff	Clients
Money/unemployment	35%	40%	60%
Education/training levels	40%	5%	25%
Discrimination/frustration	70%	50%	45%
Individual/family reasons	20%	45%	10%
Subculture	35%	20%	25%
Drugs	15%	10%	15%
Mental health problems	15%	5%	–

In Denney's (1992) Laketown Project alcohol was offered by probation officers in interview as the most frequently occurring explanation for offending among white offenders, whereas it was invoked as an explanatory factor for only two black offenders. Racism was the most frequent explanation offered for black offending (mentioned in five cases) followed by anti-authority attitudes (in four cases). By contrast, the latter was offered in only one case as a contributory factor in white offending. Difficulties relating to the client's nuclear family were more often offered as an explanation for white than for black offending.

When the explanations of offending in social inquiry reports were examined, however, a different pattern emerged. The use of alcohol was the most common explanation for white and black offending, followed by traumatic family background. Irresponsibility and anti-authority attitudes were identified as contributing to black offending only whereas white offenders were more than twice as likely as black offenders to have been 'led' into crime. Racism, the most common explanation of offending in interviews, was mentioned as a contributory factor in only two social enquiry reports.

The perceived contribution of race, culture and gender to offending behaviour among young adults was explored with participants in the INSIGHT project. Black and white participants did not differ in the

explanations they offered for offending among white men. White participants were, however, more likely than black participants to invoke race,
culture or gender as reasons for offending among and consequent imprisonment of black men.

Painter (1993) asked the young people in his survey to identify the
reasons for people they knew or had heard about getting into trouble. The
most common responses were (in this order): boredom; having no sense
of right or wrong; lack of youth clubs and discos; knowledge that they
could get away with it; lack of parental care; and in need of money for
clothes. Painter's study did not focus specifically upon race and culture
as variables but it did indicate that young people generally had a distinctive viewpoint about the reasons for crime which might usefully inform
responses to offending behaviour.

Perspectives on crime reduction

In the Black Offender Project (Lawrence *et al.* 1992) a significant clash of
perspectives emerged in relation to how black clients and probation
officers perceived the offending behaviour and associated life difficulties
experienced by the former. Black respondents generally placed an emphasis upon issues such as employment, job training and housing as central
areas of difficulty in their lives. Whilst probation staff did not deny the
significance of these issues they tended to place greater emphasis on
questions of personal relationships.

Two thirds of black clients identified a combination of employment
and income generation as a primary personal goal, a quarter mentioned
education and training and the ambition for one tenth was to have a more
settled family life. In terms of obstacles to achieving these goals, the main
emphasis was upon material issues, with half the black clients referring
to lack of employment or money and a quarter to lack of education or
training. One tenth of the remaining responses concerned drug-related
problems whilst slightly fewer than a tenth made reference to housing
problems or personal relationships and family difficulties.

By contrast, half the probation officers identified family problems
and/or relationship difficulties as the key obstacles in their black clients'
lives, a third mentioned lack of educational achievement and only one
tenth made reference to employment or financial difficulties in this context. A less marked conflict of perceptions emerged when the same questions were put to representatives of other agencies and community

groups, more than two thirds of whom identified education and training issues as the major obstacles for black offenders.

Premise development

These studies illustrate the divergence in the perceptions of offending among black people held by probation officers and by black clients with the former placing greater emphasis on issues such as racism, family and personal relationships and anti-authoritarianism and the latter attaching greater importance to material factors such as money, employment, education and training. Significantly, racism and culture were invoked relatively infrequently by black clients as explanatory factors, a finding which undermines a common premise upon which probation service groups for black offenders are built.

Drawing upon the experiences and perceptions of black people, the Inner London Probation Service Black Groups Initiative was based upon an alternative premise which recognised the discrimination and oppression, at all levels including institutional, experienced by people from British racial and cultural minority groups and the potential consequences thereof (including barriers to the development of individuals' full potential, the absence of positive images and experiences to draw upon and frustration against what is perceived as an unjust and unfair living situation) but which also acknowledged that the numbers of black people entering and re-entering the criminal justice system cannot be explained by racism alone. Group participants may have offended for a variety of reasons including peer pressure, financial stress, mental health related difficulties and poor family role models. As such, any attempts to reduce the incidence of offending among black people by enabling them to meet their personal and social needs without recourse to criminal behaviour must aim to promote increased self confidence through facilitating the development of non-oppressive lifeskills (including sexism awareness, gender diversity awareness, numeracy and literacy skill development) and through the provision of skills and training which might lead to gainful employment and/or personal satisfaction (ILPS 1993).

The Black Offender Project was initiated by the Inner London Probation Service who were concerned that they were not meeting the needs of their black clients and, more specifically, their African–Caribbean clients. The process of identifying the needs and concerns of black clients in itself highlighted a definitional problem: some clients identified as 'black' on an ILPS computer printout were found to be of Turkish and Greek Cypriot heritage. The broad definitional categories of 'black', 'white' and 'other' adopted by the Home Office and generally employed by probation services are insufficiently precise to inform the rationale for a specific form of provision. An adequate coding breakdown – which identifies, for example, clients of African–Caribbean heritage, Greek Cypriot heritage, Asian heritage, Irish heritage etc. – is required to address the cultural diversity which exists within a given probation area. Otherwise the use of the term 'black' as an umbrella phrase can hide that cultural diversity and may be used to explain away the limited provision for black and other ethnic minority clients or to perpetuate unfair racial or cultural stereotypes.

Curriculum development

In developing groupwork projects for black offenders what should be done and how it should be done are crucial questions for the probation service to address. Black clients have in the past documented feelings of isolation and disconnection in their probation groups (Denney 1992, Lawrence *et al.* 1992). As with the premise underlying groupwork practice the curriculum should be developed using the widest possible range of information sources and should be informed by the underlying premise. The INSIGHT Project (Lawrence 1994) developed its curriculum following a six-month period during which ideas and advice were sought from a range of relevant individuals and organisations including: potential students; local and national employers; local and regional voluntary projects; probation officers; and further and higher educational establishments. The initial development of the ILPS Black Groups Initiative was informed by listening to the concerns expressed by black clients in the Black Offenders Project (ILPS 1993).

The weekly sessions of the Black Groups Initiative focused upon:

- group aims and self assessment;
- people and their stressors/communication models;
- self image, role models and peer pressure;
- families and family systems;
- race and racism;
- values of society/values clarification;
- sex, sexism and sexuality;

- options, choices, consequences and personal plans.

Similar issues were addressed by the INSIGHT Project. Its curriculum consisted of the following elements:

- introduction to group/assessments;
- working in a team/communication and body language;
- learning to learn;
- dealing with stress and depression;
- authority/values of society/values clarification;
- race and racism/sex and sexism;
- drugs, alcohol and solvent abuse/personal presentation skills;
- the future/dealing with separation;
- voluntary placements.

The fact that the areas focused upon by these projects shared similarities but also some differences can be attributed to the process of consultation at various levels which preceded their development. As such, some of the concerns which have been voiced in relation to anti-racist practice – most specifically in relation to the relevance of the curriculum for black clients – were addressed.

Myths and assumptions

Myths and assumptions about black people and, in particular about black offenders, influence the criminal justice system. One such assumption, usually articulated by white probation officers, is that black people only require 'empowerment groups'. The approach adopted by the INSIGHT Project has been to stress the fundamental similarity of black people and other groups of people. Skills development (including life and social skills), education and preparation for work are of equal importance to all people regardless of their ethnicity. Where the difference lies is in the possible experience of racism, discrimination and oppression – sometimes on a daily basis – by black clients. These are issues which can be explored within empowerment groups in the first instance.

Black people can also do well in 'mixed groups' as Table 6.2 illustrates.

Table 6.2 INSIGHT 2 – 1991–4 enrolment/graduation profiles

	Total enrolment	Total to graduate	Bursary winners	Honourable mention awards
Black British	67	47	17	4
White British	61	33	16	5
Total	128	80	33	9

The outcomes for black people are affected by the combination of their tutors' personal beliefs, personal awareness, preparedness, integrity, commitment to non-oppressive casework strategies and their belief in the perpetuation of positive images, and by resource availability and motivation levels of group members.

A second myth or assumption, usually expressed by white students on each INSIGHT course, is that white people do not have culture, or have very little culture. This is addressed in the INSIGHT course curriculum by emphasising the universality of culture and diversity. The notion that white people lack culture can be traced back to the origins of the class system in the United Kingdom when the landowners took pride in their uniqueness and cultural differences and perceived it as being in their best interests to oppress the serfs by emphasising their homogeneity and lack of individuality. This process of oppression and internalisation, which has become ingrained in the British psyche over the past few centuries, is reflected in some of the current mainstream thinking about race and culture.

Conclusion
The future of groupwork with black offenders
The projects discussed in this chapter had aims and strategies that were not necessarily concerned with the process of groupwork development. They do nevertheless provide useful pointers for the development of groupwork with black and other ethnic minority clients. The main practical lessons can be summarised as follows.

Premises

Probation officers usually have explanations which they can invoke to account for their black clients' offending and they are usually different from the reasons for offending they attribute to their white clients. In developing programmes for black and other ethnic minority clients there are other viewpoints and perceptions – including those of the clients themselves – that can be drawn upon to gain a clearer understanding of black offenders, of the reasons for crime and of the means to its overall reduction. Clarity is also required as to the meaning of the term 'black'. It is essential to be explicit and clear about who programmes are targeting and why.

Curriculum

Important themes like racism, sexism and oppression should be integrated into any curriculum but specifically focused upon later in a programme, by which time groups should have developed mutual trust and skills of self expression which are a pre-requisite to tackling crucial issues such as these.

The appropriateness of the curriculum and the methods employed can be best assessed through systematic monitoring and evaluation which will include eliciting feedback from students, probation officers and significant others.

Myths and assumptions

The probation service as an institution often perpetuates myths, assumptions and stereotypes about black and other ethnic minority clients. This may occur in various ways and for various reasons, including: the existence of *some* racist officers; lack of provision within the mainstream service strategy; denying the need for and/or limiting the resources for the development of quality provision for black and other ethnic minority clients; and the use of limited coding systems. Just as some myths, assumptions and stereotypes are based upon 'reality', so are some based upon limited interpretations and incomplete information. It is essential that probation officers examine their perceptions of and assumptions about their client group, about their value to them, about their group's value to the criminal justice system and about its value to the community. Course materials should reflect the composition of the group as well as reflecting the cultural diversity which exists throughout the world and should be presented in a non-eurocentric format.

The probation service is currently providing a few groups for black and other ethnic minority clients but their development and outcomes have not been systematically documented. It is hoped that in the future, clear accounts of the development of such projects will be made available and their effectiveness carefully assessed.

In the limited space available this chapter could not address issues such as how to identify a clear mandate for black only provision (which should be derived from a mainstream probation service mandate); how to make it focused, cost effective and part of the wider community; and how to remove other obstacles such as scepticism among colleagues, clients, management and the community. These are, however, issues of crucial importance in the delivery of quality groupwork provision for black and other ethnic minority probation service clients.

References

Caddick, B. (1993) 'Using groups in working with offenders: A survey of groupwork in the probation services of England and Wales.' In A. Brown and B. Caddick (eds) *Groupwork with Offenders*. London: Whiting and Birch.

Denney, D. (1992) *Racism and Anti-Racism in Probation*. London: Routledge.

Hood, R. (1992) *Race and Sentencing*. Oxford: Clarendon Press.

Hudson, B. (1989) 'Discrimination and disparity: the influence of race on sentencing.' *New Community* 16, 21–32.

Inner London Probation Service (1993) *The Black Groups Initiatives 1992–93: A Handbook for Black Empowerment Groups*. London: ILPS Resources Unit.

Lawrence, D., Pearson, G. and Aina, C. (1992) *Black Offenders Project: Report to the Inner London Probation Service and Safer Cities*. University of London: Goldsmith's College, Department of Community Studies.

Lawrence, D. (1994) *Young Adult Offenders: Addressing Offending Behaviour Through Community/Inner London Probation Service Partnerships, The INSIGHT Project Final Report*. University of London: Goldsmith's College, Department of Community Studies.

Moxon, D. (1988) *Sentencing Practice in the Crown Court*. Home Office Research Study No. 103. London: HMSO.

Painter, K. (1993) *The Mythology of Delinquency: An Empirical Critique*. University of Cambridge: Institute of Criminology.

Chapter 7

Risk Prediction
and Criminal Justice

Anne Creamer and Bryan Williams

Background

Decision-making in the criminal justice system inevitably involves an element of prediction. For example, sentencers, in reaching a decision regarding the most appropriate disposal for an offender, will take into consideration its likely effect on his or her future behaviour (Mannheim 1965, Nicholson 1985). Similarly, in preparing a report for the courts, social workers and probation officers will invariably be making some assessment about the future behaviour of the *offender* (risk of re-offending) and of the *court* (the risk that a custodial sentence will be imposed). All such judgements will to a large extent be based on past experience, sometimes called 'practice wisdom'. In this respect, information from previous experience is utilised, correctly or incorrectly, to inform future decision-making, by a process of informal risk prediction (Gottfredson 1967).

In recent years there has been a growing interest in the use of more formalised risk prediction. In particular, statistically based prediction scales have been designed and developed which calculate, on an actuarial basis, the *risk of custody* facing an offender appearing before the court (Bale 1987, Creamer, Hartley and Williams 1992) and/or the *risk* of his/her *re-offending* (Humphrey and Pease 1991, Wilkinson 1994). Such scales claim to assist in decision-making and to provide a methodolgy for the monitoring and evaluation of decisions and practices. On the positive side, therefore, they have the potential to reduce inconsistencies in decision-making and to identify and demonstrate effective practice. These objectives receive support from various interest groups. They can be utilised to demonstrate the efficient allocation of resources (Audit Commission 1989); the appropriate use of community supervision for offenders (Home Office 1990); the avoidance of unnecessarily intrusive and controlling interventions (Harris 1992); the identification of effective intervention methods (McIvor 1990); and the monitoring of social work or probation team practice (Wilkinson 1994).

In addition to identifying the positive features of prediction scales, however, it might be prudent to consider also their potential disadvantages. In particular, it may be advisable to identify possible unintended outcomes in advance, in order to avoid preventable mistakes (Cohen 1985). Of course, in making such a judgement, much will depend on whose interests are deemed to be served and whether these interests are compatible or contradictory. It may be too naive to assume, for example, that the interests of government, social work and probation, the courts, offenders and of victims coincide (Garland 1990). Importantly, therefore, it may be that it is the *uses* to which prediction scales are put which is the crucial factor. Given the fact that they are often used in different contexts to do very different things, they cannot, despite their largely mathematical base, be considered to be politically or ideologically neutral.

Prediction methods have a relatively long history of being used in decision-making and evaluation. Historically, they have been used, for example, to inform decisions as to which prisoners should be granted parole (Tibbitts 1931); to match individuals to treatment regimes (Glueck 1951); to estimate the probability of future offending rates of boys on release from Borstal (Mannheim and Wilkins 1955); to identify children at risk of becoming delinquent (Kvaraceus 1961); and to compare the effectiveness of treatment regimes (Mannheim and Wilkins 1955).

It is worth noting that Mannheim explicitly linked the use of prediction methods to a penal philosophy which was reformative rather than retributive in character (Mannheim 1965). At that time, the rationale underpinning the use of prediction scales was the belief that a *treatment* approach to criminal justice was both socially just and potentially effective in reducing recidivism. An important adjunct to the treatment model was the use of *indeterminate sentencing* ; i.e. individuals would be released from custody at a point when the 'treatment' was considered to have been maximally effective. Such judgements were often informed by the assigning of persons to various risk categories.

Risk of re-offending and re-conviction

The early use of prediction tables and methods was primarily related to studies of the effectiveness of different sentences imposed by the court. For example, measurements of the 'success' or 'failure' of various sentencing options (e.g. open and closed Borstals), relative to a prejudiced norm, were assumed at the time to be indicators of the effectiveness of these as treatment measures. The focus of such studies was on the nature of *treatment itself* rather than on the *individuals* subject to it. This distinction is an important one. A current example of this type of approach can be seen within contemporary probation practice where a reconviction prediction scale is being used to compare the effectiveness of various probation teams and projects, by contrasting actual reconviction rates with those predicted (Wilkinson 1994).

Judgments of this type about effectiveness are, of course, characteristically focused on only one of the objectives of sentencing, namely the prevention of recidivism. The main criterion, therefore, on which success or failure is measured is the *rate of re-conviction* of offenders. In contemporary language, re-conviction rates can be used as performance indicators of practice, based on the premise that 'crime reduction is the raison d'être of the probation service' (Wilkinson 1994, p.461). There is, of course, a danger here in over-simplifying the purposes and functions of penal policies and practices (Garland 1990). Historically, one of the main criticisms of measuring the effectiveness of various treatment regimes and sentencing options in this way has been the considerable lack of agreement concerning what are to count as the indicators of success and failure (Hood and Sparks 1970).

In principle then, a comparison of actual re-conviction rates with those calculated from the application of risk of re-offending scales can play an informative role in the evaluation of penal policy and practice measures. For example, it has been found that low-risk offenders assigned to intensive probation programmes showed a recidivism rate worse than that predicted as did high-risk probationers placed on standard probation supervision (McIvor 1990). This type of information can be helpful in informing future decision-making and avoiding mistakes on ethical grounds (ensuring minimal necessary intervention); professional grounds (avoiding 'tariff escalation' and 'net-widening'); and on financial grounds (ensuring appropriate rationing and allocation of scarce resources). It is well understood, however, that, in their sentencing practices, courts are not concerned simply with the effectiveness of disposals as treatment measures in this rather limited sense (i.e. their impact on the individual's future offending) but are bound to include consideration of matters such as public disapproval of crime, the protection of society, and general deterrence (Walker 1985, Nicholson 1985). If it is accepted that penal policy serves various purposes, then it is not self-evident that the probation service or social work with offenders has the sole function of crime reduction.

It is perhaps worth pointing out that if comparative re-conviction rates were to be universally used as the only (or main) criterion for the imposition of a court sentence, then the efficacy of custodial sentences in reducing crime would require to be subjected to the same level of scrutiny as is characteristically applied to non-custodial measures.

There are well-known and fundamental problems associated with the interpretation and use of re-conviction rates, which suggest considerable caution regarding their use. For example, there is no compelling reason to assume that these are a true reflection of actual re-offending (Hood and Sparks 1970, Mair 1989). It is well understood that the formal processing of offenders is characterised by discretionary decisions and differential practices at all stages (e.g. variations in reporting rates for different crimes; police arrest and apprehension practices; charging decisions by prosecutors and so on) (Bottomley 1973). It is estimated that only three per cent overall of offences result in a criminal conviction (Barclay 1991). Furthermore, there are wide variations between different types of offence. There is thus little reason to believe that those successfully convicted and sentenced are a representative sample of offenders or offences committed. Indeed there is cause to consider that they may be significantly unrepresentative in the sense that agency practices may discriminate against disadvantage, e.g. against women, people from ethnic groups and those from lower socio-economic groups (Hood and Sparks 1970).

Risk of re-offending scales also raise problems. It is claimed that the best predictor of future behaviour is *past* behaviour (Farrington and Farling 1985), so re-conviction prediction typically involves an assessment of such factors as offending history, age of the offender at current and first offence, employment status and previous sentencing history (Wilkinson 1994). These factors are likely to reflect discriminatory practices on the part of various agencies. One of the most powerful criticisms of the treatment model of criminal justice in the past was that inherent in the discretion afforded to decision-makers was a predilection for discrimination against disadvantaged groups (American Friends 1972, Von Hirsch

1976). For example, the placing of a young offender on supervision within a welfare model (i.e. for his or her good) may have more to do with the home circumstances of the child than the nature of the offending behaviour. Similarly, the arrest and subsequent conviction of a young offender may, in large part, be related to his or her demeanour, dress and self-presentation (Piliavin and Briar 1964) and whether someone eventually receives a community disposal such as a probation or community service order may be influenced by their gender or ethnic origin (Hudson 1993, Williams, Creamer and Hartley 1988). It is not, therefore, difficult to see that if prediction scales which incorporate such factors are used in decision-making affecting individual offenders then there is at least the possibility that previous discriminatory processes are merely being reinforced.

The main issue then becomes not so much the reliability of reconviction prediction measures as monitoring tools but rather the practical implications of using them within decision-making processes. In Wilkinson's (1994) study, risk of re-offending is calculated only after a probation order is made and cannot, therefore, directly influence the decision-making process. Information about predicted reconviction risks may, however, be used in making assessments about individuals and attempting to influence courts in respect of sentencing.

Problems begin to arise when re-conviction prediction scales are used in this way to match individuals to various disposals at the pre-sentence or social enquiry stage (in effect, attempting to influence court practice by means of predictions concerning an individual's future behaviour). Even if the risk factor itself is not made available to the court, it may be used by the authors of court reports to target individuals towards or away from various disposals. (Indeed it is difficult to see the point of having a risk of re-offending scale at this stage in the process if it is not intended to influence the court disposal). In addition to the issues already referred to, the use of reconviction prediction methods is problematic on two further grounds.

First, it formalises a practice which contravenes the principle of just deserts (that individuals should be sentenced for what they *have done* in the past, not for what they *might do* in the future) (Von Hirsch 1976). Second, a fundamental feature of statistical prediction is that it does not and cannot predict for individual cases. Prediction tables, based as they are on actuarial probabilities calculated from the analysis of aggregated data, merely refer to the likely behaviour of groups or categories of individuals (Glueck and Glueck 1959). Thus, decisions made on the basis of procedures which cannot legitimately be applied to individuals, except as examples of classes or categories, but which then affect the restriction of liberty of individuals, raise serious ethical issues.

All predictive methods have a built in error rate (i.e. individual cases in which the predicted outcome does not come about) and it is these inaccurate predictions, arising from the classification of specific individuals to risk categories, which causes concern (Hudson 1993). These cases are usually known as 'false positives' (e.g. those who are catgorised as being at high risk of re-offending and who are not subsequentially re-convicted) and 'false negatives' (those who are categorised as being at low risk and yet who are re-convicted). The ethical issues come to the fore most evidently with the cases regarded as false positives. It is likely that individuals classified as being at high risk of re-offending are more likely to receive either a custodial sentence or more controlling and intrusive community supervision than they are a lower-tariff disposal. By definition, however, the false positives are not subject to verification (Castel 1991), i.e. it can never easily be known of someone classified as high risk and yet who is not re-convicted over a given period of time, whether this is because (i) they have re-offended but have escaped conviction; (ii) measures of previous or current supervision have been effective; or (iii) they fall into the proportion who were not going to re-offend anyway. The classification of individuals to high-risk of re-offending groups on the basis of statistical prediction has the potential to increase the severity of disposal for a significant number of offenders. This is made the more worrying because of the lack of a means of identifying, with any degree of accuracy, these 'system error' cases (Castel 1991, Cohen 1985).

Of course, even the most ardent promoters of the use of prediction methods advise caution in their use. Thus, despite being able to claim a remarkable validation of their Base Expectancy Score over a period of 40 years, Gottfredson and Gottfredson (1993) warn that even the best predictors (whether of the future behaviour of offenders or of systems) are quite poor. It has always been accepted that statistical predictions should not be treated as absolutely conclusive (Mannheim 1965). Although research evidence suggests that predictions made with the assistance of statistical tools may, in some circumstances, out-perform purely 'clinical' judgements (Bale 1987) they should not be used as a substitute for such judgements (Glueck and Glueck 1959).

Best practice, it is argued, includes a combination of actuarial and clinical judgements, with professional considerations coming into play in cases where there are unusual circumstances (Gottfredson and Gottfredson 1993). In relation to risk of re-offending, it is not clear what general guidance can be given to practitioners as to the circumstances which might be considered unusual, for example under what circumstances these should override a judgement suggested by the statistical tool; or who ought to make such decisions. The question 'how and on what basis are false positives to be identified by decision-makers?' remains problematic and suggests suitable caution concerning the widespread use of reconviction prediction methods in this type of context.

Risk of custody

Many of these criticisms pertain also to Risk of Custody prediction methods and scales since these too generate both false positives and false negatives; i.e. individual offenders who are classified as being at high risk of receiving a custodial sentence may not receive a custodial sentence, while other cases, classified as low-risk, will actually result in custody. Some, but not all, of the false positive cases may be accounted for as a response to the efforts of social workers and probation officers, that is, a proactive approach to making sure that the courts are aware of all the community-based alternatives and that the relative risks are explored and assessed. Similarly, some, but again not all, of the false negative cases may be considered to be due to poor risk assessments on the part of the authors of court reports. Other cases in both categories may simply reflect the variations and contingencies common in the sentencing process.

The monitoring of these 'error' cases is a relatively straightforward matter, since the use of community disposals in serious cases can readily be explored and custodial disposals in the low risk cases can be easily identified (Creamer, Ennis and Williams 1994). Regularly re-occurring variant factors will emerge and be highlighted in this monitoring process. Equally importantly, such routine analysis facilitates the regular review and revision of social work practice in relation to the courts.

The focus of risk of custody scales is on actual court behaviour, that is, their statistical base is derived from data collected over time, concerning how the sentences passed related to particular aspects of the relevant cases (e.g. nature of charges, previous sentencing history, court process etc.). Furthermore, this data can be as 'local' as required, subject only to the reliability of the statistics obtained. This potential focus on local setting is much more difficult to achieve in the case of risk of re-offending scales. Risk of custody scales also have the same worrying potential to reinforce the discriminatory practices of social agencies in the sense that, since the criminal careers of offenders are fundamentally affected by discretionary decisions in the criminal justice process, many of these decisions will be reflected as part of the statistical basis of the scales, the use of which will tend to perpetuate discrimination.

In the contemporary use of Risk of Custody scales, the main objective for authors of court reports is to engage with the prevailing sentencing policies of courts, based on reliable evidence. The primary purpose is to identify cases which are at serious risk of receiving a custodial sentence and the task is to explore and offer credible community disposals at an appropriate point on the risk scale. The emphasis is on reducing the rate of unnecessary custodial disposals by diverting some of the more serious cases from custody (Home Office 1990). Effectiveness, utilising this criterion, is not measured by the 'success' or 'failure' of treatment regimes but rather by the extent to which community supervision is targeted towards cases where courts would normally be considering custodial sentences (Bottoms and McWilliams 1979).

Such an approach to the assessment of effectiveness is realistic and achievable and it fits both with current government objectives and with the humanitarian aims of social work and probation. It facilitates routine monitoring concerning the rationing of scarce resources and the so-called net-widening and 'tariff escalation' effects of court and social work/probation practice (Creamer *et al.* 1994). Within this model the 'effectiveness' of probation and community service is measured by the extent to which these disposals are actually being used in accordance with government objectives. Thus it is possible over time to identify social work/probation teams which are proactive in recommending or suggesting community supervision to the courts in serious cases; the credibility with which the courts view reports in which this takes place; and the sentencing ethos of the court (Williams and Creamer 1989).

Moore and Wood have criticised the use of risk of custody scales to guide recommendation practice as merely reflecting and reinforcing what courts do rather than in helping influence change in court behaviour (Moore and Wood 1992). Whilst this criticism is valid given the actuarial nature of the predictive scales themselves, regular monitoring of the kind referred to, and changes in practice made as a result of it, help to avoid the worst excesses of such a reactive approach. Changes in sentencing practice can be shown to have resulted from approaches of this kind (Raynor 1988, Creamer *et al.* 1992).

Conclusion

It has been stressed that it is the context in which prediction methods and scales are used and the purposes for which they are used which are the crucial issues. Discrimination against social disadvantage occurs at various stages in the criminal justice system and this is most evident in the prison population where the poor, ethnic minorities and the mentally ill are disproportionately represented (Hudson 1993). Predictions based on historical data have the potential of increasing discrimination and of reinforcing stereotypical views of the nature of crime and of those who commit it.

The use of Risk of Custody scales, where the main purpose is to divert some offenders from custodial sentences, has at least the potential to impact on historically discriminatory practices, although it would be a mistake to over-claim the extent to which this is likely to be achieved solely through the efforts of social workers and probation officers.

The use of Risk of Reconviction prediction methods and scales to inform decisions which affect the life and liberty of individuals remains ethically dubious for the reasons adduced earlier. Their employment in the measurement of the so-called 'effectiveness' of community supervision services based mainly, or exclusively, on comparative re-conviction rates is, as discussed above, methodologically flawed. This type of development also raises vital questions concerning assumptions about the nature and functions of social work and probation within the criminal justice system.

It may be that the most cogent argument for using community disposals such as probation and community service is not that they can be shown to be more successful in preventing re-offending but rather that they are acceptably effective in this respect and more importantly that they are more humane and less brutalising than custodial sentences (Vass 1990). The level of protection which society can expect from court orders not resulting in custody is an important matter and one which should not be ignored. Exclusive concentration, however, on the 'instrumental' utility of penal policies as opposed to their 'expressive' utility misses a crucial point. Probation and community service, like other aspects of penal policy, are best evaluated in ways which take into account the wider social functions which they perform and the social values they represent (Garland 1990). Similarly, the use of prediction scales by agencies is best evaluated within a value-base which recognises their potential and actual impact on the individuals affected by such a use.

References

American Friends Service Committee (1972) *Struggle for Justice.* New York: Hill and Wang.

Audit Commission (1989) *The Probation Service: Promoting Value for Money.* London: HMSO.

Bale, D. (1987) 'Uses of the risk of custody scale.' *Probation Journal 34,* 4, 127–131.

Barclay, G.C. (ed) (1991) *A Digest of Information on the Criminal Justice System.* London: Home Office Research and Statistics.

Bottomley, A.K. (1973) *Decisions in the Penal Process.* London: Robertson.

Bottoms, A.E. and McWilliams, B. (1979) 'A non-treatment paradigm of probation practice.' *British Journal of Social Work 9,* 2, 159–202.

Castel, R. (1991) 'From dangerousness to risk.' In M. Foucault, G. Burchell, C. Gordon and P. Miller (eds) *The Foucault Effect: Studies in Governmentality.* London: Harvester Wheatsheaf.

Cohen, S. (1985) *Visions of Social Control: Crime, Punishment and Classification.* Cambridge: Polity Press.

Creamer, A., Hartley, L. and Williams, B. (1992) *The Probation Alternative: A Study of the Impact of Four Enhanced Probation Schemes on Sentencing Outcomes.* Edinburgh: Scottish Office Central Research Unit paper.

Creamer, A., Ennis, E. and Williams, B. (1994) *The DUNSCORE (University of Dundee Risk of Custody Prediction Scale): A Social Enquiry Practice and Evaluation Tool for Social Workers and Social Work Managers in Scotland.* Dundee: University of Dundee/The Scottish Office.

Farrington, D.P. and Farling, R. (eds) (1985) *Prediction in Criminology.* Albany: Suny Press.

Garland, D. (1990) *Punishment and Modern Society: A Study in Social Theory.* Oxford: Clarendon Press.

Glueck, S. (1951) 'Pre-sentencing examination of offenders to aid in choosing a method of treatment.' *Journal of Criminal Law and Criminology 41,* 717–731.

Glueck, S. and Glueck, E.T. (1959) *Predicting Delinquency and Crime.* Cambridge MA: Harvard University Press.

Gottfredson, D. (1967) 'Assessment and prediction methods in crime and delinquency.' In The President's Commission on Law Enforcement and Administration of Justice, Task Force Report: *Juvenile Delinquency and Youth Crime*. Washington D.C.: U.S. Government Printing Office.

Gottfredson, S.D. and Gottfredson, D.M. (1993) 'The long-term predictive utility of the base expectancy score.' *Howard Journal of Criminal Justice 32,* 4, 276–290.

Harris, R. (1992) *Crime, Criminal Justice and the Probation Service*. London: Tavistock/Routledge.

Home Office (1990) *Supervision and Punishment in the Community: A Framework for Action*. Green Paper, HMSO, Cmd. 966.

Hood, R. and Sparks, R. (1970) *Key Issues in Criminology*. London: Weidenfeld and Nicolson.

Hudson, B. (1993) *Penal Policy and Social Justice*. London: Macmillan.

Humphrey, C. and Pease, K. (1991) 'Effectiveness measurement in probation: A view from the troops.' *Howard Journal of Criminal Justice 31,* 31–52.

Kvaraceus, W.C. (1961) 'Forecasting juvenile delinquency: A three-year experiment.' *Exceptional Children XVIII,* 429–435.

McIvor, G. (1990) *Sanctions for Serious and Persistent Offenders: A Review of the Literature*. Stirling: University of Stirling Social Work Research Centre.

Mair, G. (ed) (1989) *Risk Prediction and Probation*. London: Home Office Research and Planning Unit.

Mannheim, H. (1965) *Comparative Criminology, Vol. 1*. London: Routledge and Kegan Paul.

Mannheim, H. and Wilkins, L. (1955) *Prediction Methods in Relation to Borstal Training*. London: HMSO.

Moore, G. and Wood, C. (1992) *Social Work and the Criminal Law in Scotland*. Edinburgh: Mercat Press.

Nicholson, C.G.B. (1985) *The Law and Practice in Sentencing in Scotland*. Edinburgh: W. Green and Son.

Piliavin, I. and Briar, S. (1964) 'Police encounters with juveniles.' *American Journal of Sociology 70,* 206–214.

Raynor, P. (1988) *Probation as an Alternative to Custody*. Aldershot: Avebury.

Tibbitts, C. (1931) 'Success and failure on parole can be predicted.' *Journal of Criminal Law and Criminology 22,* 11–50.

Vass, A. (1990) *Alternatives to Prison: Punishment, Custody and the Community*. London: Sage.

Von Hirsch, A. (1976) *Doing Justice: The Choice of Punishments*. New York: Hill and Wang.

Walker, N. (1985) *Sentencing Theory, Law and Practice*. London: Butterworths.

Wilkinson, J. (1994) 'Using a reconviction predictor to make sense of reconviction rates in the probation service.' *British Journal of Social Work 24*, 4, 461–473.

Williams, B. and Creamer, A. (1989) *Social Enquiry Within a Changing Sentencing Context*. Edinburgh: Scottish Office Central Research Unit paper.

Williams, B., Creamer, A. and Hartley, L. (1988) *The Second Chance: Scottish Probation Orders in the Late 1980s*. Unpublished report to the Social Work Services Group of the Scottish Office.

Chapter 8

What Works with Sex Offenders?

Mary Barker

Introduction

As public awareness of the incidence of sexual offencing has grown, so has the criminal justice system in England and Wales become more punitive toward sexual offenders.[1] The proportion of sex offenders in the British prison population rose steadily during the 1980s. Together, events have led to increasing demands being made on criminal justice agencies to 'do something' with the growing numbers of sex offenders coming into the system.

At the same time, there has been renewed interest in working with sex offenders, using methods more allied with rehabilitation and treatment than have been acceptable for some time. Perhaps because of the optimism sparked by the undermining of the 'nothing works' school, or perhaps because some methods of working with sex offenders have shown promising results, therapeutic programmes for sex offenders have become widespread in probation and social work circles. A survey of probation services in England and Wales in 1991 found that 43 services were running 63 programmes for sex offenders (Barker and Morgan 1993). The fact that 29 of these programmes had been set up in the previous five years, and that only three programmes had been running for more than five years, attest to the recent nature of this phenomenon and the speed with which many programmes have been set up. What unifies these therapeutic programmes is their subscription to a broadly 'cognitive–behavioural'

---

1 Since the overwhelming majority of sexual offenders known to the criminal justice system is male, sex offenders will be referred to by the male pronoun in this chapter.

approach to working with sex offenders, despite the fact that the efficacy of this method of working has only recently begun to be tested.

The following pages review some of the methods that have been used in work with sex offenders, and attempt to draw from the research conclusions about the efficacy of therapy.

Sex offender therapies

It is self-evident that methods for working with sex offenders reflect practitioners' theoretical approaches, and a variety of treatment types is currently available for sex offenders. Physical, psychoanalytic, behavioural and cognitive therapy models are all used, and whilst therapies often combine a variety of methods (Marshall *et al.* 1991a), a review of such programmes is valuable for assessing what is known about the outcome of various therapies.

Assessment of the success of any programme, whatever its theoretical orientation, is invariably couched in terms of its ability to reduce the severity or frequency of sexual offences, over and above that which would have occurred without treatment (Perkins 1991). Although conclusive evaluations are few, there is some evidence as to the relative success of each type of treatment.

Physical therapies

Evidence on the efficacy of physical therapy with sex offenders seems unequivocal. Psychosurgery, as reported by Marshall and Barbaree (1990a), appears to have been an abysmal failure as well as ethically disastrous. Castration by surgery can reduce sexual re-offending. However, it does not do so in every case. The side effects can be very damaging: it appears to result in an increase in non-sexual re-convictions and is personally and emotionally disrupting. Chemical castration, through the use of anti-libidinal drugs such as Depoprovera, has been shown to be of value in reducing sexual urges but does not constitute effective treatment on its own. As Perkins (1991) argues, many sex offenders commit offences for motives other than sexual gratification: simply reducing sex drive will not necessarily reduce offending. Where such medication appears to be most beneficial is in conjunction with effective psychological therapies.

Psychoanalytic therapies

Broadly psychoanalytic therapies appear to have variable outcomes as far as offending is concerned, some programmes claiming to have reduced recidivism and some not. Results from a series of evaluations of programmes run in the United States in the 1960s and early 1970s suggested that recidivism rates can even be higher for those who have been through psychoanalytic therapies than for those who have not (see Thornton 1992a for a review of these). Marshall and his colleagues have little confidence in treatments based on a self-help philosophy (Marshall *et al.* 1991b) and conclude that self-help programmes should be 'terminated forthwith' (p.8). The general thrust of their argument is that a purely psychoanalytic approach seems at best ineffective and at worst positively harmful.

Behavioural therapies

The behavioural therapy programmes of the 1960s were based on the assumption that sexual behaviour was entirely sexual in motivation, and hence that if sexual preferences could be changed then the problem behaviours would stop (Marshall and Barbaree 1990a). This produced a variety of treatment procedures and techniques – for example, aversion therapy, covert sensitisation and masturbatory reconditioning – that aimed to change deviant sexual preferences. In general such techniques rely on repeatedly associating the problematic sexual arousal with a consequent unpleasant image or sensation, such that arousal will eventually become inhibited. For example, covert sensitisation refers to a procedure in which an offender is taught to imagine a scene relevant to his offending – such as imagining himself committing an offence – and follow it with imagined unpleasant consequences, such as being arrested or publicly humiliated. Imagined pleasant alternatives to the offending behaviour have also been employed in order to help inhibit an offence (Salter 1988). For example, in masturbatory reconditioning, the offender is encouraged to replace a deviant masturbation fantasy with a non-deviant one, the point being to associate the pleasant sensation of orgasm with non-deviant, legal sex, so reinforcing the experience.

All these procedures have been found to be useful and successful in modifying the deviant arousal of some offenders, and some programmes continue to employ only these techniques (Marshall and Barbaree 1990b, Perkins 1991). However, used on their own, these techniques do not address any of the motives activating and maintaining deviant sexuality, and provide offenders with no insight into their offending behaviour. In addition, aversion therapies are felt by some to be ethically dubious on account of their supposed unpleasantness for offenders. In common with other behaviour modification techniques, there is some suggestion that their effects may not be lasting unless they are supported by other types of therapy.

Cognitive–behavioural therapies

These programmes draw upon the increasingly sophisticated multi-factorial theories of sexual offending generated by Finkelhor and associates, and by Bill Marshall and his colleagues. As a consequence, therapeutic methods with a variety of theoretical origins are often included in cognitive–behavioural programmes. The philosophy appears to be that until more is known about which methods are effective, then it is safest to use a combination of different types of therapy.

Typically, therapy begins with an assessment of the nature of the individual's offending and associated problems. The broad objectives of cognitive–behavioural therapy are: to make the offender take responsibility for his offending and his behaviour generally; to help him, as a consequence of this, to become more motivated to stop offending; and, finally, to equip him with behavioural controls to exercise over the temptation to offend. It is widely believed that unless there is some acknowledgement from the offender of responsibility for his abusive behaviours, therapy cannot proceed successfully. A large part of any sex offender programme is therefore devoted to overcoming denial of responsibility and reality. To assist this process, the cycle of behaviour, involving the antecedents and consequences of offending, are worked out with the offender. The more thorough these initial investigations are, the more appropriate the treatment can be made. In order that blatantly distorted attitudes to women and children can be worked on, offenders first have to increase their ability to empathise with victims and others. Sex education and some understanding of the emotional aspects of sexual activity are often necessary at this stage, and are best related closely to the problems involved in subjects' offending. This is important in order to avoid the risk of simply helping offenders to become more informed offenders. It is suggested that behavioural techniques are best introduced when the offender really wishes to stop offending, since they rely on offenders' asserting control over their impulses. All parts of a therapeutic programme are said to be necessary to the success of all others. In addition, some programmes include training in relapse prevention. Based on principles derived from work undertaken with people with addictions, re-lapse prevention aims to help offenders to avoid the situations they identify as problematic, and improve their self-management in such situations when unavoidable.

Groupwork forms an important part of most cognitive–behavioural treatment programmes. Its primary advantage is said to be that group members can provide each other with insights into others' problems on the basis of personal experience, and can confront and challenge each others' distorted thinking.

The effectiveness of cognitive–behavioural therapy

Much has been claimed for broad-based cognitive–behavioural treatment programmes, though, as Marshall *et al.* (1991b) report, evaluations are few and recent because such programmes are a relatively new development. Marshall's review concludes that all but one evaluation of this type of programme provides support for the belief that cognitive–behavioural programmes are of clear benefit. However, Perkins (1991) sounds a note of caution in suggesting that this may be simply because cognitive–behavioural programmes have been made the subject of more sophisticated evaluations than other types of therapy.

Methodological problems have tended to limit the extent to which programmes have been able to produce rigorous, and hence reliable, evidence of the efficacy of their work. Chief among these problems is the difficulty of obtaining accurate measures of the recidivism of sexual offenders. Another pervasive problem has been the failure of evaluators to take into consideration the nature of their client group when making claims of therapeutic success. The use of comparison or 'control' groups of untreated sex offenders against which the recidivism rate of the treated sex offenders can be measured is a feature of evaluation often overlooked. Without comparison between similar treated and untreated groups of sex offenders it is impossible to say whether therapy has had any independent effect. Little attempt has been made in evaluation of sex offender programmes to distinguish between types of sexual reconviction (Thornton 1992a). For example, if following treatment a child molester stops molesting children but instead exposes himself, can treatment be judged to have been a success?

One programme evaluation that has overcome many of these crucial methodological problems is the Sex Offender Treatment and Evaluation

Project (SOTEP) currently running at the Atascadero State Hospital, California. Those who have gone through the programme so far have been assessed and have shown a variety of positive short-term changes (Marques *et al.* 1989). In addition, a one year follow-up of official police records showed relatively low recidivism rates: eight per cent for treated compared to 20 per cent for untreated offenders (Marques 1988, Marques *et al.* 1989, Miner *et al.* 1990). A three-year follow-up found few subjects from either the treated or the untreated groups had been arrested or returned to custody for sexual or non-sexual crimes (Marques *et al.* 1991). However, the untreated offenders were re-arrested after a much shorter period of time than the treated offenders, and on average, the treated group presented a lower risk of both violent and sexual offences than the untreated group. This gives the therapists some grounds for cautious optimism, but from what is known about sex offender recidivism, follow-up needs to be done for some years longer to confirm the success of the approach.

Thornton (1992b) conducted a useful review of such comprehensive evaluations as there are of cognitive–behavioural programmes in which he compared their effects in terms of recidivism rates with those of other modes of treatment, excepting physical treatments. Table 8.1 presents a summary of these evaluation results. Re-offending as recorded here refers

Table 8.1: Long-term outcome for treated and untreated sex offenders

Study	Percent known to re-offend sexually		
Cognitive–behavioural programmes	Treated	Untreated	Apparent effect
Davidson (1979–80)	11.0	35.0	treated 69% better
Marques *et al.* (1987–91)	5.0	7.8	treated 36% better
Marshall and Barbaree (1988)	17.9	42.9	treated 58% better
Rice *et al.* (1990)	37.0	31.0	untreated 16% better
Other types of programme			
Florida (1984)	13.6	6.5	untreated 52% better
Frisbie (1969)	19.4	11.5	untreated 41% better
Peters Institute (1980)	13.6	7.2	untreated 47% better
Sturgeon and Taylor (1980)	15.4	25.0	treated 38% better

Source: Thornton 1992a

only to further convictions for sexual offences. The 'apparent effect' is the difference in reconviction rates between treated and untreated offenders, expressed as a percentage of the rate for the untreated group.

Table 8.1 shows clearly that those cognitive–behavioural programmes Thornton reviewed are associated with lower sexual reconviction. In the one evaluation that did not show this effect, the programme had never been fully implemented (Rice, Quinsey and Harris 1991). Therapy of other types, for example the psychoanalytic approach taken by the Peters Institute, seems on the whole to have failed in reducing re-offending.

Features of therapeutic programmes associated with success

Although evidence for the general success of comprehensive cognitive–behavioural sex offender programmes is beginning to accumulate, very little is currently known about which features of programmes contribute to their success in reducing re-offending. The current basis of much programme design is conventional wisdom, based on the experience of a few widely read practitioners. However, there are several evaluations in progress, and assessments of the importance of different aspects of therapeutic programmes are beginning to be published.

Types of offender

Some types of offenders appear to respond better to therapy than others. Marshall *et al.* (1991a) report a number of programmes that appear to be more successful with child molesters and exhibitionists than they are with rapists. There is, however, no discussion of why this might be. The California Sex Offender Treatment Evaluation Project reported the failure of the aversion therapy component of their programme with rapists, and, as a result, decided to replace it with a covert sensitisation procedure (Marques *et al.* 1989). Again, the authors present no discussion of why the therapy might have failed with this group. There may be any number of reasons for such failures. Pro-rape attitudes probably have wider social support than does the idea of sex between adults and children. Rapists may find social reinforcement for their distorted ideas about women and sex, such that their willingness to accept responsibility for their offences, and consequently their motivation to engage, is reduced. Given the increasing numbers of convictions for rape, it seems important for future research to address the failure of interventions with this group.

Within the population of child molesters coming to sex offender programmes, it is possible to identify those more likely to succeed in therapy than others. The STEP study, carried out recently in the UK, found that entrenched offenders – characterised by sexual and emotional preferences for children, and seriously inadequate personalities – required significantly more therapeutic input to achieve any level of change than did offenders with less entrenched offending habits (Beckett *et al.* 1994). Careful assessment of the nature of those entering therapy seems a prerequisite for success.

Length of programme

Early results from an analysis of data collected on juvenile sex offenders undergoing a programme of therapy in the United States suggest that the longer offenders are in treatment, the lower their risk of re-offending, and the higher the chance of achieving treatment goals (Ryan *et al.* 1987). This study suggests that nine to twelve months should be the minimum duration of treatment. Unfortunately, no information was given about the conditions under which treatment was delivered, or how many hours of treatment this nine- to twelve-month period should involve. However, the same general conclusion is supported by a study reported in Fordham (1992), which found that offenders' gains from therapy increased over a six-month period. The researchers in the latter study suggested that a 30 to 40 per cent further improvement was possible if the programme had continued.

The STEP study found that short-term programmes – those of approximately 60 hours duration – had some success in reducing denial and minimisation of offences in some sex offenders. However, they were found to have made little progress in addressing the problems of relapse prevention, and to have had little or no effect with the more entrenched child molesters. In fact, the STEP report recommends that this latter group of offenders would be best dealt with in a residential therapeutic environment, so that not only can they receive a much higher number of hours of therapy but can also be monitored during the time they are not being worked with (Beckett *et al.* 1994).

Therapeutic tasks

From follow-up data on 69 juvenile sex offenders, Ryan and Miyoshi (1990) were able to reach tentative conclusions about the association of certain tasks in therapy with a reduction in re-offending. The post-therapy follow-up period was anywhere between 12 to 30 months after completion of the programme, and during this time 9.2 per cent of the sample were either rearrested or questioned in relation to a sexual offence. The achievements in therapy found to be associated with non-offence were the ability of offenders to interrupt the offence cycle identified during therapy and their ability to identify factors that might trigger an offence. On the basis of these findings, Ryan and Miyoshi suggest that therapists and researchers should place particular importance on helping offenders understand their offending as part of a cycle of behaviour, and teaching them methods of interrupting that cycle. This message supports the work of the large number of programmes for sex offenders in which understanding the cycle of offending is the cornerstone.

Impressions of success in therapy

Ryan and Miyoshi make the additional important point that clinicians' general impressions of offenders' success in a programme for sex offenders do not necessarily predict the ability of those offenders to prevent themselves from committing further assaults. This supports the idea that some objective evaluation of the success of the intervention is a vital part of any programme that attempts to reduce risk. Clearly, if those running treatment programmes are to make recommendations in relation to the likelihood of an individual re-offending on completion of a programme then these are best made on the basis of objective assessments of change in addition to professional judgement.

Relapse prevention

A relapse prevention module may also be an important part of therapy. The SOTEP study at Atascedero State Hospital in California employs relapse prevention techniques to consolidate and maintain therapeutic changes. The programme's researchers found that the strongest predictor of the offender's likelihood to re-offend was his ability to apply the relapse prevention skills learnt in the programme (Marques *et al.* 1991). Imparting to the offenders a sense of responsibility for their behaviour was not enough on its own to lower their risk of committing further sexual offences. Findings from the STEP study support the importance of teaching relapse prevention strategies (Becket *et al.* 1994). Pithers (1990) reports a five-year follow-up of 167 sex offenders (147 child molesters and 20 rapists) treated using a relapse prevention model, which revealed only a four per cent recidivism rate. He suggests that a critical component of such a programme is to organise a network of friends and family to supervise the offender outside the therapeutic context. The members of this network meet regularly with therapists to monitor the offender's progress. This rather elaborate process is believed to give offenders additional support in managing their 'lapses' so as to prevent them becoming 'relapses'. Though both Pithers and Ryan *et al.* are reporting early findings, it seems intuitively sensible to believe that providing offenders with techniques for coping with their lapses, and structures to help them monitor and control their behaviour, will increase their chances of not re-offending.

Programme implementation and management

There is evidence to suggest that the implementation and management of programmes is important for their success in reducing recidivism. A report on eight community-based sex offender programmes running in the Pacific Region of Canada concluded that 'a rigorous, tough-minded approach (to delivering treatment) has a measurable positive effect on recidivism rates' (Stephenson 1991, p. 29). In a generally pessimistic evaluation of the effectiveness of these programmes, only the programmes that met prescribed standards for therapist training and experience and efficient record keeping, were found to result in reductions in recidivism. The researchers reported that in the programmes not found to be effective there was no treatment plan drawn up for the group or for individuals. Discussions in these 'non-effective' groups did not challenge denial by the offenders or even focus on offences, and cycles of offending were not identified or followed-up. Offenders were disruptive and disrespectful towards therapists in these groups. The groups that appeared to be reducing recidivism were also those that inspired confidence in the parole officers whose clients were on the programme. The Canadian experience, moreover, was that the effective programmes were also financially less costly than the other, less well-managed programmes.

The STEP study had several interesting observations to make in this respect. The researchers were concerned with examining group leadership skills and the cohesiveness of the sex offender groups they evaluated, since previous research had indicated that these factors may be important to successful therapy. It transpired that programmes that achieved the most change in their clients were those that group members rated highest in cohesiveness, and where there was agreement between leaders and members as to group goals and expectations.

Together, these findings suggest that good management and group leadership skills should be a much higher priority for sex offender programmes than they may have been up to now. The Canadian discovery of a direct relationship between these factors and recidivism is tremendously helpful in promoting proper support and resourcing of sex offender programmes. The relative cheapness of effective programmes lends additional weight to this argument.

There remain a number of features common to cognitive–behavioural programmes, the contribution of which to reducing recidivism has yet to be demonstrated. For example, there are as yet no data relating to the optimal number of hours of treatment for delivery over the suggested minimum period of nine to twelve months. Further, the research so far undertaken provides no advice on the proportion of group work to individual work most likely to benefit different types of offender. Studies tell us that the training of staff, resourcing of programmes and support of management are important to the success of therapeutic programmes. However, research is currently not in a position to tell us precisely how and to what degree these features are important.

Conclusion

Research supports the contention that cognitive–behavioural therapies can significantly reduce the recidivism rate of sexual offenders. Effective programmes appear to be those that are comprehensive and include interventions aimed at reducing deviant sexual arousal, modifying distorted cognitions and beliefs and enhancing offenders' abilities to interrupt their own cycles of offending, and which provide relapse prevention training.

In summary, there are a number of features of programmes which the research suggests are associated with reduced offending:

(1) The type of offender on the programme can produce differential effectiveness: child molesters and exhibitionists seem to respond better to cognitive–behavioural treatment as currently applied than do rapists.

(2) Longer-term programmes seem generally to be more effective than shorter programmes.

(3) Teaching offenders techniques for identifying and interrupting their own offence cycles seems to be important, as does including a relapse prevention component in treatment.

(4) Good management and thorough implementation of programmes appears positively to affect the resulting recidivism rates of programme graduates. It is difficult to see how offenders can benefit from treatment that does not actually take place or is delivered by those not qualified for such work.

References

Barker, M. and Morgan, R. (1993) *Sex Offenders: A Framework for the Evaluation of Community-based Treatment.* London: Home Office.

Beckett, R., Beech, A., Fisher, D. and Fordham, A.S. (1994) *Community-based Treatment for Sex Offenders: An Evaluation of Seven Treatment Programmes.* Occasional Paper Series. London: Home Office.

Finkelhor, D. with Araji, A., Beron, L., Browne, A., Peters, S.D. and Wyatt, G.E. (1986) *A Sourcebook of Child Sexual Abuse.* California: Sage.

Fordham, A.S. (1992) 'Evaluating sex offender treatment programmes.' Paper presented to British Psychological Society Conference, Harrogate.

Marques, J.K. (1988) 'The Sex Offender Treatment and Evaluation Project: California's New Outcome Study.' In R. Prentley and V. Quinsey (eds) *Human Sexual Aggression: Current Perspectives. Annals of New York Academy of Sciences 528,* 235–243.

Marques, J.K., Day, D.M., Nelson, C. and Miner, M.H. (1989) *The Sex Offender Treatment and Evaluation Project: Third Report to State Legislature in response to PC 1365.* California: California Department of Mental Health.

Marques, J.K., Day, D.M., Nelson, C., Miner, M.H. and West, M.A. (1991) *The Sex Offender Treatment and Evaluation Project: Fourth Report to the State Legislature in Response to PC 1365.* California: California Department of Mental Health.

Marshall, W.L. and Barbaree, H.E. (1990a) 'An integrated theory of the etiology of sexual offending.' In W.L. Marshall, D.R. Laws and H.E. Barbaree (eds) *Handbook of Sexual Assault: Issues, Theories and Treatment of the Offender.* New York: Plenum.

Marshall, W.L. and Barbaree, H.E. (1990b) 'Outcome of comprehensive cognitive–behavioural treatment programmes.' In W.L. Marshall, D.R. Laws and H.E. Barbaree (eds) *Handbook of Sexual Assault: Issues, Theories and Treatment of the Offender.* New York: Plenum.

Marshall, W.L., Jones, R., Ward, T., Johnson, P. and Barbaree, H.E. (1991a) 'Treatment outcomes for sex offenders.' *Clinical Psychology Review 11,* 465–485.

Marshall, W.L., Ward, T., Jones, R., Johnson, P. and Barbaree, H.E. (1991b) 'An optimistic evaluation of treatment outcome with sex offenders.' *Violence Update 1*, 7, 8–11.

Miner, M.H., Marques, J.K., Day, D.M. and Nelson, C. (1990) 'Impact of relapse prevention in treating sex offenders: preliminary findings.' *Annals of Sex Research 3*, 165–185.

Perkins, D. (1991) 'Clinical work with sex offenders in secure settings.' In C.R. Hollins and K. Howells (eds) *Clinical Approaches to Sex Offenders and their Victims.* Chichester: John Wiley and Sons.

Pithers, W.D. (1990) 'Relapse prevention with sexual aggressors: a method for maintaining therapeutic gain and enhancing external supervision.' In W.L. Marshall, D.R. Laws and H.E. Barbaree (eds) *Handbook of Sexual Assault: Issues, Theories and Treatment of the Offender.* New York: Plenum.

Rice, M.M., Quinsey, V.L. and Harris, G.T. (1991) 'Sexual recidivism among child molestors released from a maximum security psychiatric institution.' *Journal of Consulting and Clinical Psychology 59*, 3, 381–386.

Ryan, G. and Miyoshi, T. (1990) 'Summary of a pilot follow-up study of adolescent sexual perpetrators after treatment.' *Interchange 1*, 90, 6–8.

Ryan, G., Davis, J., Miyoshi, T., Lane, S. and Wilson, K. (1987) 'Getting at the facts: the first report from the uniform data collection system.' *Interchange* June, 5.

Salter, A.C. (1988) *Treating Child Sex Offenders and Victims: A Practical Guide.* California: Sage.

Stephenson, M. (1991) 'A summary of an evaluation of the Community Sex Offender Programme in the Pacific Region.' *Forum on Corrections Research 3*, 4, 25–30. Canada: Correctional Service.

Thornton, D. (1992a) 'Long-term outcome of sex offender treatment.' Paper delivered at Third European Conference on Psychology and the Law, Oxford, September.

Thornton, D. (1992b) 'A framework for the assessment of sex offenders.' Paper delivered at Third European Conference on Psychology and the Law, Oxford, September.

Chapter 9

Intensive Probation

George Mair

Intensive probation (IP) in one form or another has been one of the most significant developments in dealing with offenders in the community during the last decade. Although the move towards intensive probation only began in the early 1980s in the USA, by 1990 every state had at least one IP programme. In England and Wales a major policy initiative encouraged several probation areas to set up IP programmes on an experimental basis for a period of two years, beginning in April 1990. Other countries, too, have set up forms of IP. There is, therefore, a sense in which the intensive probation movement has come along and swept all before it but it would be a mistake to jump to such a conclusion too easily. IP cannot be characterised as a coherent approach and there are still too many unanswered questions about it, but in terms of its rapid growth it cannot be ignored.

This paper aims to provide an overview of intensive probation, focusing on the USA and on England and Wales. It contains four sections: first, a description of the background to IP; second, a brief review of the American experience; third, the results of the IP initiative in England and Wales; and finally, a discussion of the policy and practice issues which have emerged from IP.

Background

Perhaps the first thing to be clear about is that intensive probation is not new. During the 1960s and 1970s various forms of IP were tried both in the USA and in the UK; in this country the best-known of these was the IMPACT (Intensive Matched Probation and After-Care Treatment) experiment set up by the then Home Office Research Unit (see Folkard *et al.*

1974, Folkard, Smith and Smith 1976). These early efforts at IP tended to focus upon providing more of what was on offer in the first place – social work counselling – by either delivering more to offenders or by reducing caseloads. In the event, results were by no means as positive as had been hoped for and IP was labelled as a failure. This crude conclusion contributed to the notorious claim associated with Robert Martinson that 'nothing works' – a claim about the efficacy of court sentences which continues to dog community penalties as well as custody today (see Mair 1991). IP, then, does not appear as a brand-new approach to probation; it comes with a history which carries with it (rightly or wrongly) a sense of failure.

The reasons for the revival of IP in the USA in the early 1980s lie in what has been called 'America's Correctional Crisis' (Gottfredson and McConville 1987). Essentially, this consisted of three factors which make up what Petersilia and Turner (1993) refer to as the practical argument in favour of IP: first, prisons and jails were seriously overcrowded to the point where many were under court orders to reduce the numbers incarcerated; second, there was a fiscal crisis which meant that building more custodial institutions, even if it was desirable, was not possible as a solution; and third, there was a feeling that the public had lost confidence in probation as offering any measure of safety from offenders in their care. A further argument – the 'argument from principle' (Petersilia and Turner 1993) – in favour of IP has subsequently emerged which states that the USA has very little to offer offenders between probation and prison; more intermediate punishments are needed and IP offers a useful additional choice (see Morris and Tonry 1990).

These arguments do not, it should be noted, point necessarily to intensive probation as the only possible solution and this may be one reason why there is no such thing as a generic IP programme. Petersilia and Turner (1991) point out that:

> 'So many programs call themselves [IP] that the acronym alone reveals little about any program's particular character. The only common characteristic of [IP] programs is that they involve more supervision than routine probation programs.' (p.611)

Starting from this foundation, IP in America can vary according to its target population, its aims, organisation and operation. It can include the following features in any combination: curfew/house arrest (with or without electronic monitoring), special conditions made by the sentencer (such as employment or counselling), team supervision, drug/alcohol monitoring, community service, probation fees, split sentences/shock incarceration, community sponsors, restitution, objective risk/need assessment (Byrne 1990). The key difference between IP now and IP 20 to 30 years ago is that now the emphasis is on control and surveillance and not on more social work or counselling.

In England and Wales the origins of IP lie in a variety of factors which are impossible to rank in order in terms of their significance. Prison overcrowding was, of course, a factor as it had been for so many penal innovations since the mid-1950s (the suspended sentence, community service, and day centres being only three examples). Also, in the second half of the 1980s there emerged two closely related themes about the need for effective punishment and the necessity of restoring the confidence of sentencers in the work of the probation service. The influential Green Paper *Punishment, Custody and the Community* (Home Office 1988) pointed out that prison 'was not the most effective punishment for most crime' (p.2), whilst also making the point that there was a need for rigorous and demanding community penalties which would effectively reduce offending. The large decrease in the number of juveniles involved in court proceedings was an important example of what might be achieved (between 1980 and 1990 the number of juveniles proceeded against in magistrates' courts dropped by around 85,000 – partly as a result of demographic changes). Costs were another factor: prison is expensive and community penalties are assumed to be markedly cheaper, although if IP did not in fact act to divert offenders from custody any cost advantage would be lost. Finally, there was the example of IP in the USA. As with so many innovations, this had been hailed as the answer to any number of problems by criminal justice professionals when it began, and early research tended to confirm this feeling. It was only a matter of time before this wonderful new approach to dealing with offenders in the community made its way across the Atlantic.

IP in England and Wales was intended to be an experimental initiative and there were relatively few guidelines about what it should look like and how it should be put into practice. It was intended for high-risk offenders aged between 17 and 25 who were likely to receive a prison sentence. It was expected to include a day centre or specified activities requirement and frequent reporting to probation officers. Rigorous referral and selection procedures were to be set up; indivualised programmes were to be worked out with the offender and presented to the court; there was to be a focus on offending behaviour; a multi-agency approach was to be used; and the participation of ethnic minority and female offenders was to be ensured.

These guidelines are rather vague and left a considerable amount of discretion to individual probation services as to the kind of IP schemes they would set up. As with the American experience, there is no clear model of IP. Both American and British IP schemes were expected to satisfy a variety of demands – such as reducing offending, diversion from custody, reduction in costs, and so forth – and it would be very surprising indeed if a court disposal could satisfy such demands equally well. IP, like so many innovations, was the subject of considerable claims (particularly in the USA) and therefore suffered to a certain extent from having high expectations thrust upon it. This problem was exacerbated by many jurisdictions in the USA deciding to set up IP schemes without any clear rationale for doing so; IP was fashionable and seemed to offer solutions to many of the difficulties facing probation. But how far was IP successful in practice?

Intensive probation in the USA

There are three main types of IP in the USA – enhanced probation, enhanced parole, and prison diversion (and the last of these can be either 'front-door', which means diverting offenders from prison before they get there, or 'back-door' which means that offenders who have been sentenced to prison are released early on to an IP programme); some IP schemes can include all three types. Our interest here lies primarily in enhanced probation and prison diversion, and three examples of such IP programmes will be described: the Massachusetts scheme which is probation enhancement; the Georgia IP programme which is a 'front-door' diversion scheme; and the New Jersey scheme which uses the 'back-door' method. In addition, the major RAND study of IP will be discussed briefly.

The Georgia IP scheme is commonly credited as being the first significant scheme in the new generation of intensive probation programmes. It is a prison diversion programme which was begun in response to continuing severe levels of overcrowding in the state's prison system. IP participants can be directly sentenced to the programme or placed on it following review by IP staff of those sentenced to custody. Caseloads of 25 offenders are supervised by a probation officer and a surveillance officer; as their titles suggest, these two officers were expected to have different tasks, although in practice it has been found that their work can overlap almost completely. In the early phase of the programme, five face-to-face contacts per week are made; offenders have to comply with conditions of employment (or education or job search), drug/alcohol testing, the payment of probation fees, and house arrest. The programme lasts a minimum of six months.

The Georgia IP scheme was widely perceived to be highly successful and has been used as a model for many other IP programmes. Over time, however, questions have been posed about its perceived success which make the issue less clear-cut. For example, while the programme was claimed to divert offenders from custody, the fact that judges could sentence direct to IP weakens this claim; in addition, a large proportion of those on IP had essentially similar characteristics to those sentenced to regular probation. It should also be noted that as Georgia was traditionally a very heavy user of prison it may be that many of those incarcerated were not particularly serious offenders, thus the scope for diversion was high. While recidivism rates for IP look good, the comparison groups are not similar; and the cost-effectiveness claims for the scheme do not stand up, as many IP cases do not look like diversions from custody (for discussion of the Georgia scheme see Clear, Flynn and Shapiro 1987, Erwin 1986, Erwin 1987, Erwin 1990, Petersilia 1987a, Petersilia 1987b, Petersilia and Turner 1993).

The New Jersey IP scheme is also a prison diversion scheme, but unlike Georgia uses a 'back door' approach whereby after several months in custody prisoners are encouraged to apply for intensive probation. A detailed screening process is carried out and those who are recommended for IP are finally considered by a panel of judges for re-sentencing. This approach is likely to result in the best bets being chosen for IP, but they have been sentenced to prison and served some time so that net-widening should be minimised. The features of the programme are very similar to those of the Georgia scheme, and it too has been hailed as a success. Again, however, questions can be raised: judges may sentence to prison offenders who they would not normally have done so with the expectation that they will apply for IP; and the comparison groups of prison and IP cases are not similar in terms of their characteristics (for more on the New Jersey scheme see Pearson 1987a, Pearson 1987b, Pearson and Bibel 1986, Pearson and Harper 1990 and Petersilia 1987a).

The Massachusetts IP programme is an example of a probation enhancement model. Here, the objective is to make probation more effective by assigning higher-risk offenders to more intensive forms of supervision;

the probation caseload is re-allocated using a risk/needs classification system. Instead of using a self-selected group of probation officers to supervise IP offenders, all probation officers (specifically those included in the study areas) had to be involved in the Massachusetts scheme and this raised serious implementation difficulties. Only around one quarter of offenders received the supervision which they should have under the programme design. Recidivism rates showed little improvement, although there was some evidence that higher levels of supervision (including surveillance and treatment) did lead to a reduction in recidivism (see Byrne and Kelly 1989, Cochran, Corbett and Byrne 1986, Corbett, Cochran and Byrne 1987 and Petersilia 1987a).

The RAND Corporation has carried out a major study of a series of IP programmes in 14 jurisdictions across the USA (see Petersilia and Turner 1991, 1993 and Turner, Petersilia and Deschenes 1992). These studies fail to show that IP is an unequivocal success – reconviction rates did not decrease as expected, technical revocations were high (with consequent implications for the cost of programmes) – but they do point to the kinds of issues raised by earlier studies, for example the need to be clear about what IP was for, how to structure programmes, the balance between surveillance and treatment, the problem of technical revocations, the costs of IP programmes. While the RAND study is an important one, its methodological problem should not be ignored: it is difficult to talk about IP in general as each of the programmes was different; the implementation of the programmes is not covered in detail; the follow-up period was only 12 months; it is quite possible that some parts of programmes are more effective than others but this cannot be dealt with in the research design; and questions remain about the appropriateness and effectiveness of the random allocation design used.

Intensive probation in England and Wales

IP programmes in England and Wales ran officially in eight probation areas for 24 months from 1 April 1990, and the Home Office Research and Planning Unit set up a study to examine its operation and impact. The design of the research was dictated by the belief that a process evaluation was a vital prerequisite to any outcome evaluation insofar as it was impossible to interpret the meaning of an outcome measure without some understanding of the processes which gave rise to it. There is an easy assumption made too often in research that the programme planned is the programme which is delivered, but this is by no means always the case for a variety of reasons both good and bad.

A monitoring system was set up to collect information on all referrals to IP schemes (the term referrals is used to cover those who were either referred for assessment to IP schemes, recommended for IP in a social inquiry report, or sentenced to IP), and data were collected at three points: first at the point of sentence; second, when the intensive part of the IP scheme was completed; and third, when the order was terminated successfully or unsuccessfully. Three IP programmes were chosen for detailed study in terms of their implementation, operation and organisation: Durham because it was a small area and was starting up its IP programme from scratch; West Yorkshire because it had two IP schemes which had been running for some time prior to the official starting date; and the West Midlands because it was a large metropolitan area. In each of these areas probation officers (both those involved in working on IP as well as others not involved directly) and offenders were interviewed, and a mail questionnaire was sent to all magistrates in those petty sessional divisions which had access to IP.

Two sets of outcome measures were devised. Primary measures were recidivism (during the course of IP as well during subsequent supervision, and covering time to reconviction, the reconviction offence, and the sentence on reconviction), diversion from custody, financial costs, the views of sentencers and the views of offenders. Secondary measures were specific to IP programmes or to the individualised packages put together for offenders and might include finding suitable accommodation or employment, help with tackling drug misuse or the use of leisure facilities.

Overall, a total of 1677 offenders were referred for IP in the eight areas. Almost all of these were male (95%) and more than three quarters were aged 25 or less (half were between 17 and 20 years old). Around six per cent were from ethnic minorities. The most common offence was burglary of a dwelling (26%), with other forms of burglary (16%), theft/handling (16%) and violent offences (14%) also common. Only six per cent were first offenders, whilst 51 per cent had six or more previous court appearances leading to a guilty finding. Fifty four per cent had served a previous custodial sentence and 42 per cent had spent at least some time on remand in custody in connection with their current offence. Almost two thirds (64%) were sentenced at the Crown Court. In all, 45 per cent of referrals were sentenced to IP whilst 37 per cent were sentenced to custody. These figures suggest that IP was successfully targeting offenders at risk of a custodial sentence (they were young, had previous convictions, experience of custody, and were dealt with in the Crown Court). However, these figures hide wide variations amongst areas as the following table shows.

Table 9.1 Referrals to IP schemes by area

Area	% 17–20	% male	% Crown Court	% 6+ pre-cons	% previous custody	Total No.
Durham	52	98	50	61	67	95
Leeds	47	97	73	50	58	532
West Midlands	86	96	47	29	41	187
Berks	88	94	60	35	32	94
Gwent	36	99	55	68	68	186
Hants	40	98	85	63	62	351
Manchester	82	88	35	59	65	17
Northumbria	35	81	39	43	38	215
Total	50	95	64	51	54	1677

Some areas had far more referrals than others (and this was not necessarily a function of size as the Manchester figure of 17 shows; this programme closed down within a year), and some were more successful than others at targeting high-risk offenders, for example Hampshire had more than twice as many sentenced at the Crown Court as Northumbria; Durham was more than twice as likely to have offenders with six or more previous convictions as the West Midlands; and Gwent was more than twice as likely to have offenders with previous custodial experience as Berkshire. Some differences were due to the design of IP schemes; the Northumbria scheme, for example, did not conform to Home Office guidelines in that it was voluntary and not tied to any conditions attached to a probation order (and this may have had something to do with the fact that Northumbria was most successful in targeting female offenders).

Sentencer satisfaction with IP appeared to be very high (although only a few judges were interviewed). There was little agreement about the position of IP among the various sentencing options available to the courts, however, and relatively minor offences were mentioned as being suitable for IP. Overall, the advantages of IP were perceived as either system-oriented (reducing the numbers going into custody) or welfare-oriented (it had strong rehabilitative potential); any mention of the possible more punitive aspects of IP were rare. There was a good deal of agreement about the major potential disadvantage of IP – that it might be seen by offenders or the public as a soft option.

Probation officers who worked on IP schemes were enthusiastic about them (with the exception of West Midlands officers). Non-IP staff were not quite so positive, although the longer that schemes had been running and the more consultation that had taken place, the more likely they were to be satisfied. Negative comments focused upon the elitist nature of IP, claims that ordinary officers could have achieved the same objectives if they had been given the resources allocated to IP, and apprehensions about the use of voluntary organisations. Such organisations were used in all IP programmes to a certain extent, but some probation officers worried that this was a 'thin end of the wedge' scenario whereby voluntary organisations might begin to take work from the probation service, leading eventually to its marginalisation.

Offenders who participated in IP programmes were positive about them. They appreciated the attention which was given to them and felt that someone was taking an interest in them for the first time. They commented very positively about their project workers (who were not professionally qualified probation officers) but saw their probation officers as rather less helpful. This is almost certainly due to the dominance of the project worker who might see an offender several times a day, whereas the supervising officer might see the offender once a week.

The process evaluation of IP raised some key issues about the implementation process of schemes. First, it took some areas quite a few months to get their IP programme up and running; detailed consultations and negotiation were necessary with maingrade officers and with the National Association of Probation Officers (NAPO). The trial period was scheduled to last for 24 months but if some programmes took six to twelve months to become operational, this had implications for the success of the programme. Second, for those areas which had been running IP programmes under another name, time to develop a scheme carefully meant that problems were resolved and mistakes were rectified before the research began; other areas had to grapple with problems while their projects were being studied. Third, an IP scheme with a specific location and dedicated staff seemed to be a better proposition than setting up a general programme which could be applied by any maingrade officer (this is not to suggest that the former is without problems). Finally, and perhaps surprisingly, there was very little evidence of innovation (Northumbria being the honourable exception) in the IP schemes which were developed; most were simply based around existing day centre or specified activities programmes with increased reporting.

IP in England and Wales has been reasonably successful. It has demonstrated that probation services can develop rigorous and demanding programmes which successfully target high-risk offenders; equally, it has shown that not all services may be capable of setting up such programmes efficiently and effectively. The reconviction rates of those subject to IP will be an important indicator of their success and work is underway on this (for a full report of the IP initiative see Mair *et al.* 1994).

Conclusion

Whatever one might think about intensive probation, it does appear to be filling a gap in the community corrections market. The problem may lie in that expectations for IP are pitched so highly that any achievements which do not reach that level are dismissed and IP accounted a failure. Much of the US research into IP in the last few years has stressed the dangers of expecting IP to be able to achieve all of the claims which have been made for it (see, e.g. Byrne, Lurigio and Petersilia 1992). If a community penalty could effectively reduce prison overcrowding as well as re-offending, at the same time as satisfying public safety concerns, and doing all of these things at reasonable cost, it would indeed be a well-deserved success. It would be enough of a challenge to design such a penalty in an ideal world; unfortunately, the complexities of criminal justice systems, the difficulties of trying to change the attitudes and practices of very different individuals, the relative lack of knowledge about successful modes of intervention, and the lack of adequate resources render it impossible. But this is not a counsel of despair; it is more an acknowledgement of the very real problems which exist.

The research into IP may have flaws (what research is not immune from criticism?), but it has supplied a considerable amount of information which, if used properly, could lead to more effective IP programmes. The need for planning and rationalising the introduction of IP rather than a simple knee-jerk reaction to a problem is one common-sense injunction. Petersilia (1990) has set out a list of nine conditions for effective change which she argues are vital for the successful implementation of IP programmes; these are factors which need consideration prior to the introduction of the programme. So far there is relatively little material on the content of effective IP programmes, but increasingly there is agreement that schemes which focus solely upon surveillance and deterrence do not work; a healthy dose of treatment/rehabilitation is necessary (although how much and what kind remains unclear). Simply delivering more – whether it be control, treatment, or whatever – to a group of offenders is not enough; relevant services have to be delivered to appropriate offenders (McIvor 1992). Research has a key role to play in all of this, and better evaluations of IP would be helpful.

Michael Tonry (1990) has argued that even if IP cannot successfully meet all of its stated aims, it very successfully meets various latent aims which ensures its continued growth. IP increases the credibility of probation in the eyes of sentencers and the general public; it increases the self-esteem of probation staff; and it helps satisfy demands for tougher punishment while permitting probation officers to carry on with their functions. Similarly, in England and Wales, the symbolic function of IP should not be ignored. The initiative delivered a message to the probation service about the need to provide demanding programmes which could deal with offenders in the community. From this perspective IP can be read as another move from central government to encourage the service to change direction and culture – a move which has been going on since at least 1984 with the introduction of the Statement of National Objectives and Priorities (Home Office 1984).

Although the formal experiment in this country ended in March 1992, IP remains significant. Many probation areas run IP schemes of one kind or another, and, as noted above, the expressive value of the initiative is important. IP is here to stay for the foreseeable future.

References

Byrne, J.M. (1990) 'The future of intensive probation supervision and the new intermediate sanctions.' *Crime and Delinquency 36*, 1, 6–41.

Byrne, J.M. and Kelly, L. (1989) *Restructuring probation as an intermediate sanction: an evaluation of the Massachusetts Intensive Probation Supervision Program*. Final report to the National Institute of Justice, Washington, DC.

Byrne, J.M., Lurigio, A.J. and Petersilia, J. (eds) (1992) *Smart Sentencing: The Emergence of Intermediate Sanctions*. Newbury Park, CA: Sage.

Clear, T.R., Flynn, S. and Shapiro, C. (1987) 'Intensive supervision in probation: a comparison of three projects.' In B.R. McCarthy (ed)

Intermediate Punishments: Intensive Supervision, Home Confinement and Electronic Surveillance. New York: Criminal Justice Press.

Cochran, D., Corbett, R.P. and Byrne, J.M. (1986) 'Intensive Probation Supervision in Massachusetts: a case study in change.' *Federal Probation L,* 2, 32–41.

Corbett, R.P., Cochran, D. and Byrne, J.M. (1987) 'Managing change in probation: principles and practice in the implementation of an intensive probation supervision program.' In B.R. McCarthy (ed) *Intermediate Punishments: Intensive Supervision, Home Confinement and Electronic Surveillance.* New York: Criminal Justice Press.

Erwin, B.S. (1986) 'Turning up the heat on probationers in Georgia.' *Federal Probation L,* 2, 1724.

Erwin, B.S. (1987) *Evaluation of Intensive Probation Supervision in Georgia: Final Report.* Atlanta, GA: Department of Corrections.

Erwin, B.S. (1990) 'Old and new tools for the modern probation officer.' *Crime and Delinquency 36,* 1, 61–74.

Folkard, M.S., Fowles, A.J., McWilliams, B.C., McWilliams, W., Smith, D.D., Smith, D.E. and Walmsley, G.R. (1974) *IMPACT. Vol. I – The design of the probation experiment and an interim evaluation.* HORS 24. London: HMSO.

Folkard, M.S., Smith, D.E. and Smith, D.D. (1976) *IMPACT. Vol. II – The results of the experiment.* HORS 36. London: HMSO.

Gottfredson, S.D. and McConville, S. (eds) (1987) *America's Correctional Crisis: Prison Populations and Public Policy.* New York: Greenwood Press.

Home Office (1984) *Probation Service in England and Wales: Statement of National Objectives and Priorities.* London: Home Office.

Home Office (1988) *Punishment, Custody and the Community.* Cm 424. London: HMSO.

McIvor, G. (1992) 'Intensive probation supervision: does more mean better?' *Probation Journal 39,* 1, 2–6.

Mair, G. (1991) 'What works – nothing or everything?' *Home Office RSD Research Bulletin 30,* 3–8.

Mair, G., Lloyd, C., Nee, C. and Sibbitt, R. (1994) *Intensive Probation in England and Wales: An Evaluation.* HORS 134. London: Home Office.

Morris, N. and Tonry, M. (1990) *Between Prison and Probation: Intermediate Punishments in a Rational Sentencing System.* New York: Oxford University Press.

Pearson, F.S. (1987a) *Research on New Jersey's Intensive Supervision Program. Final report to the National Institute of Justice.* Washington DC: National Institute of Justice.

Pearson, F.S. (1987b) 'Taking quality into account: assessing the benefits and costs of New Jersey's Intensive Supervision Program.' In B.R. McCarthy (ed) *Intermediate Punishments: Intensive Supervision, Home Confinement and Electronic Surveillance*. New York: Criminal Justice Press.

Pearson, F.S. and Bibel, D.B. (1986) 'New Jersey's Intensive Supervision Program: what it is like? How is it working?' *Federal Probation L, 2*, 25–31.

Pearson, F.S. and Harper, A.G. (1990) 'Contingent intermediate sentences: New Jersey's intensive supervision program.' *Crime and Delinquency 36, 1*, 75–86.

Petersilia, J. (1987a) *Expanding Options for Criminal Sentencing*. Santa Monica, CA: Rand.

Petersilia, J. (1987b) 'Georgia's intensive probation: will the model work elsewhere?' In B.R. McCarthy (ed) *Intermediate Punishments: Intensive Supervision, Home Confinement and Electronic Surveillance*. New York: Criminal Justice Press.

Petersilia, J. (1990) 'Conditions that permit intensive supervision programs to survive.' *Crime and Delinquency 36, 1*, 126–145.

Petersilia, J. and Turner, S. (1991) 'An evaluation of intensive probation in California.' *Journal of Criminal Law and Criminology 82, 3*, 610–658.

Petersilia, J. and Turner, S. (1993) 'Intensive probation and parole.' In M. Tonry (ed) *Crime and Justice: A Review of Research. Vol. 17*. Chicago: University of Chicago Press.

Tonry, M. (1990) 'Stated and latent features of ISP.' *Crime and Delinquency 36, 1*, 174–191.

Turner, S., Petersilia, J. and Deschenes, E.P. (1992) 'Evaluating intensive supervision probation/parole (ISP) for drug offenders.' *Crime and Delinquency 38, 4*, 539–556.

Chapter 10

Evaluating Work with Offenders
Community Service Orders

Jean Hine and Neil Thomas

The growth of community service

If numbers of orders made is the indicator of the success and effectiveness of a sentencing disposal, there is no doubt that community service is a runaway success. Since its introduction in England and Wales in 1975, and in Scotland in 1979, the disposal has prospered beyond all expectation: 1992 (the last year for which published figures are available) saw 10 per cent of all offenders who were sentenced for indictable offences in England and Wales being given a community service order – the same proportion as were given a probation order. This phenomenal success is undoubtedly attributable to the chameleon-like character of the disposal – its ability to appeal to a wide range of penal philosophies and viewpoints.

> '...contemporary penality exists within societies which are themselves marked by pluralism and moral diversity, competing interests and conflicting ideologies. In such a context, and with the need to appeal to a range of different audiences at one and the same time, it is no surprise to find that penality displays a range of rhetorical identifications and a mosaic of symbolic forms.' (Garland 1990, p.275)

Garland was writing about the full range of penal options, but he might easily have been commenting on one particular sentencing option – the community service order. The wide appeal was well described in the Wootton Report (HMSO 1970, paras 33–37), and the author of the report herself said the sentence was 'an undisguised attempt to curry favour with everybody' (Wootton 1978, p.178).

To a Conservative Home Secretary facing a crime wave, a fiscal crisis, an overcrowded and outdated capital stock of prisons and little power to stem the flow of new recruits, it offered a cheap and potentially tough alternative to set before the courts and the party conference. For Labour it maintained a link with its rehabilitative ideals while avoiding claims that it was soft on crime. For Probation Service managers it offered an insurance against the decline of the probation order, a claim on greater resources, a 'liberating catalyst...for new methods' (Mathieson 1977, p.731) and a means of exerting greater managerial control whilst staying true to the mission of avoiding harsh custodial sentences. And sentencers gained a valuable antidote to the perceived weaknesses of probation, prison and fines, with no check on their discretion.

At a deeper level too the order has resonances. In an age of discontinuity and threats to the social order from economic restructuring and social dislocation 'community' spoke variously of mutuality and social order and 'service' envisaged the person responsible for criminal actions responsibly paying back and restoring the balance of social order through the negative wage of free service. Furthermore, the inculcation of work discipline and even skills into those who might not otherwise be subject to it had particular symbolic significance (Foucault 1977). Hoggarth (1991) suggests that the range of features associated with 'work' can equally apply to community service, adding to its attractions.

Here then was a penalty for all seasons, perfectly adaptable to the seasoned and unseasoned offender, and perfectly adaptable to any microclimate. Thus all the pilot schemes could be judged successful and viable, despite considerable differences in approach (Pease *et al.* 1975). Thus probation officers might express views which contradicted their service's avowed policy and perhaps behave accordingly (Pease *et al.* 1975, Young 1978, Skinns 1990). Thus the same scheme could cover benches with contrasting sentencing practices. This adaptability and wide appeal has been the cornerstone of its success and continued growth, a growth accelerated by the implementation of the Criminal Justice Act 1991 with its emphasis on community disposals and introduction of the combination order (a probation order with a short community service order combined).

The introduction of national standards

Community service was the main offspring of a report which marked 'a retreat from penal optimism' of scientific rehabilitation (Hood 1974, p.376) and the emergence of penological pragmatism, lacking a clear philosophical base or overarching goals. Guidance about the operation and organisation of community service was minimal when legislation was introduced, and it remained that way until the imposition of National Standards for Community Service in England and Wales in 1989. At this time John Patten, then Minister of State at the Home Office with responsibility for the introduction of National Standards, acknowledged that guidance issued by the Home Office in 1974 had actually encouraged probation areas to develop working practices 'along lines suited to their local conditions', but he felt this was appropriate then as:

'It is risky to prescribe working practices in too much detail until practical experience and knowledge has accrued.' (Patten 1990)

The Association of Chief Officers of Probation had taken the initiative in 1986 with the publication of Guidelines for the Operation of Community Service, and the National Standards aimed to build on these, but with an emphasis on 'punishment in the community'. As John Patten said at the time, 'If we want the courts and the public to accept that CS is a credible alternative to custody, it must involve punishment.' National standards for Community Service in Scotland were also introduced in 1989, but they took a different and less overtly punitive approach.

National Standards for England and Wales were revised in 1992 (when National Standards were introduced for a range of other aspects of work of the Probation Service) and with them the core characteristic changed:

'the main purpose of a CSO...is to re-integrate the offender into the community through: positive and demanding unpaid work, keeping to disciplined requirements; and reparation to the community by undertaking socially useful work which, if possible, makes good damage done by offending.' (Home Office 1992a, p.67)

However, the procedures laid down to achieve this modified vision were not much changed, reflecting, as Garland suggests, that:

'...penal discourse is as much concerned with its projected image, public presentation and legitimacy as it is with organising the practice of regulation.' (Garland 1985)

The chameleon-like nature of the disposal requires evaluation that is similarly multi-faceted, in order to assess the wide range of indicators of success necessitated by the range of interested parties. Most evaluative

exercises in community service have addressed just one or two of the
many facets of the chameleon, with just two research projects attempting
to evaluate a wide range of the elements of community service – one in
Scotland and one in England. This review will focus particularly on those
two pieces of work by Gill McIvor in Scotland and by Neil Thomas, Jean
Hine and Mike Nugent in England (McIvor 1992, Thomas, Hine and
Nugent 1990). National Standards for England and Wales 1992 provide
us with a good framework for assessing effectiveness, allowing us at the
same time to test some of the assumptions inherent within those standards. A detailed resume of the standards will not be provided, but in
summary the intentions appear to be:

- To instil confidence in sentencers, who will then impose orders on
  serious offenders committing serious offences and not on people for
  whom less onerous sentences are appropriate – thus diverting them
  from costly custodial sentences.

- To make properly targeted offenders appreciate and conform to the
  tight discipline imposed, acknowledge CS as a means of making
  amends and benefit from the discipline, skills and self-esteem that can
  be derived. They become less alienated and more law-abiding, not
  least by working with or on behalf of those less fortunate than
  themselves.

- To help the community – especially its most vulnerable members –
  reap practical benefits as well as seeing the positive contributions
  which offenders can make, reducing fear of criminals and facilitating
  community reintegration.

Sentencers

Sentencer confidence

Measuring sentencer confidence is not easy. In Scotland, Carnie (1990)
interviewed sentencers soon after the introduction there of National
Standards for Community Service, at which time the sentencers themselves said that they would have little direct impact on their sentencing
practice. No such study has been undertaken with sentencers in England
and Wales, and thus we have to look for other data which might indicate
the impact of the National Standards here.

Criminal Statistics England and Wales 1991 (Home Office 1992b) show
that sentences of community service increased proportionately and in raw

numbers in the early 1980s, but then remained relatively stable for the rest of the decade. There was no substantial change in pattern following the introduction of National Standards in 1988–89. It could be argued that National Standards were not intended to increase the overall numbers of community service orders made, rather they were meant to encourage sentencers to make more orders on more serious offenders and fewer orders on less serious offenders. If this was effective, the overall numbers of orders made could well have fallen.

Probation Statistics England and Wales (Home Office 1993) provide two possible indicators of 'seriousness' of offenders: current offence and previous sentences experienced. The figures show very little change in the nature of the offences for which community service was made. The most common offence type in 1992 was theft and handling stolen goods, and has been so since 1981. There was a slight increase in 1992 in the proportion of orders which were made for violence and burglary offences, but nothing which can be attributed to the introduction of National Standards in 1989.

The previous sentencing history of offenders has actually become less serious over time rather than more so, with the proportion of first offenders increasing from 10 per cent in 1981 to 14 per cent in 1991 (the last year for which this information is available) and the proportion of offenders with a previous custodial sentence falling from 40 per cent in 1981 to 34 per cent in 1991, neither trend being interrupted by the introduction of National Standards. There is thus no evidence here that sentencer confidence was increased by the introduction of National Standards.

Sentencing figures also call into question the effectiveness of National Standards in achieving another stated aim: that of fairness and consistency. The Standards themselves relate to delivery of the service rather than to sentencing, but there are clear gender differences in sentencing to community service orders. Table 10.1 shows the percentage of offenders sentenced to community service for indictable offences in different age and gender groups. The different sentencing rates between the four groups have remained constant over time and have not been affected by National Standards.

There are also significant differences in both the previous criminal history and the type of offence for men and women on community service. Figure 10.1 shows the different proportions of first offenders amongst men and women between 1981 and 1991, and also the way in which the trends changed in the last two years illustrated. The proportion of first offenders amongst women increased, whilst the proportion of first offenders amongst men slightly decreased. There is some tentative evidence here that National Standards did affect the extent to which less serious offenders were sentenced to community service, but only in the desired direction with respect to males.

Table 10.1 Percentage of offenders sentenced for indictable offences only in England and Wales, who were sentenced to community service orders 1981–1991, by gender and age group

	Males		Females	
Type of order and Year	*Aged 17–20 years*	*Aged 21 and over*	*Aged 17–20 years*	*Aged 21 and over*
	%	%	%	%
1981	11	5	4	2
1982	11	6	4	2
1983	13	7	4	2
1984	13	7	5	3
1985	13	7	5	3
1986	14	7	5	3
1987	13	7	5	3
1988	13	7	6	3
1989	13	6	5	3
1990	13	7	6	4
1991	14	8	6	4
Total number sentenced 1991, all sentences	**82,400**	**190,000**	**10,300**	**29,200**

Source: Criminal Statistics England and Wales, 1991, Tables 7.10–7.13, pp.151–152 (Home Office 1993)

The Study of Community Service Orders in England (Thomas *et al*. 1990) examined practice in detail in five community service schemes around the country. The schemes were chosen to represent the spectrum of organisation and approaches to community service in operation at that time (prior to National Standards). The assumption that stricter community service would result in greater sentencer confidence and thus more orders on

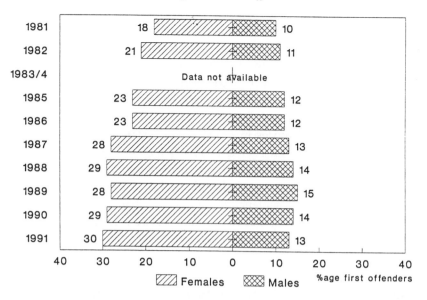

Source: Probations Statistics 1991, Table 3.5, pp.45–46 (Home Office 1992c)

Figure 10.1 Percentage of males and females sentenced to community service 1981–91 who were first offenders

more serious offenders can be tested by comparing 'strictness' of the regime with the nature of the offenders who were given community service. There were indeed differences between the schemes studied in terms of both the proportion of first offenders (7% to 18%) and the proportion of offenders with previous custodial experience (35% to 39%). However there was no real correlation between these rates, nor between the rates and the 'tightness' of the scheme.

The immediate impact of the National Standards in England and Wales was monitored in a study commissioned by the Association of Chief Officers of Probation (Wilkinson and Thomas 1991). The study included detailed interviews with staff in nine probation areas in England and Wales. The results from this survey concerning the impact of National Standards on sentencing practice are mixed. Four areas reported a decrease in the number of orders made, whilst five reported an increase. The seriousness of the offence and the previous criminal history of the offenders also showed variations in the nature of the changes which occurred. In many ways this is not surprising. A detailed examination of offence and previous sentencing based on the Bale Risk of Custody Scale (Hine 1991) showed considerable agreement among sentencers about the 'core' group of offenders to whom community service was given in terms of the seriousness of the offence and their previous criminal history. About 75 per cent of the offenders in every scheme fell into the mid range of offence seriousness and previous criminal history. The variation which did occur was in relation to the remaining 25 per cent of offenders, and here there were substantial differences in practice. For instance, one scheme had more offenders with serious current offences and very few offenders with minor offences, whilst another had a minority of first offenders and more offenders with a previous custodial sentence. The scope for significant and consistent impact upon sentencing practice was therefore limited. Elizabeth Hoggarth also found that community service is used mainly 'at the middle levels of offending score' (Hoggarth 1991).

Table 10.2 Offenders breaching community service orders in England and Wales 1981–91, number and percentage breached and number and percentage sentenced to immediate custody

| | | Community Service | | |
Year	Number offenders breaching order	Breaches as %age of offenders sentenced	Number sentenced to immediate custody	%age use of immediate custody
1981	4500	18%	1700	37%
1982	5300	18%	2000	38%
1983	5600	16%	2100	37%
1984	6400	16%	2500	38%
1985	6500	17%	2600	41%
1986	6200	18%	2300	36%
1987	6600	18%	2300	35%
1988	8200	23%	2600	31%
1989	9600	28%	2500	26%
1990	11,000	30%	2300	21%
1991	11,900	29%	2400	21%

Source: Criminal Statistics England and Wales 1991, Table 7.28, p.169 (Home Office 1993)

NB Percentages are based on raw figures and this may not correspond exactly to percentages obtained from the rounded figures in this table.

Another measure of sentencer confidence can be obtained from looking at the numbers of breaches processed by the courts and the outcomes of those breaches.

The figures in Table 10.2 do show a striking impact of National Standards on the number of offenders returned to court for breach of their community service order. The figures had been relatively stable since 1984, but then in 1988 there was a sharp rise in both the number of people proceeded against for breach, and the rate of breaches. Whilst National Standards did not take official effect until early 1989, draft standards were circulated to probation services early in 1988 with encouragement to begin to implement them as soon as possible. We thus see the Standards beginning to have an effect on enforcement policy even before they were finalised. The increase in numbers has continued, though the rate has remained steady at between 28 per cent and 30 per cent of orders in a year.

The outcome of these breach proceedings is of considerable interest, indicating as it does sentencer response. The numbers of people who have been given a custodial sentence in England and Wales following breach proceedings for community service has been very stable across each of the ten years in Table 10.2, despite the huge increase in numbers of people dealt with for breach since 1988. Courts have therefore been much more likely to allow the order to continue since the introduction of National Standards, the proportion receiving an immediate custodial sentence having fallen from 35 per cent in 1987 to 21 per cent in 1991. Is this a sign of increased confidence? Is giving the offender back to the community service scheme a demonstration of the sentencer's belief that the order will be completed? These figures confirm a view expressed by community service staff during the study of community service orders in England, that breach proceedings changed from being a 'last resort' measure with a high likelihood of the order being revoked, to a 'first resort' measure with an accompanying expectation that in most cases a warning would be given and the order allowed to continue. This is a policy which was undoubtedly successful, as a high proportion of orders which were allowed to continue were subsequently completed successfully, but not without significant cost. The costing exercise in the English study estimated that breach proceedings cost between £103 and £231. The question remains as to whether this has been a cost worth paying – a conservative estimate of the total national cost of breaches would be approximately £2 million in 1991.

The role of the Probation Officer in sentencing

Most community service orders are made following the preparation of a pre-sentence (previously social inquiry) report by a probation officer. These reports are influential, and thus the role of the probation officer in targeting community service orders must be considered. The study of community service orders in England found that in the four schemes where this data was available, between 85 and 98 per cent of orders had a report prepared. Around a half of these had community service as the main proposal and a further ten per cent of orders had CS as a secondary proposal, with a further 25 per cent of reports proposing a disposal other than CS but stating that community service was available. This meant that roughly 15 per cent of the orders made had no report or had a report which did not mention community service (a few did have a report which said that the offender was not suitable for community service).

Whilst courts frequently make community service orders where probation officers have felt that another (usually lesser or equal) penalty would be more appropriate, we also know from studies of social inquiry Reports that many proposals for community service are rejected by sentencers in favour of a custodial sentence. Thus probation officer attempts to implement local or national policies in relation to targeting will meet with limited success. Unfortunately we have no information to indicate whether there was any change in the nature of recommendations or sentencers' agreement rates following the introduction of National Standards. There was significant impact by the Criminal Justice Act 1991 on both counts, but this was part of a much broader restructuring of sentencing practice and is likely to have had much greater impact than National Standards which were geared to affecting the way a particular sentence was operated within an unchanged sentencing framework.

Offenders

The impact of 'discipline'

An assumption embedded in National Standards is that tight schemes inculcate discipline, and that over time this will improve compliance with the requirements of the order and thereby the completion rates. The evidence for this is patchy.

Table 10.2 shows that the breach rate increased to a level of 28 per cent in 1989 following the initial introduction of the Standards, and since then has been 30 per cent and 29 per cent. If this assumption had held true we would have expected that the breach rate would reduce after an initial high, rather than showing a slight increase as it has.

Some positive data confirming this view comes from the study of Community Service Orders in Scotland (McIvor 1992). In this study of 12 community service schemes six schemes were identified as 'more strict' and six identified as 'less strict'. These schemes were then compared for their level of absences, both acceptable and unacceptable. Absence levels were lower in the strict schemes, suggesting that stricter enforcement increased compliance with requirements. However when this analysis was taken one step further to look at the eventual outcomes of orders, there was no real difference between the schemes in terms of their successful completion rates:

> 'Even in the absence of rigidly enforced guidelines, however, it appeared that offenders were well able to gauge the tolerance of community service staff. This would explain why schemes achieved similar levels of completion despite wide variations in the levels of unacceptable absences from work.' (McIvor 1992, p.72)

Whilst there was no relationship between the number of absences and the likelihood of completing the order satisfactorily, there was a relationship with the time taken to complete – more absences were related to longer time to complete the order – but unfortunately it is not clear in which direction the causal link might be. Thus it may be that the longer it takes to complete the order the more absences there will be.

These findings were confirmed in our study of community service orders in England (Thomas *et al.* 1990). Around 70 per cent of orders were completed satisfactorily in each of the five schemes studied. There was some difference in whether the remaining 30 per cent of orders ended because of breach proceedings or because of a further conviction, although to some extent this distinction was false. We found that failure to attend for community service and the commission of a further offence often went together, with differences in recording practice between the schemes accounting for the different figures. It may also be a matter of timing which leads to one outcome rather than the other.

Table 10.3 overleaf compares each of the five schemes in the study of community service orders in England on a range of factors. We can see from this table that a high breach rate (a measure of strict enforcement) does not correlate with a high completion rate. Both scheme C and scheme E have a high rate of breach: in the former the overall successful rate of completion was just 56 per cent but in the latter it was 75 per cent. The key factor here is the courts' responses to the breaches. Scheme C had a low rate of orders allowed to continue, whereas scheme E had a high rate of continuance. This in turn led to a much higher average cost per order. In both schemes with a high breach rate there was a low proportion of orders completed within six months. The evidence is therefore confusing about the impact of stricter enforcement of the requirements of community service orders.

Table 10.3: Comparison of five community service schemes in England

Item	Scheme A	Scheme B	Scheme C	Scheme D	Scheme E
Mean length of order (hours)	127	129	123	135	135
% orders hours completed	71%	68%	56%	67%	75%
% orders with one or more breach proven	22%	18%	29%	22%	28%
% of orders allowed to continue following breach	7%	9%	8%	8%	21%
% orders where further offence committed	30%	30%	15%	15%	19%
% of orders completed with 6 months	68%	53%	36%	56%	35%
% of orders with more than 3 failures to attend	69%	69%	35%	39%	43%
% of orders with lst work appointment within 7 days	4%	0%	24%	10%	59%
% of orders with personal problems recorded	56%	69%	43%	31%	56%
Average cost breach proceedings	£204	£104	£103	£188	£231
Average cost per order (weighted, 1988–9 costs)	£750	£712	£494	£566	£715
Average cost per hour of CS worked	£7.95	£7.55	£6.85	£6.06	£6.57

Source: Thomas, Hine and Nugent 1990

There is evidence from the work in Scotland and England that some of the components of National Standards are not related to the eventual outcome of the community service order. Both McIvor (1992) and Thomas *et al.* (1990) found no relationship between the completion rate and either time to start work or being given the first appointment. Orders which took a long time to start were just as likely to be successfully completed as those where the offender started work within a day or two of the order being made. Other features of the experience of community service had more direct bearing on the outcome of the order, as is witnessed by the comments made by offenders during interviews.

Offenders' views
The tasks which offenders undertook during their community service orders were important, but they did not differentiate work in the way in which it is usually described within the Probation Service, for instance as 'group' task or 'individual' task, as 'manual' work or 'caring' work. In talking to offenders it was clear that an important factor for them was that the work they were doing was worthwhile: that they could see that someone would benefit from the work that they were carrying out. It was not necessary for them to enjoy the work to feel that it was worthy, nor did they necessarily need to have direct contact with the beneficiary to feel this: it was important that the worth of their work was apparent from the task, or that it was explained to them by their supervisor. A similar conclusion emerged from both the Scotland and the England research.

Supervision by a community service supervisor whom the offender respected was another key factor. In Thomas *et al.*'s (1990) study it was apparent from interviews that on the whole offenders had a very positive view of community service staff and that respect was lost or confirmed by contact with them. The value of good CS supervisors was not lost on scheme managers either. Each scheme seemed to have one or two outstanding supervisors who could be trusted to win over difficult offenders and help them through their order.

A high proportion of offenders in both the Scottish and English studies felt that they gained something from their experience of community service. Some felt they had acquired new skills (such as decorating), whilst others had refreshed old skills. Some unemployed offenders felt that the experience was helpful in 'getting the feel of the tools again' whilst many employed offenders resented having to give up 'free' time, especially at weekends, to undertake their work. Many had a sense of satisfaction with a 'job well done', whilst others were content to have helped someone in a very constructive way. These sorts of responses were common among all offenders, no matter what the type of work which was undertaken or whether it was carried out in an individual agency or a group project. Tasks which researchers expected offenders to experience as tedious (e.g. counting buttons into small bags for sale in a charity shop) the offenders were often able to justify in terms of the value to the agency, group or individual for whom the task was done. Some welcomed the opportunity to meet new people and quite a few felt their self-esteem and self-confidence had increased from the experience, especially where they felt they had been trusted or given some responsibility.

Many offenders actually enjoyed their experience of community service, probably because they were getting something constructive out of it. Some level of enjoyment or value was essential to maintain attendance rates on community service: without this there was no incentive to turn up other than the sanction of a further court appearance attached to non-attendance. It is much more constructive to hear an offender say that he (rarely a she) had forced himself to attend his community service placement because he didn't want to let the beneficiary down.

Reconviction

Reconviction rates following a community service sentence have been addressed by a range of studies, with remarkably similar results. McIvor (1992) describes these studies in some detail, with reconviction rates of between 36 and 44 per cent within 12 months of sentence and 51 per cent within two years. Her own work suggested 40 per cent were reconvicted within one year and 58 per cent reconvicted within two years of the original community service sentence. She went on to suggest that the first six months was the period of greatest risk (29% reconvicted within this period), but cannot clarify what proportion of these reconvictions relate to offences committed prior to the sentence of community service. It was possible in this study however to look at those offenders sentenced within the first six months and look at subsequent reconvictions. This revealed that a very high proportion of these offenders had a second reconviction within the full four years of follow-up.

The Home Office undertook a study of reconviction rates among offenders sentenced to probation or to community service in England and Wales during 1987 and published the results in a Statistical Bulletin (Home Office 1993). This survey also did not distinguish reconvictions for offences prior to the order being made, nor did it try to assess the possible impact of this feature. The analysis revealed that 54 per cent of those receiving a community service order that year had a reconviction within two years: a remarkably similar figure to that derived from other research. This would suggest that overall around 55 per cent of offenders sentenced to community service orders can be expected to be reconvicted within two years of sentence.

McIvor (1992) explores in some detail relationships between reconviction and a range of other features examined in the research. Several important features which emerged from this were unrelated to the offenders' experience of community service: age of offender, number of previous convictions, and time between last conviction and community service conviction. However there was some indication that the community service experience can influence outcome:

> 'Offenders whose experiences of community service had been particularly rewarding were less often reconvicted and fewer were convicted of offences involving dishonesty, such as burglaries and thefts.' (McIvor 1992, p.173)

The community

The overwhelming response from agencies and beneficiaries for whom community service work is carried out is of appreciation and gratitude. Beneficiaries were interviewed by Thomas et al. (1990) whilst McIvor (1992) conducted a large postal survey of placement-providing agencies and individual recipients of community service work. Much of this appreciation was due to the fact that few beneficiaries would have been able to get the work done if it had not been for the intervention of community service schemes: individuals and agencies did not have the finances to be able to pay for the work to be undertaken, and did not have people (volunteers, family, friends) who could do it for them. Pensioners were particularly appreciative, be it of their garden being tended, a room being decorated or a lunch being provided at a lunch club.

In both the English and Scottish studies most beneficiaries reported that the work which was undertaken was of a high standard with which they were very satisfied. There were occasional complaints about messy working such as paint being spilled on the floor. On the whole, however, work was experienced as being well done and where necessary people were neat and tidy. Quite a few beneficiaries befriended or were befriended by the offenders who were working with them: for instance the woman who appreciated the advice of the offender whilst they were wheelchair shopping; the pensioner who insisted on making too frequent cups of tea for a group of offenders decorating his home; or the group of offenders who always bought an extra portion of fish and chips so that the pensioner for whom they were tending the garden could join them for lunch.

It might have been expected that the experience of direct contact with offenders may have helped to reduce beneficiaries' fears of crime and of offenders. Interestingly, however, Thomas *et al.* (1990) found that questions in this area led to responses which suggested that beneficiaries frequently felt that the offenders whom they knew were not typical of other offenders, and often forgot that the community service workers were in fact offenders performing a sentence of the court.

Conclusion

Press reports suggest that procedures will be toughened in the current redrafting of National Standards. Early drafts show the aims of CS to be unchanged, but particular attention has been given to detailed specification of the criteria for work placements, such as some placements 'providing manual work'. More generally, work must 'restrict the offender's liberty, and...take account of his or her responsibilities but not convenience.' They could again be an exercise in 'projected image', made more likely in current times of political uncertainty. McNair (1993), commenting on the 1992 standards, noted that those aspects which were tightly defined and monitored were the process aspects such as pace of work, frequency of attendance and unacceptable absences, whereas those aspects left loose concerned substance and outcomes (students of the 'effectiveness' literature might question whether this is the right way round). Whilst the newest standards for community service may be trying to impinge more on the substance, they should still be seen as:

> '...a framework for the expectation and requirements of supervision. They are there to enable professional judgement to be exercised within a framework of accountability, by encouraging imagination, initiative and innovation in the development of good practice and by ensuring that supervision is delivered fairly, consistently and without discrimination.' (McNair 1993, p.116)

In 1987, the report of a national survey of probation area views about community service orders identified a constant counter-balance between administrative efficiency and professional effectiveness (Adair, Harman and Hine 1987). To work efficiently and effectively community service must be flexible and able to bring together the interests of the sentencer, the offender and the community. The Probation Service has demonstrated its ability to manage that tension effectively and to add to the equation public accountability. The three major stakeholders – sentencer, offender, community – are always in evidence, but the relative importance of each has shifted over time.

In the early years of the order there was an emphasis on the offender, displayed through a concern for the rehabilitative aspects of community service, and an emphasis upon providing the most appropriate work for the offender. National Standards marked the peak of a phase concerned with the sentencer: the need for punishment in the community, the need to target orders and the need to provide a disciplined experience. The focus shifted therefore to the retributive or correctional aspects of community service. There is evidence that we are now moving into a phase where the balance is shifting towards the community aspect, with a concern for the reparative potential of community service. This move is fed by central and local initiatives towards working in partnership, both formal and informal, with voluntary and statutory agencies, and through the Citizens and Victims Charters. The draft version of the new national standards also draws attention to the importance of work which has a crime prevention or crime reduction element and to the views of community representatives.

All three strands remain important in the evaluation of community service, as all three strands are working towards the same end – the reduction of re-offending. The Probation Service is uniquely positioned to provide the bridge between these three interest groups. It is not an easy role, but the Service has shown that it can 'Find the Balance, Manage the Tensions' (Adair, Harman and Hine 1986).

References

Adair, H., Harman, J. and Hine, J. (1986) 'Finding the Balance, Managing the Tensions.' *Interim Report of a National Survey – Planning for the Future of Community Service.* London: ACOP.

Adair, H., Harman, J. and Hine, J. (1987) *Community Service in the 80s.* London: ACOP.

Carnie, J. (1990) *Sentencers' Perceptions of Community Service by Offenders.* Edinburgh: Scottish Office Central Research Unit.

Foucault, M. (1977) *Discipline and Punish: The Birth of the Prison.* London: Allen Lane.

Garland, D. (1985) *Punishment and Welfare.* Aldershot: Gower.

Garland, D. (1990) *Punishment and Modern Society.* Oxford: Clarendon Press.

Hine, J. (1991) 'Standards and sentencing: a magical mystery tour.' Paper to conference 'Community Service Orders: The Impact of National Standards.' Nottingham Polytechnic, September 1991.

Hoggarth, E. (1991) *Selection for Community Service Orders.* Aldershot: Avebury.

Home Office (1970) *Report of the Advisory Council on the Penal System (The Wootton Report).* London: HMSO.

Home Office (1992a) *National Standards for the Supervision of Offenders in the Community.* London: HMSO.

Home Office (1992b) *Criminal Statistics England and Wales 1991.* London: HMSO.

Home Office (1992c) *Probation Statistics England and Wales 1991.* London: HMSO.

Home Office (1993) *Probation Statistics England and Wales 1992.* London: HMSO.

Home Office (1993) 'Reconvictions of those given probation and community service orders in 1987.' *Statistical Bulletin 18,93.* London: Home Office.

Hood, R. (1974) 'Criminology and penal change: A case study of the nature and impact of some recent advice to governments.' In R. Hood (ed) *Crime, Criminology and Public Policy: Essays in Honour of Sir Leon Radzinowicz.* London: Heinemann.

Mathieson, D. (1977) 'Community service.' *Justice of the Peace 141,* 730–731.

McIvor, G. (1992) *Sentenced to Serve, Evaluative Studies in Social Work.* Aldershot: Avebury.

McNair, I. (1993) 'Developing good practice.' In D. Whitfield and D. Scott (eds) *Paying Back: Twenty Years of Community Service.* Winchester: Waterside Press.

Patten, J. (1990) 'The need for change?' Unpublished paper to conference 'Managing Community Service: National Standards and Beyond'. University of Birmingham.

Pease, K., Durkin, P., Earnshaw, I., Payne, D. and Thorpe, J. (1975) 'Community service orders.' *Home Office Research Study No. 29.* London: HMSO.

Skinns, C.D. (1990) 'Community service practice.' *British Journal of Criminology 30,* 65–79.

Thomas, N., Hine, J. and Nugent, M. (1990) 'Study of Community Service Orders: Summary Report.' Unpublished report to Home Office.

Wilkinson, C. and Thomas, N. (1991) 'Community Service Orders: Monitoring National Standards.' A Final Report to the Association of Chief Officers of Probation, University of Birmingham.

Wootton, B. (1978) *Crime and Penal Policy: Reflections on Fifty Years Experience.* London: George Allen and Unwin.

Young, W. (1978) *Community Service Orders: The Development and Use of a New Penal Measure.* London: Heinemann.

Chapter 11

Widening Circles
Mediation in Criminal Justice

Tony F. Marshall

The development of practice

The recent appearance of 'mediation and reparation' programmes across
the world (in just the last two decades) has been marked by the sudden-
ness with which surprising new ideas have caught on, very patchy
development in different parts of the world, and a confusing history of
diverse origins and influences. The result is a mix of methods and aims
which are difficult for the newcomer to absorb and which are often not
reconciled even within individual programmes. The typical 'something
for everyone' approach has been pointed out by Dignan (1992) and Snare
(1993) among others.

Some of this confusion is deliberate. In the practical world, innovations
become accepted and survive only if they can demonstrate that they serve
the interests of a variety of parties, each of which is capable of obstructing
development. Clarity of purpose and priorities often make it difficult to
reconcile different interest groups.

It is not just a matter of political obscurantism, however. Some of the
confusion is inherent in the complexity of the ideas behind these innovations, and the challenge they present to orthodox philosophies of criminal
justice. This can best be understood by looking at the development of
current practice over time in different countries.

All the programmes to be considered here have this much in common:
they all involve negotiation between victims and offenders with the
assistance of a (neutral) third party. The idea that victims might want to
talk with those that have injured them is surprising at first sight. After all,
traditional criminal justice systems are predicated on keeping both apart

and taking decision-making out of their hands. For the victim this has obvious advantages – avoidance of danger, anxiety, and emotional stress and the minimisation of secondary impact from the crime. Such a system does not, however, necessarily serve the interests of all victims. Some actually desire more involvement, as a means of working through the bad feelings resulting from the crime. There is also the question of appropriate compensation.

Traditional legal processes focus upon the offender and his or her punishment. While the concept of compensation to the victim antedates these processes and survives as a component of popular ideas of 'natural' justice, justice systems do not recognise it as a major function. There are two major philosophies of compensation in modern society. One sees it as a state welfare function, much in the way individuals may be compensated from state funds for, say, industrial injury. The alternative view is that compensation is essentially a private concern between the offender and the victim. In Britain a typically hybrid response has evolved. Criminal injury, unless minor, can be compensated from State funds through the Criminal Injuries Compensation Scheme. Other losses are solely a matter of civil claim against the offender, although this principle is again compromised by allowing criminal courts to assess and award compensation to the victim and to impose this on the offender as part of the sentence.

Such state involvement has been much less significant in the United States, where, moreover, compensation claims might be greatly increased by hospital and medical bills in the absence of a free national health service. It was as a result of this, and the difficulty of making civil claims against offenders, that restitution programmes began to provide facilities for negotiation of compensation on referral from the court (in conjunction with sentence). Such programmes were simple in conception and operation. They would consult with victims to assess what was due and with offenders to assess their means of making reparation. They would then try to negotiate a package deal that would satisfy both sides, often using creative features such as the offender carrying out work on behalf of the victim (or some social cause selected by the victim) when the offender had no money or earnings to make financial compensation. Most of the time a simple go-between process was all that was needed, without victim and offender having to meet.

In these early programmes, mediation was used simply as a means of negotiating reparation. In certain cases, however, matters would prove more complex. There might be a dispute between the main parties over the offender's liability; there might be many victims, or many offenders, or both; there may have been a history of relationship between victim and offender that introduced other considerations; there might be emotional feelings obstructing negotiation. In such cases it would often prove efficacious to arrange a meeting between victim and offender, with a mediator from the programme. Through such meetings it became apparent that the needs of victims were more far-ranging than material compensation. Such needs included the desire to express anger or upset to the perpetrator, a personal apology and explanation, resolution of remaining fears, the mending of broken relationships, or the symbolic 'ending' of a bad experience through agreement and even the offer of forgiveness. This expansion of the concept of compensation has often been demonstrated by research on mediation and reparation programmes (Marshall and Merry 1990, Umbreit 1990), both in terms of what occurred at such meetings and what was valued by the victims taking part, when interviewed subsequently. Whilst the aim of simple reparation programmes was to effect restitution by offenders, on the assumption that this was what victims needed, practice showed that in some cases such an assumption was not valid, that other needs were paramount and that material compensation might even be rejected by the victim on the basis that offenders should not simply be able to 'buy themselves out' of responsibility for their actions.

This changed view of victims' needs provided the stimulus for a widening of the concept of reparation programmes themselves. In Kitchener, Ontario, a particularly complex case of vandalism and nuisance involving a large group of offenders and many victims was resolved through a series of victim-offender meetings and led to a continuing programme of mediation which survived for many years. The idea was also picked up in other Canadian and United States communities, especially ones where a large Mennonite contingent already stressed the resolution of crime within the community rather than resort to official authorities. In these new programmes, which came to be called VORPs, or Victim Offender *Reconciliation* Programmes, the idea of resolving victim needs was combined with a positive value placed upon personal participation, community problem-solving, offender atonement and victim forgiveness. These values challenged traditional criminal justice practice of avoiding direct participation, whether by victim or offender, and the emphasis it placed on punishment rather than 'healing'. Practice in fact led to the development of a distinct philosophy of justice, 'restorative justice', most fully developed by Zehr (1990). This philosophy replaced traditional concerns with a central concern for the healing of the victim, the need for the offender to assume direct personal responsibility for putting things right, and healing the rift a crime created in the community by reconciling victim and offender. A balance of atonement and forgiveness, with Christian religious overtones, assumed a symbolic core to this philosophy, but it was found to be acted out in actual meetings, even in cases where the parties had no religious allegiance, as a natural psychological process of reconciliation.

Others were to seize upon the reparation programme as a means to serve further ends. Court overloads at the time had created a climate favourable to diversion of minor offences to alternative means of resolution, particularly in the case of juvenile offenders. If victims' concerns could be satisfied through negotiated compensation, then more cases could be diverted from court. Juvenile diversion programmes based on reparation exist in the United States, Britain, Austria, Belgium and Germany. Whilst ostensibly offering a service to victims, some of these programmes in fact operated with a hidden agenda of negotiating diversion. When, as in Britain especially, the diversion programmes were influenced by social workers whose dominant concern was to reduce the impact of criminal justice on juveniles, the double aims often resulted in trying to persuade victims to accept minimal reparation (often an apology alone) in exchange for the offender being cautioned rather than prosecuted (see Marshall and Merry 1990, Davis 1992). As a result, the leading organisation representing victims in Britain, Victim Support, was decidedly cautious about the impact of these programmes and stressed the danger that they might serve the interests of offenders (or the courts) rather than those of victims.

That reparation programmes on behalf of juvenile diversion were a strange animal indeed was highlighted not only by the above fears, but also by the converse fear expressed by many commentators that offering something more than just cautioning would lead to overall net-widening rather than a diversionary effect, with many offenders who would previously have been cautioned or informally 'warned' being drawn into the programmes and greater involvement in order to satisfy victims. This problem has been confirmed by research in Norway (Falck 1992), America (Hudson 1992) and Scotland (Warner 1992), although the latter questions whether net-widening is necessarily a bad thing, apart from cost implications.

Whilst many social workers were primarily trying to reduce the impact of criminal justice on their charges, others were experimenting with new means of trying to rehabilitate offenders, especially probation officers and social workers working with serious repeat offenders, often, in Britain, in the context of Intermediate Treatment programmes (a last ditch attempt to prevent recidivist offenders being placed in custody). A feature of such work was the analysis with offenders of the reasons why they got into trouble and confronting them with the reality of their behaviour, including its consequences. Many offenders denied the importance of what they had done (see Sykes and Matza 1957, 'Techniques of neutralization'), but encounters with their victims prevented such denial and encouraged more socially responsible attitudes that might help rehabilitation. Many probation-run reparation programmes in Britain, plus others based in IT schemes, began from such experimental work. Whilst the personnel involved stressed the importance of serving victims' interests as well as providing a resource for reforming offenders, the primary impetus for such programmes inevitably again led to the suspicion that victims could be 'used' on behalf of reforming offenders, possibly compounding their victimisation. On the other hand, Marshall and Merry (1990) found that many victims welcomed the chance to be involved in trying to influence their offenders and help prevent further victimisation of others.

In Germany and Austria reparation programmes have become common for juvenile offenders, with the main initiative coming from the courts. These programmes appear to stress both diversion and the reformative experience of confronting offenders with the harm they have caused. Messmer (1990) in particular stresses the latter aspect of German victim-offender programmes, concluding from detailed audio transcripts of meetings that they challenge offenders' justifications of their behaviour in a way that the courts fail to do.

In Norway and Finland a major emphasis has been, as with the American VORPs, on community involvement. Norway, for instance, has embarked on a major programme of community-based mediation programmes as an alternative to prosecution. Their main orientation is to the resolution of conflict without official intervention. Similar community mediation programmes have been set up in the last couple of decades in North America, Britain, and Australia. Apart from the British schemes, which are still trying to persuade courts to provide referrals, they regularly receive cases where offences result from interpersonal disputes rather than anti-social intent. These programmes are primarily concerned with parties who have some form of relationship and wish to resolve their problems. Reparation programmes for victims and offenders, however, have found a high proportion of their cases, too, involve some kind of relationship, past or present; about half in the case of Marshall and Merry (1990) and as high as 70 per cent in the case of Warner (1992).

In the last few years there have been quite separate developments in Australia and New Zealand. In New Zealand, the Criminal Justice Act of 1985 introduced a sentence of reparation, ordered by the courts, with the responsibility for negotiating the reparation given to the probation service. As with the first American reparation programmes, Galaway (1992) found that few of these negotiations (just 10%) involved victim-offender meetings. This was because it was administratively simpler and less time-consuming for the probation officers. Interviewing victims who had not met with the offender, Galaway found that 43 per cent would have liked a chance to meet, and a further 33 per cent would at least have liked a chance to consider it. Whilst some probation officers in New Zealand promote victim-offender meetings, because of the further benefits for both the victim and offender-reform, they are still relatively infrequent in many districts.

A separate initiative in New Zealand was far more innovative. This developed from Maori critiques of 'white' justice and a demand for more community involvement in cases affecting Maori juveniles. A major cause of crime was identified as the breakdown of traditional cultural and family controls. The modern justice system did nothing to re-establish these, and was seen as reinforcing the social disadvantages faced by Maori youth. The Children Young Persons and Their Families Act 1989 introduced new procedures. A new Youth Court was established, but access to the court was predicated on first referring a case to a Youth Justice Co-ordinator, who would convene a Family Group Conference. The Conference is attended by the accused and his or her family (including any influential relatives beyond the nuclear family), other community figures of significance to the young person, a police officer and a youth advocate. The main intention of these meetings is that the accused and their families should share responsibility for putting right the harm done, determining appropriate penalties and planning for future rehabilitation (McElrea 1993).

Many of these Conferences are also attended by the victims, so that apart from family and community involvement in resolving an offender's behaviour, responsibility for the harm done is shared by the offender and the offender's family, and similar negotiation and reconciliation processes occur as in the VORP programmes. Although the 1989 Act gave victims the right to attend such Conferences, it did not particularly feature their role in serving victims' needs and in many cases Conferences were arranged without informing victims or taking into account their preferences. Maxwell and Morris (1993) carried out research into the early working of this scheme and were critical of general practice with regard to victims' interests. There are now attempts to reinforce victims' rights in this respect, especially in view of the fact that they have assumed a far greater role in such Conferences than was originally envisaged.

Similar Family Conferencing has been introduced into some areas of Australia, with offenders, victims and offender's family playing equal roles. These programmes are operated by police departments (see Alder and Wundersitz 1994). The same principles underlay the establishment of the Cardiff Juvenile Justice Centre in Wales in 1993, which was intended to conciliate both between offenders and victims and between offenders and their families.

The effect of these diverse practices and ideologies, focused around the core idea of negotiation between victims and offenders, has been to identify common ideas concerned with reconciliation and social healing, which have come to supersede the more limited intentions with which innovations in particular places started out. While the original practitioners in the experimental schemes were probation officers, youth workers, social workers, police officers, and so forth, a new professional identity has usurped these roles – that of the neutral or independent mediator in criminal justice. In Britain and America this identity has been reinforced by organised generalist mediation movements. MEDIATION UK (an umbrella voluntary organisation) has published practice guidelines for mediators, including those in reparation programmes (Marshall 1989). These were influenced by research on early practices, such as Marshall and Merry (1990), and they attempt to counteract, through appropriate safeguards, dangers of serving one party more than another, as well as more practical features such as confidentiality and power-balancing. In 1993 a handbook on victim-offender mediation practice was published in collaboration by the charity Save the Children and the West Yorkshire Probation Service (Quill and Wynne 1993). Similar handbooks and guidelines exist in the United States.

This emerging professional identity has led to a reframing of the reparation programme as a conflict-resolution or collaborative problem-solving tool, and as an opportunity for all parties to take control of their own interests and to determine the ends they want to achieve, rather than having these thrust upon them. The restorative justice theories of such as Zehr have been provided with a base in conflict-resolution theory and thus laicised, as in MEDIATION UK's (1990) paper on 'Criminal Justice Policy' and in Wright (1991), although the re-expression of the ideas as 'relational justice' by the Jubilee Policy Group (1992) retain a base in Christian theology. The traditional philosophies of criminal justice are criticised for their abstraction from real life and refusal to allow the parties to participate and assume responsibility, thus denying them a therapeutic and learning experience. It is also criticised for its reliance on punishment alone as the major reformative influence. The new programmes emphasise the necessity of providing opportunities, encouragement and support for rehabilitation, alongside sanctions.

These ideas have been criticised from a number of perspectives. The major flaw is their focus on the interpersonal, taking insufficient cognisance of the social and cultural contexts of crime and social control (see, for example, Mika 1992). How can one expect an offender who sees him or herself as a victim of social disadvantage to take sole personal responsibility for the results? Can one really expect to resolve crime solely through reconciliation of individual offenders and victims? The recent New Zealand and Australian initiatives point the way to a further widening of the mediation concept to include reconciliation between the offender and his or her family and community, a reconciliation that may be even more difficult to achieve, but which could have more far-reaching implications for reform. Even these programmes, of course, cannot deal with fundamental social inequalities that affect whole communities. To achieve this would involve even more basic initiatives, including the resourcing of those family groups and communities expected to re-assume social control functions that have been eroded by their experience of disadvantage, discrimination and powerlessness. Recognition of these issues is included in some of the latest reformulations of the restorative justice idea (Marshall 1991, 1994, Weitekamp 1992b).

Research and major issues

The recency and diversity of developments in mediation in criminal justice have made it difficult to build a solid underpinning in research. Much of the research carried out has occurred during the early years of different programmes, while they were still finding their feet and in a period of maximum change. This applies to the most substantial British research (Marshall and Merry 1990), to the Maxwell and Morris (1993) critique of the New Zealand Family Group Conferences, and so on. Even these pieces of work yield substantial information on problems and possibilities, outcomes and obstacles, influences and implications, but they have not so far been sufficient to provide the definitive evaluation of such practices demanded by funders and policy-makers, in terms of hard cost-effectiveness. Many studies are also confined to single programmes, which makes generalisation impossible. The main multi-programme studies so far are Coates and Gehm (1985), Weitekamp (1992a) and Umbreit (1994) in the USA; Marshall and Merry (1990) and Warner (1992) [the latter covering two similar projects only] in Britain; Trenczek (1990) and Kerner, Marks and Schreckling (1992) in Germany; Falck (1992) in Norway; and Maxwell and Morris (1993) in New Zealand.

The research evidence so far clearly shows the practicality of bringing victims and offenders together (a matter of some doubt in the early days) and the ability of adequately trained mediators to control such encounters. It also shows that the great majority of those who take part, victims and offenders, see it afterwards as a constructive and satisfactory exercise. The naturalness of owning up, apologising and making amends has substantial appeal. Umbreit's work on victims' perceptions of the fairness of the process (Umbreit 1990, 1992), in particular, demonstrates the popularity of the idea. Studies of public attitudes also indicate general receptivity to the negotiation of reparation, even as an alternative to custody (Galaway 1984, Wright 1989, Bae 1992).

Nevertheless, most programmes suffer from sub-optimal caseloads (in the case of the Scottish projects studied by Warner (1992), failure to obtain enough cases was, according to Knapp and Netten (1992), the main reason for their inability to attain cost-effectiveness). In part this difficulty stems from the voluntariness of the process and the number of parties on which it is dependent. For instance, if half of all offenders would co-operate, and half of all victims, only a quarter of all cases would be possible. Practical problems of arranging meeting places and times further reduce the possibilities, especially if there are time constraints imposed by other criminal justice agencies (e.g. Marshall 1990). The major reason for limited caseloads, however, is almost certainly the reluctance of criminal justice agencies to refer more cases. The reasons for this reluctance, the restrictions placed on referrals, the nature of cases referred and not referred are all vital subjects for further research.

This problem is part of a wider one of obtaining acceptance within traditional criminal justice processes for innovations that have very different aims and methods and which, on occasion, may even contradict normal practices. This issue permeated the bulk of the research contributions to the book compiled by Messmer and Otto (1992) on victim-offender projects across the world. Whilst programmes operated by, or in close association with, justice agencies often found their aims subverted by those of the agencies (e.g. diversion taking precedence over victims' needs), those which attempted to operate from an independent community base found it hard to survive or to obtain cases at all. Whilst the justice philosophy assumed by the victim-offender programmes remains peripheral to mainstream ideas, it may prove impossible to operate such programmes on any organisational basis in a cost-effective way. While this continues, it is impossible for these programmes to demonstrate the positive achievements they need to show to obtain greater acceptance of their approach – a double-bind common to many types of innovative practice.

One partial escape from this problem is for programmes to concentrate their work on the cases where they can achieve the greatest effects relative to the effort involved. Marshall and Merry (1990) were critical of the British programmes they studied for the high proportion of cases where go-between (or 'indirect') mediation occurred, on the basis that direct mediation involving meetings between victims and offenders offered much greater potential for satisfying victims' needs and changing offenders' attitudes. Indirect mediation is most appropriate for simply negotiating reparation – a service for which there certainly exists a demand, but which may not justify the cost involved. The resort to indirect mediation, despite an emphasis on the advantages of face-to-face meetings by the operators of these programmes, may be a consequence of resistance to the idea of a meeting among many victims. But if the result of this is to engage in less cost-effective work, it does not help the cause of the projects (Trenczek 1990, Warner 1992). Current research by Umbreit on a comparative basis across several countries, including the two longest established British programmes (Leeds and Coventry) may help to elucidate some of the pros and cons of these competing types of mediation. One also would like to see more research on the attitudes of those victims who show a reluctance to meet the offender although they are willing to negotiate reparation. It may be that the stress, inconvenience and time involved in such a meeting is only justified from the victim's point of view when there has been major hurt and upset from which they are still suffering. If this means that only a small proportion of victims really have sufficient to gain from taking part in a face-to-face meeting, then it draws into question the efficacy of reparation schemes as means of reforming offenders, as very few will get the chance to be involved. The number of cases in which both the victims have much to gain and the offenders are liable to be particularly influenced by the experience could be very small indeed.

If these are proved to be real dilemmas, then the worth of mediation in criminal justice will depend on the widened concept of its employment envisaged in restorative justice theory. Adoption of a participative problem-solving approach to offences, rather than a simple punitive-blaming response, as is being attempted in Family Group Conferences and the like, could bear much more experimentation and research. This will itself depend on the willing acceptance of such ideas by the major criminal justice agencies in order to give them a chance to succeed. Even in New Zealand and Australia, where there has been widespread enthusiasm for such attempts, there is also a great deal of resistance and scepticism.

A further problem for research is posed by the multiplicity of aims and aspirations associated with criminal justice mediation programmes. This makes it difficult to define criteria for success. In one case a great deal of relief may have been provided for the victim, in another an offender may have been persuaded to change the course of his or her life, whilst in yet another case, minor effects on victim and offender may have been achieved at a great saving in the costs that would otherwise have been incurred. Totalled across all cases, any one criterion may not yield particularly impressive results, even though each meeting may have produced some worthwhile outcome. For instance, it is the usual finding in relation to later offending that victim-offender programmes have a positive but slight effect (Marshall and Merry 1990, Dignan 1991, Warner 1992, Umbreit 1994) – encouraging, perhaps, but not enough to stimulate major funding of such programmes or to sway sceptics. Impacts on victims are well-documented in terms of their self-assessments, but there is no real quantitative evidence, and such achievements, in any case, do not promise obvious cost-savings further down the line as crime reduction does. While one needs more careful economic analysis of programmes, an emphasis on cost-minimisation may lead them into areas of work where their effect is more limited. Costs are easily quantified, but achievements are not. Many programmes have been side-lined into minor offences where risks are low and throughput high (Pate and Peachey 1988, Trenczek 1990, Marshall and Merry 1990, Weitekamp 1992a), despite the fact that the highest achievements may be associated with the more serious offences, such as those of violence (Umbreit 1994). Cost-effectiveness may also vary with the level of resources invested – real achievements may depend on a certain minimum level of resourcing, as the evaluation of the Scottish projects by Warner (1992) seems to indicate.

References

Alder, C. and Wundersitz, J. (1994) *Family Conferencing and Juvenile Justice: The Way Forward or Misplaced Optimism?* Canberra, Australia: Australian Institute of Criminology.

Bae, I. (1992) 'A survey on public acceptance of restitution as an alternative to incarceration for property offenders in Hennepin County, Minnesota, USA.' In H. Messmer and H-U. Otto (eds) *Restorative Justice on Trial: Pitfalls and Potentials of Victim Offender Mediation – International Research Perspectives.* Dordrecht: Kluwer.

Coates, R.B. and Gehm, J. (1985) *Victim Meets Offender: An Evaluation of VORPs.* Valparaiso, Indiana: PACT Institute of Justice.

Davis, G. (1992) 'Reparation in the UK: dominant themes and neglected themes.' In H. Messmer and H-U. Otto (eds) *Restorative Justice on Trial: Pitfalls and Potentials of Victim Offender Mediation – International Research Perspectives.* Dordrecht: Kluwer.

Dignan, J. (1991) *Repairing the Damage: An Evaluation of an Experimental Adult Reparation Scheme in Kettering, Northamptonshire.* Sheffield: University of Sheffield.

Dignan, J. (1992) 'Repairing the damage: can reparation be made to work in the service of diversion?' *British Journal of Criminology 32*, 4, 453–520.

Falck, S. (1992) 'The Norwegian community mediation centres at a crossroads.' In H. Messmer and H-U. Otto (eds) *Restorative Justice on Trial: Pitfalls and Potentials of Victim Offender Mediation – International Research Perspectives.* Dordrecht: Kluwer.

Galaway, B. (1984) *Public Acceptance of Restitution as an Alternative to Imprisonment for Property Offenders: A Survey.* Wellington, NZ: Department of Justice.

Galaway, B. (1992) 'The New Zealand experience implementing the reparation sentence.' In H. Messmer and H-U. Otto (eds) *Restorative Justice on Trial: Pitfalls and Potentials of Victim Offender Mediation – International Research Perspectives.* Dordrecht: Kluwer.

Galaway, B. and Hudson, J. (eds) (1990) *Criminal Justice, Restitution and Reconciliation.* Monsey, NY: Criminal Justice Press.

Hudson, J. (1992) 'A review of research dealing with views on financial restitution.' In H. Messmer and H-U. Otto (eds) *Restorative Justice on Trial: Pitfalls and Potentials of Victim Offender Mediation – International Research Perspectives.* Dordrecht: Kluwer.

Jubilee Policy Group (1992) *Relational Justice: A New Approach to Penal Reform.* Cambridge: Jubilee Policy Group.

Kerner, H.-J., Marks, E. and Schreckling, J. (1992) 'Implementation and acceptance of victim offender mediation programmes in the Federal Republic of Germany: a survey of criminal justice institutions.' In H. Messmer and H-U. Otto (eds) *Restorative Justice on Trial: Pitfalls and Potentials of Victim Offender Mediation – International Research Perspectives* Dordrecht: Kluwer.

Knapp, M. and Netten, A. (1992) 'Reparation, mediation and prosecution: comparative costs.' In S. Warner (1992) *Making Amends: Justice for Victims and Offenders.* Aldershot: Avebury.

Marshall, T.F. (1989) 'A FIRM view of practice standards.' *Mediation 6, 1, 1–5.*

Marshall, T.F. (1990) 'Results of research from British experiments in restorative justice.' In B. Galaway and J. Hudson (eds) *Criminal Justice, Restitution and Reconciliation.* Monsey, NY: Criminal Justice Press.

Marshall, T.F. (1991) 'Criminal justice in the new community'. Paper to British Criminology Conference, York.

Marshall, T.F. (1994) 'Grassroots initiatives towards restorative justice: the new paradigm?' In A. Duff, S. Marshall, R.E. Dobash and R.P. Dobash (eds) *Penal Theory and Practice: Tradition and Innovation in Criminal Justice.* Manchester: Manchester University Press.

Marshall, T.F. and Merry, S. (1990) *Crime and Accountability: Victim Offender Mediation in Practice.* London: HMSO.

Maxwell, G. and Morris, A. (1993) *Family Participation, Cultural Diversity and Victim Involvement in Youth Justice: A New Zealand Experiment.* Wellington, NZ: Department of Social Welfare and Institute of Criminology, Victoria University.

McElrea, F. (1993) 'A new model of justice.' In B.J. Brown and F. McElrea (eds) *The Youth Court in New Zealand: A New Model of Justice*. Aukland, NZ: Legal Research Foundation.

MEDIATION UK (1990) *Criminal Justice Policy*. Bristol: MEDIATION UK.

Messmer, H. (1990) 'Reducing the conflict: An analysis of victim offender mediation as an interactive process.' In B. Galaway and J. Hudson (eds) *Criminal Justice, Restitution and Reconciliation*. Monsey, NY: Criminal Justice Press.

Messmer, H. and Otto, H.-U. (eds) (1992) *Restorative Justice on Trial: Pitfalls and Potentials of Victim Offender Mediation – International Research Perspectives*. Dordrecht: Kluwer.

Mika, H. (1992) 'Mediation interventions and restorative justice: responding to the astructural bias.' In H. Messmer and H-U. Otto (eds) *Restorative Justice on Trial: Pitfalls and Potentials of Victim Offender Mediation – International Research Perspectives*. Dordrecht: Kluwer.

Pate, K. and Peachey, D. (1988) 'Face to face: victim offender mediation under the Young Offenders Act.' In J. Hudson, J. Hornick and B. Burrows (eds) *Justice and the Young Offender in Canada*. Toronto: Wall and Thompson.

Quill, D. and Wynne, J. (1993) *Victim and Offender Mediation Handbook*. London: Save the Children Fund.

Snare, A. (1993) 'Psychosocial interventions aimed at resolving the conflict between the perpetrator and the victim, for example within the framework of mediation and compensation programmes.' Paper to Twentieth Criminological Research Conference, Council of Europe, Strasbourg, 22–25 November.

Sykes, G.M. and Matza, D. (1957) 'Techniques of neutralisation: a theory of delinquency.' *American Sociological Review* 22, 664–670.

Trenczek, T. (1990) 'A review and assessment of victim-offender reconciliation programming in West Germany.' In B. Galaway and J. Hudson (eds) *Criminal Justice, Restitution and Reconciliation*. Monsey, NY: Criminal Justice Press.

Umbreit, M. (1990) 'The meaning of fairness to burglary victims.' In B. Galaway and J. Hudson (eds) *Criminal Justice, Restitution and Reconciliation*. Monsey, NY: Criminal Justice Press.

Umbreit, M. (1992) 'Mediating victim offender conflict: from single-site to multi-site analysis in the United States.' In H. Messmer and H-U. Otto (eds) *Restorative Justice on Trial: Pitfalls and Potentials of Victim Offender Mediation – International Research Perspectives*. Dordrecht: Kluwer.

Umbreit, M. (1994) *Victim Meets Offender: The Impact of Restorative Justice and Mediation*. Monsey, NY: Criminal Justice Press.

Warner, S. (1992) *Making Amends: Justice for Victims and Offenders*. Aldershot: Avebury.

Weitekamp, E. (1992a) 'Can restitution serve as a reasonable alternative to imprisonment? An assessment of the situation in the USA.' In H. Messmer and H-U. Otto (eds) *Restorative Justice on Trial: Pitfalls and Potentials of Victim Offender Mediation – International Research Perspectives*. Dordrecht: Kluwer.

Weitekamp, E. (1992b) 'Reparative justice'. Paper to Third European Colloquium on Crime and Public Policy in Europe, Noordwijkerhout, 5–8 July.

Wright, M. (1989) 'What the public wants.' In M. Wright and B. Galaway, B. (eds) *Mediation and Criminal Justice: Victims, Offenders and Community*. London: Sage.

Wright, M. (1991) *Justice for Victims and Offenders*. Milton Keynes: Open University Press.

Zehr, H. (1990) *Changing Lenses: A New Focus for Criminal Justice*. Scottdale, PA: Herald Press.

Chapter 12

Social Work with Prisoners

Brian Williams

Introduction

Social work with prisoners has repeatedly been described, over the years, as the 'Cinderella' of the social services (Dawtry 1963, Monger, Pendleton and Roberts 1981, Williams 1991). Despite the introduction of national standards for through-care, there has been little reason to challenge this description. There has, however, been a growing recognition of the important consequences of imprisonment for offenders' families, and recent legal changes have also led to an increase in statutory supervision of prisoners after release. To this extent, through-care is becoming a higher priority for social workers and probation officers – particularly at times when imprisonment is increasingly used in preference to community penalties. Increased workloads and diminishing resources are likely to lead to increased use of groupwork and of collaborative work with other professionals.

This chapter will briefly review the arguments for and against a social work presence in prisons. It will assess the evidence on the merits and drawbacks of specialisation in through-care work by field probation officers and social workers, and review some recent practice developments and the research evidence for and against them. Some of the material on the impact of imprisonment upon offenders' families will also be reviewed. Most of the literature relates to England and Wales: the legal and prison systems in Scotland are distinctive, and this chapter does not necessarily apply to them, except where explicit reference is made to Scotland.

Lord Justice Woolf, in preparing his report (Woolf and Tumim 1991) following the Strangeways riots, showed a welcome respect for research evidence, and made good use of expert criminological assessors. For a time after the publication of his report in 1991, there was considerable optimism about the prospects for improving the prison system and the possibility of providing better through-care services in England and Wales. The report had its weaknesses – not least its neglect of women prisoners (Liebling 1991, Player 1994), of race issues (Sim 1994, Williams 1994) and of anything but the narrowest view of what justice in prisons might entail (King 1994). Nevertheless, it moved official thinking and action on prison matters forward for a period.

This broadly reformist agenda was at least partially reversed by politicians seizing on (or creating) moral panics around offending on bail (Sampson 1993, Williams 1993), offending by prisoners on home leave (Mathiesen 1993) and juvenile offending (Sampson 1993, Pearson 1994) to justify the ill-informed assertion that 'prison works'.

A strategy based on this misconception was vigorously pursued despite clear evidence that almost all other western criminal justice systems base their policies on scepticism about the effectiveness of imprisonment (Hudson 1993). Many of the lessons of Woolf were officially discarded in favour of another prison-building programme, although some positive changes were well-entrenched by that time. In Scotland, for example, the whole culture of the prison service was being challenged, with enormous implications for sentence planning and the roles of staff (Frizzell 1993, King 1994).

For a time, the prison system in England and Wales was able to take advantage of the breathing space created by lower numbers after the implementation of the 1991 Criminal Justice Act. Some experimentation became possible, regimes were improved and positive developmental work began in many prisons. Prison overcrowding was back within a year, however, and it became necessary to revert to crisis management. Probation caseloads decreased as more offenders were imprisoned, but over a period, the balance of probation officers' caseloads changed, with increasing emphasis on meeting the bureaucratic requirements of the national standards on through-care. As longer-term prisoners are released under statutory supervision, this will form an increasingly dominant part of probation officers' work.

Groupwork with prisoners

The research evidence on groupwork with prisoners suggests that although this can be effective, most innovative group work has been experimental and relatively short-lived (Badham *et al*. 1993, Fisher and Watkins 1993). As one worker put it, 'Regrettably, in prisons generally, groupwork is relatively uncommon and often sporadic largely because of institutional and resource constraints' (Towl 1993, p.78).

There has been a large scale experiment with courses for sex offenders in prisons in England and Wales, although this has yet to be fully evaluated. It appears to have had mixed results, partly because of the way in which it was introduced: a number of prisons withdrew from the programme at an early stage, for example, when it became clear that no additional resources would be made available for its implementation (Sampson 1994).

The preparation of staff to run such groups has also been problematic: the prison service appears to have seen no need to provide specific training for uniformed staff involved in delivering the courses. As one observer saw it, 'there seems to be an entrenched belief in the prison system that the provision of a training package automatically enables anyone to deliver it' (Sabor 1992, p.16), when there is clearly a need for sophisticated preparation of staff to enable them to use such material effectively (Nicholson and Cowburn 1990, Brown 1993, Cowburn 1993).

One of the arguments used by the advocates of withdrawal of probation officers from working inside prisons was that they should be freed from everyday 'welfare' work in order to concentrate upon more specialist tasks, including groupwork (Ashe 1993). At present, although there is a huge expansion of groupwork with sex offenders, systematic groupwork by probation officers with prisoners seems not to be the norm. For example, 21 per cent of prisons surveyed in 1993 reported no groups running at all, and most of the provision relating to drug and alcohol misuse was facilitated by staff of outside agencies (Towl 1993). The survey did find, however, that the level of groupwork activity had increased, and that probation officers were the professionals most likely to be running groups. This trend is likely to continue for a number of reasons: the sex offender programme alone will involve enormous numbers, the Throughcare Framework document makes a variety of demands upon prison staff which will most easily be met by working with clients in groups, and it also encourages greater use of local community agencies (Home Office/Prison Service 1994).

The most common type of groupwork was on offending behaviour, influenced by the work of Priestley and McGuire (Priestley *et al*. 1984). Alcohol and drug issues followed closely, then anger management, lifer groups, social skills, sex offending and anxiety management. Apart from the provision of a national programme of group work with sex offenders, the largest growth area was anger management (Towl 1993). The selection of themes for groupwork with prisoners may be led, to some extent, by probation officers' and other professionals' interests and expertise: consumer studies show some disparities between clients' and probation officers' views of their main problem areas (Williams, Nooney and Ray 1987, Williams 1991).

Benefits of working with prisoners in groups include standardising the information they are given, for example about parole, and avoiding repetitive individual interviews in giving such information (Ashe 1993). Prison-based groupwork can also, in some circumstances, bring different professionals together for the benefit of their clients: 'A holistic approach – viewing prisoners and staff as whole people not restricted by their respective roles – underpins this work and thrives on the multidisciplinary and multicultural perspectives brought to the course.' (Towl 1993a)

Sabor (1992) suggests that probation officers are usually well-trained in groupwork, but it seems unlikely that most of those involved in the prison groups under consideration in her article have received any special preparation for groupwork with sex offenders.

Much groupwork by probation officers in the UK is done without proper evaluation (Barker and Morgan 1991, Cowburn 1993), but comparatively full and systematic research is being carried out into the prison sex offender programme (Sampson 1994). Unfortunately, resource constraints are built into the model chosen for the programmes, and probation officers have felt excluded from the programme (Brown 1993). Issues of racism, sexism and homophobia do not appear to have been properly addressed either in staff training or in the groupwork itself, and the programme may prove to be limited by its adherence to a particular model of training and delivery which is very different from that already established within the probation service (see Brown 1993, Cowburn 1993). The failure to follow prisoners up effectively after release, predicted by some observers (Sampson 1994), would severely discredit the scheme.

Research in North America has claimed considerable success for groupwork using cognitive skills training (e.g. Fox 1989, Ross and Fabiano 1985), although this has only been used to a limited extent in the UK so far (Thornton 1987).

Work with prisoners: withdrawal or engagement?

Since 1963, the Prison Officers' Association has argued that the welfare role in prisons ought to be undertaken by uniformed staff. In 1981, the National Association of Probation Officers decided to work towards the withdrawal of prison-based probation staff, and the two associations reached agreement in 1984 on the protection of members' jobs when this policy came to fruition. In the 1990s, however, NAPO became concerned about other changes (including the reduction in the use of community penalties after the 1993 Criminal Justice Act, and prison governors' greater powers under devolved budgeting), and gave this campaign low priority. As a result, there has been a lengthy period of uncertainty about the future of probation work inside prisons in England, Wales and Northern Ireland, while Scottish social workers have been largely untouched by the withdrawal debate.

At the same time, shared work between prison officers and other professionals has greatly increased. This is perhaps most advanced in Scotland, although there, as elsewhere, it has developed in a piecemeal way (SWSIS 1993). The initiative for such inter-disciplinary work has sometimes come from governors, and schemes are vulnerable when the key staff move on to other jobs, unless social work has been built into the regime (Williams 1992, Smith 1992). There are, however, increasing signs of a policy 'steer' towards shared working. The Woolf report strongly supported an enhanced role for prison officers, and also praised specific inter-disciplinary initiatives such as bail information schemes. The Chief Inspector of Prisons had been saying for some time that shared welfare work was a matter of public policy, referring to the relevant Circular Instructions, and this approach has also been advocated by the prison service and the Social Work Services Group in Scotland (SPS/SWSG 1990).

All the same, uncertainty about the future of social work in prisons has meant that the provision of one-to-one services to prisoners by probation officers working inside prisons has been rather reactive in recent years. Governors are reviewing the kind of 'welfare' services they require under the new contracting arrangements, and probation departments in prisons have been challenged to provide the kind of services the governors regard as relevant. The end result may be that prison-based probation officers are drawn more deeply into functions which involve servicing the needs of prisons, rather than concentrating on direct work with prisoners. This trend merely echoes the move towards working as 'case managers' already seen in the field and in social work more generally, and will be difficult to resist.

A danger has been identified by a number of researchers: prison-based probation officers can become excessively embroiled in the day-to-day running of prisons, and field staff can become unduly preoccupied with form-filling and lose touch with the more creative aspects of through-care work. These trends are not confined to work with prisoners, or indeed to social work (McWilliams 1992, Hudson 1993, Nellis 1993).

Studies of work with lifers suggest that probation officers tend to treat prisoners as cases rather than individuals, inhibiting 'a more relevant response to the lifer's desire for dignified independence and recognition of his [sic] capacity for self-control' (Coker and Martin 1985, p.235). Another study notes the difficulties inherent in probation officers' position where lifers' parole applications are concerned, and the peripheral role of probation staff in the process, complicated by financial constraints imposed by probation services (Mitchell 1992). Similarly, a small study of prisoners' views of the probation service argued that many of the policies and practices of probation services prevent a client-centred, personal approach to through-care work. Clients were dissatsfied with what they saw as bureaucratic and impersonal ways of working, and the study concluded that unfashionable notions such as befriending and caring might need to be rehabilitated (Williams 1992b).

Probation officers working with young offenders in custody also did so predominantly in a reactive and unenthusiastic way, missing opportunities to engage with clients who were expressing social work needs (McAllister, Bottomley and Liebling 1992). In an earlier consumer study in Northern Ireland, probation officers were seen as helpful with practical problems, but the author concluded that 'the systematic social work practice inherent in throughcare policy is virtually non-existent' (Craig 1984, p.49).

The evidence of an increase in joint work between probation officers and prison officers, and the benefits and pitfalls of such an approach, have been reviewed elsewhere (Smith 1992, Williams 1991). There is clearly considerable suspicion between the two occupational groups (Peelo *et al.* 1991, Mitchell 1992), and indeed between them and psychologists, chaplains and others who might collaborate in providing through-care services to prisoners (Mitchell 1992, Brown 1993), although it has been argued that 'with the commitment of prison managers and the willingness of different staff groups to look at ways of developing an effective throughcare system, the conditions for groupwork can be found' (Ashe 1993, p.50). It may be that efforts to co-work should be concentrated on focused group-work with prisoners, and on differentiating between the roles of probation and other staff (Ashe 1993, Kett *et al.* 1992).

The Woolf report and the 1992 and 1995 national standards were welcomed by many in England and Wales, on the grounds that their emphasis on due process and systematic intervention might offer a means to achieve more purposeful through-care work (Williams 1992b, Stern 1994). Most of the research reviewed above does not bear out this opti-mism, although it largely pre-dates the introduction of national standards.

On the question of specialisation, there are conflicting views. Some have argued that specialist through care teams are a retrograde step because they allow probation management to limit the resources devoted to through-care work (Liebling 1989, McAllister *et al.* 1992), whilst others have suggested that such teams can provide a more systematic service, particularly to clients from inner-city areas (Legget and Devlin 1986). McAllister *et al.* (1992) researched through-care of young offenders and listed the advantages and disadvantages. Where clients are concerned, the former seem to outnumber the latter but specialist teams are only practi-cable in urban areas. According to another researcher, 'specialisation may be an advantage in providing an effective throughcare service, but it is by no means essential. It can be done effectively by the "ordinary" probation officer as well' (Bridges 1988, p.19). There seems likely to be increased official encouragement of specialisation on the grounds that it produces more focused work (Whitehead, Turver and Wheatley 1991, Smith 1994).

Suicide prevention

Recent research on prison suicides has some implications for through-care. Liebling (1992) noted that young prisoners attempting suicide were 'amongst those least likely to be receiving regular contact and support from the outside probation service. They are also less likely to perceive this contact as useful' (p.156). Restricted access to outside agencies, includ-ing the probation service, was also identified as a factor in self-injury and suicides among women prisoners (Liebling 1994), whose lives could be saved if appropriate, individual attention were given to their problems in time.

A 'listener scheme' set up in Swansea prison preceded a halving of the incidence of recorded self-harm by prisoners. Initiated by the probation team and the local Samaritans, this project has been emulated in a number of other prisons, and demonstrates successful co-operation between prisons and the voluntary sector, with strong probation involvement (Davies 1994). It is interesting that the report on suicides in Feltham recommended the establishment of specialist probation teams to avoid vulnerable young people slipping through the net of services (Howard League 1993).

There is clearly a role for purposeful through-care work in helping isolated and depressed prisoners to avoid self-harm and suicide.

Temporary release

There are increasing opportunities for prisoners to attend resettlement courses in their home areas during the latter part of sentences. The probation service has been proactive in setting up such courses in many areas, although coverage is patchy. Apart from the obvious benefit of removing the clients temporarily from the custodial environment (Liebling 1989), such courses seemed to improve relationships between prisoners and probation officers, but they were often poorly planned and staff were unclear about their purpose (McAllister et al. 1992). It appears, however, that properly planned temporary release schemes can complement individual through-care contact in a constructive way (Liebling 1989, Whitehead et al. 1991).

Anti-oppressive through-care practice

There is insufficient space here to do full justice to all the issues relating to anti-racist and anti-sexist practice in through-care work. Research on these areas is summarised elsewhere (Dominelli et al. 1995, Kett et al. 1992, Eaton 1993, Carlen 1990). Some of the implications of the Woolf report for women have also already been discussed in other publications (Liebling 1991, NACRO 1991). The probation service's resistance to special attention being paid to the needs of women prisoners and black prisoners is also documented in other, recent research (Carlen 1990, Eaton 1993, Kett et al. 1992). There is very little material relating to discrimination against lesbian and gay prisoners, but see Preece (1993), Eaton (1993) and NAPO (1989).

Some concern has been expressed in recent years about a consequence of the narrower definition of through-care being applied in the era of cash-limited probation budgets and the national framework for through-care, namely the reduction in work with prisoners' families. This has coincided, somewhat paradoxically, with the publication of a series of research findings about the effects of imprisonment on prisoners' families and their consequent needs.

Male prisoners' partners are increasingly marginalised by probation officers, who seem worried about whether any time spent helping prisoners' families is a legitimate part of their work. It seems that 'prioritising "tackling offending" actually undermines probation officers' ability to achieve, in practice, the reduction of offending behaviour' (Peelo *et al.* 1991, p.318). Helping prisoners' partners to resolve debt problems, for example, might enable probation officers to form a relationship which would be the basis for continuing work and more obviously offence-related work.

Other research shows that the needs of prisoners' children have also been neglected. Most of it does not specifically relate to probation work, but has clear implications for it. Catan (1992), for example, has reviewed earlier research and conducted her own on the relative rates of development of babies in women's prisons with their mothers and in the community, and she endorses Wilkinson's earlier (1988) findings on after-care. Women on release from prison tended to be so preoccupied with practical problems that they were unable to concentrate initially on what, for many of them, would have been a higher priority, re-establishing contact with and custody of children taken into local authority care during their imprisonment. McDermott and King's (1992) study has implications for through-care also: families' communication and financial problems during men's imprisonment could be alleviated if the findings were sensitively applied by probation officers and social workers, or appropriate referrals made to voluntary agencies (Light 1993).

The Scottish experience

Scotland has a distinctive legal system, a separate prison service and a different set of through-care arrangements, although there are similarities between the situations in Scotland, in England and Wales and in Northern Ireland. A common theme is the need for effective liaison between prison and field social workers, particularly in the period prior to prisoners' release, and the difficulties in achieving this. The Scottish system was set out, after a thorough review of the previous arrangements, in a document called *Continuity Through Co-operation* (SPS/SSWG 1990), published in 1990. A set of *National Objectives and Standards for Social Work Services in the Criminal Justice System* was published in 1991, addressed mainly towards the role of field social workers.

The Scottish prison service has gone further down the road towards a welfare role for prison officers than in England and Wales, although its implementation has been patchy in practice (SWSIS 1993). An inspection of prison-based social work services carried out in 1992 by the Social Work Services Inspectorate for Scotland (SWSIS) found considerable variation in the progress being made towards developing the welfare role of prison officers. There is a clear determination in the Scottish inspectorate to keep up the impetus towards a two tier system, with prison officers undertaking 'first line welfare tasks' and 'freeing social workers to devote their time to those social work tasks requiring professional qualifications' (SWSIS 1993, p.3). Interestingly, these are defined to include liaison with social workers and other professionals outside the prison, although some prison officers elsewhere in the UK have developed considerable skills in these areas when working in inter-agency projects such as bail information schemes.

The inspectorate argues that it will only be possible for prison social workers to focus to an appropriate extent upon clients' offending behaviour when they have off-loaded their 'welfare' tasks and developed more groupwork programmes. There are other problems preventing the implementation of effective and coherent through-care in Scotland, however. As in England and Wales, funding constraints and the pressure of other work make it difficult for field staff to visit prisoners as often as they might wish, and the early signs are that it is proving extremely difficult for Scottish social workers to comply with the national standards (which require, for example, that a three-way meeting is arranged between prisoners, their prison social worker and the field colleague before release) (SWSIS 1993). The picture is further complicated by local government reorganisation, which raises questions about the future source of funding for through-care and parole supervision. Current attempts to shift the culture of Scottish prisons in the direction advocated by the Woolf report, towards 'a more enlightened Prison Service' (Frizzell 1993, p.203) include an aspiration to improve relationships between prison officers and inmates by increasing use of personal officer schemes – but this is expressed by Frizzell, the Chief Executive of the Scottish Prison Service, in the future tense.

Further reading

The research on post-release work was thoroughly and succinctly summarised by Haines (1990). Research and prisoners' writing on the experience of imprisonment was summarised by Williams (1991), whilst Priestley's anthology (1989) provides a variety of contemporary and historical views. Research findings on race and gender issues relating to throughcare are discussed in Dominelli *et al.* (1995). The research on the effectiveness of probation work with various client groups is summarised by Raynor, Smith and Vanstone (1994); for an account of what little work has been done on the effectiveness of through-care, see Haines (1990).

Acknowledgements

Considerable help was received in preparing this chapter from Val Cox and Jane Watt, to whom I am most grateful.

References

Ashe, M. (1993) 'Meeting prisoners' needs through groupwork.' In A. Brown and B. Caddick (eds) *Groupwork with Offenders*. London: Whiting and Birch.

Badham, B., Blatchford, B., McCartney, S. and Nicholas, M. (1993) '"Doing something with our lives when we're inside": self-directive groupwork in a youth custody centre.' In A. Brown and B. Caddick (eds) *Groupwork with Offenders*. London: Whiting and Birch.

Barker, M. and Morgan, R. (1991) 'Surveying probation practice with sex offenders.' *Probation Journal 38*, 4, 171–176.

Bridges, A. (1988) 'South-west youth custody survey.' *Probation Journal 35*, 18–19.

Brown, A. (1993) 'Suggested reforms to the sex offender treatment programme.' (Mimeo) London: Prison Reform Trust.

Carlen, P. (1990) *Alternatives to Women's Imprisonment*. Milton Keynes: Open University Press.

Coker, J.B. and Martin, J.P. (1985) *Licensed to Live*. Oxford: Blackwell.

Cowburn, M. (1993) 'Groupwork programme for male sex offenders: establishing principles for practice.' In A. Brown and B. Caddick (eds) *Groupwork with Offenders*. London: Whiting and Birch.

Craig, J. (1984) *The Probation Through-care Services – A Report on a Consumer Survey*. Occasional Paper 3. Belfast: Policy, Planning and Research Unit, Stormont.

Davies, B. (1994) 'The Swansea Listener Scheme: views from the prison landings.' *Howard Journal 33,* 2, 125–136.

Dawtry, F. (1963) 'A new look for after-care?' *Justice of the Peace 127,* 702–704.

Dominelli, L., Jeffers, L., Jones, G., Sibanda, S. and Williams, B. (1995) *Anti-racist Probation Practice.* Aldershot: Arena.

Eaton, M. (1993) *Women After Prison.* Buckingham: Open University Press.

Fisher, K. and Watkins, L. (1993) 'Inside groupwork.' In A. Brown and B. Caddick (eds) *Groupwork with Offenders.* London: Whiting and Birch.

Fox, T.A. (1989) 'The necessity of moral education in prisons.' *Journal of Correctional Education 40,* 1, 20–25.

Frizzell, E.W. (1993) 'The Scottish prison service: changing the culture.' *Howard Journal 32,* 3, 203214.

Haines, K. (1990) *Aftercare Services for Released Prisoners: A Review of the Literature.* London: Home Office Research and Planning Unit.

Home Office (1995) *National Standards for the Supervision of Offenders in the Community.* London: HMSO.

Home Office/HM Prison Service (1994) *National Framework for the Throughcare of Offenders in Custody to the Completion of Supervision in the Community.* London: Home Office.

Howard League for Penal Reform (1993) *Suicides in Feltham.* London: Howard League.

Hudson, B. (1993) *Penal Policy and Social Justice.* London: Macmillan.

Kett, J., Collett, S., Barron, C., Hill, I., and Metherell, D. (1992) *Managing and Developing Anti-racist Practice within Probation, a Resource Pack for Action.* St. Helens: Merseyside Probation Service.

King, R.D. (1994) 'Order, disorder and regimes in the prison services of Scotland and England and Wales.' In E. Player and M. Jenkins (eds) *Prisons after Woolf: Reform through Riot.* London: Routledge.

Legget, B. and Devlin, M. (1986) 'You reap what you sow – shared approach to working with YC clients while inside and in the community.' In NAPO *Probation: Engaging with Custody.* London: NAPO.

Liebling, A. (1989) 'Temporary release: getting embroiled with prisons.' *Howard Journal 28,* 1, 51–55.

Liebling, A. (1991) 'Where are the women in Woolf?' *Prison Report 15,* 4–5.

Liebling, A. (1992) *Suicides in Prison.* London: Routledge.

Liebling, A. (1994) 'Suicide amongst women prisoners.' *Howard Journal 33,* 1, 1–9.

Light, R. (1993) 'Why support prisoners' family-tie groups?' *Howard Journal 32,* 4, 322–329.

Mathiesen, T. (1993) 'Contemporary penal policy: a study in moral panics.' *Criminal Justice 11*, 1, 4–6.

McAllister, D., Bottomley, K. and Liebling, A. (1992) *From Custody to Community: Throughcare for Young Offenders.* Aldershot: Avebury.

McDermott, K. and King, R.D. (1992) 'Prison rule 102: "stand by your man": the impact of penal policy on the families of prisoners.' In R. Shaw (ed) *Prisoners' Children: What are the Issues?.* London: Routledge.

McWilliams, B. (1992) 'The rise and development of management thought in the English probation system.' In R. Statham and P. Whitehead (eds) *Managing the Probation Service.* Harlow: Longman.

Mitchell, B. (1992) 'Preparing life sentence prisoners for release.' *Howard Journal 31*, 3, 224–239.

Monger, M., Pendleton, J. and Roberts, J. (1981) *Throughcare with Prisoners' Families.* Nottingham: University of Nottingham Department of Social Administration and Social Work.

NACRO (1991) *A Fresh Start for Women Prisoners, the Implications of the Woolf Report for Women.* London: NACRO.

National Association of Probation Officers (1989) *Working with Lesbians and Gay Men as Clients of the Service: Good Practice Guidelines.* London: NAPO.

Nellis, M. (1993) Review of Statham and Whitehead's Managing the Probation Service. *Howard Journal 32*, 3, 265–268.

Nicholson, R. and Cowburn, M. (1990) 'Offence-based work with long-sentence sex offenders.' *Probation Journal 37*, 1, 10–13.

Pearson, G. (1994) 'Youth, crime and society.' In M. Maguire, R. Morgan and R. Reiner (eds) *The Oxford Handbook of Criminology.* Oxford: Clarendon.

Peelo, M., Stewart, J., Stewart, G. and Prior, A. (1991) 'Women partners of prisoners.' *Howard Journal 30*, 4, 311–327.

Player, E. (1994) 'Women's prisons after Woolf.' In E. Player and M. Jenkins (eds) *Prisons after Woolf: Reform through Riot.* London: Routledge.

Preece, A. (1993) 'Being gay in prison.' *Probation Journal 40*, 2, 85–87.

Priestley, P., McGuire, J., Flegg, D., Helmsley, V., Welham, D. and Barnitt, R. (1984) *Social Skills in Prison and the Community.* London: Routledge.

Priestley, P. (1989) *Jail Journeys.* London: Routledge.

Raynor, P., Smith, D. and Vanstone, M. (1994) *Effective Probation Practice.* London: Macmillan.

Ross, R. and Fabiano, E. (1985) *Time to Think: A Cognitive Model of Crime and Delinquency Prevention and Rehabilitation.* Johnson City: Academy of Arts and Sciences.

Sabor, M. (1992) 'The sex offender treatment programme in prisons.' *Probation Journal 39*, 1, 14–18.

Sampson, A. (1993) 'Truth is the first casualty in the war on juvenile crime.' *Prison Report 22*, 16–17.

Sampson, A. (1994) *Acts of Abuse: Sex Offenders and the Criminal Justice System.* London: Routledge.

Scottish Office (1991) *National Objectives and Standards for Social Work Services in the Criminal Justice System.* Edinburgh: Scottish Office.

Scottish Prison Service/Social Work Services Group (1990) *Continuity through Co-operation.* Edinburgh: SPS/SWSG.

Sim, J. (1994) 'Reforming the penal wasteland? A critical review of the Woolf Report.' In E. Player and M. Jenkins (eds) *Prisons after Woolf: Reform through Riot.* London: Routledge.

Smith, D. (1992) 'Social work in prisons.' *Practice 6*, 2, 135–145.

Smith, G. (1994) 'Throughcare: the inspectorate's view.' Unpublished paper given at conference, 'Throughcare: Raising the Profile', February.

Social Work Services Inspectorate for Scotland (1993) *National Inspection of Prison-based Social Work Units.* Edinburgh: SWSIS.

Stern, V. (1994) 'The future of the voluntary sector and the pressure groups.' In E. Player and M. Jenkins (eds) *Prisons after Woolf: Reform through Riot.* London: Routledge.

Thornton, D.M. (1987) 'Moral development theory.' In B.J. McGurk, D.M. Thornton and M. Williams (eds) *Applying Psychology to Imprisonment: Theory and Practice.* London: HMSO.

Towl, G. (1993) 'Groupwork in prisons.' *Probation Journal 40*, 1, 42.

Towl, G. (1993a) '"Culture" groups in prison.' In A. Brown, A. and B. Caddick (eds) *Groupwork with Offenders.* London: Whiting and Birch.

Towl, G. (1993b) 'Groupwork in prisons.' *Probation Journal 40*, 4, 208–209.

Whitehead, P., Turver, N. and Wheatley, J. (1991) *Probation, Temporary Release Schemes and Reconviction.* Aldershot: Avebury.

Wilkinson, C. (1988) 'The post-release experience of women prisoners.' In A. Morris and C. Wilkinson (eds) *Women and the Penal System.* Cropwood Conference Series No. 19. Cambridge: Institute of Criminology.

Williams, B. (1991) *Work with Prisoners.* Birmingham: Venture.

Williams, B. (1992) *Bail Information: An Evaluation of the Scheme at H.M. Prison Moorland.* Bradford: Horton.

Williams, B. (1992) 'Caring professionals or street-level bureaucrats? The case of probation officers' work with prisoners.' *Howard Journal 31*, 4, 263–275.

Williams, B. (1993) 'Bail bandits: the construction of a moral panic.' *Critical Social Policy 37*, 104–112.

Williams, B. (1994) 'Towards justice in probation work with prisoners.' In D. Ward and M. Lacey (eds) *Towards Greater Justice: the Probation Service in the 1990s*. London: Whiting and Birch.

Williams, M., Nooney, K. and Ray, I. (1987) 'Social work needs of prisoners: a survey.' In B.J. McGurk, D.M. Thornton and M. Williams (eds) *Applying Psychology to Imprisonment: Theory and Practice*. London: HMSO.

Woolf, Lord Justice, and Tumim, Judge S. (1991) *Prison Disturbances April 1991*. London: HMSO. Cm1456.

Chapter 13

Effectiveness Now
A Personal and Selective Overview

Peter Raynor

The purpose of this short final chapter is to provide a personal and inevitably somewhat subjective overview of the current state of research in Britain on the effectiveness of social work with offenders. My comments will be necessarily selective, reflecting my own interests and preoccupations; I hope this will not be seen as an indulgence, given the careful objectivity of other contributions. My main purpose is to attempt some assessment of where we now stand and where we might usefully go in the future. In particular, I am concerned that some real but modest successes in the area of effectiveness should not constrain us within a narrow and utilitarian band of activity dominated by reconviction studies, but that we should build on these achievements to locate our research on effectiveness in a wider context, informed by a broad view of the linkage of criminal justice activity with wider interests, institutions and policies.

First, however, the context must be established by a recognition of how far we have moved. From around the mid-1970s to the late 1980s the field of social work with offenders was dominated by the doctrine that 'nothing works' (Martinson 1974, Brody 1976), and the consensus was that nobody (or only presumed naive practitioners) could reasonably expect different sentences to result in different levels of recidivism for otherwise comparable offenders. The story of the 'nothing works' era has been told and retold many times, and does not need to be repeated here (see, for example, Raynor, Smith and Vanstone 1994). The exaggeration and pervasiveness of the message was matched by similar findings in other areas of social work (for example Fischer 1976) which, sometimes in spite of their authors' intentions, lent themselves to deployment as part of the

New Right's attack on welfare institutions and the professionals who staffed them (as in Brewer and Lait 1980).

Even Bottoms and McWilliams (1979), writing from a position much more friendly to social work, tended to take for granted that probation had little impact on offending, and concentrated on developing a model of probation practice which aimed for other outcomes such as practical help and diversion from custody. In England and Wales, the Home Office Research Unit virtually abandoned research on the effectiveness of probation after the rather discouraging results of the IMPACT experiment (Folkard, Smith and Smith 1976), and concentrated instead on measures such as Community Service, which was intended to affect levels of custodial sentencing rather than the subsequent behaviour of offenders. The effectiveness of probation did not make a significant reappearance in the Home Office research agenda until the late 1980s. The main penal policy successes of the 1980s concerned changes in sentencing, such as the dramatic reduction in custodial sentencing for young people (Rutherford 1986), rather than improvements in the rehabilitation of offenders.

In some other countries and in some British university departments the assumptions of the 'nothing works' doctrine were less dominant, and a series of findings began to emerge which challenged this approach. Research reviews from Canada and Scotland (Gendreau and Ross 1979, McIvor 1990) and meta-analytic statistical studies from Canada and the United States (Andrews *et al.* 1990, Lipsey 1992) began to identify types and components of programmes which were consistently associated with better results, whilst evaluation studies of innovative supervision programmes in various countries provided further evidence of what could be achieved in practice (Clear, Flynn and Shapiro 1987, Petersilia 1990, Raynor 1988, Raynor and Vanstone 1994a, Roberts 1989, Ross, Fabiano and Elwes 1988).

Awareness of this material was promoted in Britain by the need to respond to Government policies which aimed to increase the proportion of offenders supervised in the community rather than in prison. In Scotland this took the form of central funding for work with offenders undertaken by social work departments, whilst in England and Wales the new policies were embodied in the rather short-lived 1991 Criminal Justice Act. The emerging consensus from this wide range of work is well represented already in this volume: broadly speaking, if we want to design and implement community-based programmes which have the best chance of reducing subsequent offending, recent and current work tends to support particular approaches to targeting, delivery and management. Programmes should be aimed at high-risk offenders rather than those at little risk of reoffending; they should focus on characteristics or circumstances which have contributed to offending; they should have a structured approach to learning with an emphasis on cognitive–behavioural methods; they need appropriately trained and committed staff, adequate resources and supportive management; and they should be continuously evaluated to maintain consistency of delivery, to monitor effectiveness and to promote organisational learning.

It is not the purpose of this chapter to elaborate further on the current state of knowledge about 'what works', but rather to comment on some aspects of the context in which such findings have emerged and on some possible further developments. It is of course clear that we know far more about 'what works' that we did ten years ago, and for the first time we have a realistic prospect of offering supervision programmes which can be both expected and demonstrated to have an impact on future offending. This represents a major achievement and potentially a dramatic change in the credibility and performance of agencies working with offenders in the community. My concern is that this may lead to a restricted view of the future research agenda. Now that we are beginning to make some progress with the topic of effectiveness, it is tempting to see future work as primarily an accumulation of longer, better-designed, more sophisticated evaluation studies unpacking in finer detail the links between particular programme characteristics and reductions in reconviction, in the hope that this will translate straightforwardly into improved policy and practice. This would, however, be too simple a view, and the remainder of this chapter is concerned with some issues which we risk neglecting if we plunge too uncritically into a brave new world of effectiveness research.

Warnings about over-commitment to empiricism in social work evaluation research always run the risk of being caricatured as indifference to facts or as a preference for comforting professional myths (see Raynor 1984a, Sheldon 1984, Smith 1987). It is therefore a wise precaution to state at the outset that there is no substitute for an empirical (although not necessarily empiricist) heuristic approach to testing claims of effectiveness, and I hope that the volume and quality of such studies will continue to grow rapidly. We are only at the beginning of developing a knowledge-base about effective methods for work with offenders. However, we also need to think critically about the type of effectiveness research we are doing, and about how it might develop in the future. The need for a critical view stems partly from politics, partly from criminology and partly from considerations of ethics and values.

The political questions are partly about how we use information about effectiveness; partly about how we expect others to use it; and partly about how the policy context can influence the kind of research we undertake. For example, anyone undertaking effectiveness research on probation in England and Wales is likely to encounter a number of paradoxes in the relationship between research, policy and politics. The first paradox is that the 'nothing works' era was actually a good time for the probation service: there was steady expansion in the 1970s and 1980s, and fairly general support for the idea that a good job was being done. It can be argued that there were genuine successes, particularly during the 1980s in diversion from custody for young offenders, whilst the 'nothing works' doctrine primarily concerned effects on future offending rather than influences on sentencing, but these distinctions were not widely recognised at the time in the working culture of the probation service, and both penal policy and public expenditure policy were favourable to probation even when other services suffered spending cuts. The 1984 Statement of National Objectives and Priorities emphasised reduction in custodial sentencing without raising any difficult questions about effectiveness (Home Office 1984). The Home Office's research agenda fitted in with this general pattern: positive findings on Community Service reflected widespread support and some diversionary effects (Pease, Billingham and Earnshaw 1977) without much attention to reconviction rates, and the policy decision to make Community Service available to all courts was taken before such results were available.

This generally positive attitude to community-based supervision was maintained as a component of the debates which preceded the 1991 Criminal Justice Act, but with an important shift of emphasis: the strategy set out in the Government statements (Home Office 1988, 1990) was essentially similar to that of 1984, but for public consumption included a tougher rhetoric ('punishment in the community') and the claim that it was a strategy to reduce crime, not simply a strategy to reduce expensive custodial sentencing. This in turn entailed commitment to the view that 'community sentences' would be more effective than custodial sentences in reducing crime. This was a bold and positive step after a decade and a half of 'nothing works' findings, and although undertaken for reasons we should applaud, it may well have offered some hostages to fortune. In reality the available stock of positive findings on the effectiveness of community sentences was rather smaller than it was five years later. As far as probation programmes for persistent offenders in England and Wales were concerned, it consisted largely of studies (such as Raynor 1988 and Roberts 1989) which demonstrated reductions in reconviction following involvement in special projects; these were encouraging but arguably not typical of the generality of probation practice. Comprehensive evidence about the effectiveness of everyday average probation practice in reducing crime was simply not available, and this is still largely the situation today, although some broad comparative studies of the outcomes of probation and other sentences (for example, Copas 1992) fall well short of making a general case for the superior efficacy of community sentences. Earlier studies such as Walker, Farrington and Tucker (1981) conveyed the same message, and we need to distinguish carefully between evidence that probation *can be* effective and evidence that it *is normally* effective.

The most recent paradox in England and Wales (not yet replicated, fortunately, in Scotland) is that the Government seems to be turning its back on probation, having decided that there are more votes to be gained by asserting that 'prison works' and that more offenders should be locked up, including children as young as 12 years old. The Home Secretary's new policy, announced to the cheers of Conservative party activists in October 1993, shows little sign of being affected by new studies (such as Raynor and Vanstone 1994a, 1994b) showing much lower reconviction rates for burglary following a cognitively-based probation programme than for comparable offenders released from prison. At a time when our knowledge about the potential crime-reducing effects of community sentences is advancing rapidly, the government has lost its enthusiasm and is looking in other directions. The Home Secretary has even expressed his regret that Britain does not have a significant caucus of Conservatively inclined criminologists who could be relied upon to discover 'facts' more in line with his own theories. The general lesson, familiar from other areas of policy-related research, is that the evidence generated by researchers on effectiveness does not normally influence policy in a straightforward rational way, but contributes to a stock of arguments which can be deployed by policy-makers from time to time in support of decisions made largely for other reasons. This deployment will often be in a simplified or selective form. Conversely the evidence can be as easily ignored by policy-makers when other political considerations are perceived as salient; at such times, the main political use of research will be as a component in opposition to new policies by practitioners and professional interest groups. Rather than expecting research to guide policy, it may currently be more realistic to regard knowledge as a resource on which policy-makers may draw when it suits them. Our primary obligation seems to be the development and dissemination of the knowledge-base in readiness for those times when temporary political shifts provide a window of opportunity for knowledge-based policies. Similarly the integration of new knowledge into the procedures and practices of social work agencies will be influenced by existing interests, commitments and patterns of work, and is likely to be uneven. Our research, our dissemination strategies and our expectations of impact need to be realistically attuned to these political contexts.

A second set of questions to be asked about current developments in 'effectiveness' research stems from criminology rather than politics. In bald summary, we need to remember to ask ourselves the questions 'effective for what?' and 'effective for whose purposes?'. The 'nothing works' era, although unproductive of ideas about useful supervision programmes, was in fact very productive in other areas of theory and research, raising questions about the nature of crime and its definition, the social meaning of criminal justice processes, the nature and construction of criminal statistics and the functions of social control in a society characterised by uneven distribution of resources and power. Disenchantment with the idea of treating individual offenders did not lead to a general disenchantment with penal reform but to other approaches such as decriminalisation, diversion and decarceration which have had a significant influence on policy and on the thinking of practitioners. It would be particularly unfortunate if research on effectiveness were now to enter a new phase of criminological amnesia, concentrating exclusively on experimental and quasi-experimental studies of the rates of officially recorded reconvictions following different sentences or programmes. Our evaluation methodologies need to guard against this kind of narrowing of the field of enquiry. From my own experience of evaluative work in this field (particularly Raynor 1988, Lucas, Raynor and Vanstone 1992, Raynor and Vanstone 1994a, 1994b) I would offer the following suggestions.

(1)   A pluralistic approach to evaluation design, recognising that there are a range of 'stakeholders' (Smith and Cantley 1984) including offenders, agency managers, practitioners, sentencers and the

community, who may have different investments and ideas about what would count as success.

(2) A range of outcome indicators, not confined to reconvictions but including offenders' attitudes, opinions and self-reported problems (see, for example, Mair 1991), and other contextual measures such as changes in sentencing.

(3) An attempt to 'unpack' reconviction rates to consider not only incidence but also seriousness, the extent of harm to personal victims, and the social reaction to reconviction. Reconviction, although not an accurate measure of re-offending, is arguably the most relevant measure as perceived by other actors in the criminal justice process, but if our interest in crime reduction is also an interest in the reduction of harm we need to consider the nature of the reconvictions and their consequences. For example, graduates of one programme have shown a greater reduction in serious offending and in offending with personal victims than in overall offending (Raynor and Vanstone 1994a, 1994b), and their very low level of custodial sentences on reconviction provides a further indication of the low perceived seriousness of the new convictions.

(4) An awareness of social context and its influence on the opportunities and priorities of offenders and practitioners (see, for example, Stewart and Stewart 1993). What difficulties do people actually face and what would count for them as improvement?

(5) An awareness of the context of development. For example, the introduction of a major innovative project in an agency has consequences for other work and for the development of the organisation and its staff, which may in turn impact on its effectiveness (Petersilia 1990); sometimes a programme has been introduced in order to achieve goals for the organisation as well as for offenders, and this also should be a component in its evaluation.

(6) Attention to the perceived meaning of involvement in the programme: what are the subjective dimensions of effectiveness or ineffectiveness? If it is seen as helpful, how or why is it helpful?

(7) An awareness of limitations and of specific features of the programme which may limit the replicability of findings. To take a rather obvious example, many available programme evaluations predominantly measure the effects on young white men, and other

groups of people in trouble with the law will have different needs and resources.

This kind of evaluative approach requires a range of research methods and some investment in planning and resources, but can be far more instructive for all parties than approaches based simply on counting officially recorded infractions without getting close to either offenders or practitioners. It also has certain practical advantages: for example, a programme evaluation incorporating a substantial follow-up reconviction study can easily take four or five years from the initial planning of the programme to final delivery of results, and the capacity to communicate interesting interim data based on other indicators is important in maintaining the interest and commitment of practitioners. Wide involvement in the evaluation process maintains awareness and commitment to effectiveness. It is also quite possible that a Government's own priorities and policies will change during the process of evaluation (for example, from diversion to rehabilitation to punishment) and the use of a range of indicators of outcome increases the possibility that the exercise will be as interesting when it is completed as it was when it was planned.

A broad evaluative strategy also lends itself to the development of new areas for investigation, and it is useful to consider where some future efforts might be directed. For example, attention has tended to concentrate on special programmes which required evaluation because they were innovative or experimental; we still know little about the effectiveness of 'normal' probation, where the diversity and individualisation of practice presents considerable challenges to research. Not only practices but also practitioners are diverse, and little work has been done in Britain concerning the comparative effectiveness of different practitioners in different kinds of situation. Some Australian research (Trotter 1993) suggests that different practitioner characteristics and behaviour (such as pro-social modelling and empathy) can have a considerable influence on effectiveness. Different practitioners may be effective at different tasks: for example, pre-sentence reports have been shown to be quite variable in quality (Gelsthorpe and Raynor 1992), and recent research on helping problem drinkers shows possible benefits in matching clients and helpers who have similar beliefs and expectations (Keene and Raynor 1993). The time is surely ripe for evaluations of 'normal' probation which pay adequate attention to practitioner variables. We also know little about the effects of help with personal, practical and 'welfare' problems, which offenders clearly value and many practitioners deliver, but which has tended to be

undervalued by a more fashionable focus on confronting offending behaviour. As Haines (1990) has pointed out, criminological control theorists
such as Hirschi (1969) would predict that helping offenders with problems
of social integration could have an impact on the level of offending, and
others have argued for a focus on criminogenic need rather than simply
on offending; studies of normal probation and through-care activities
could contribute usefully to an investigation of these possibilities.

My final comments relate to some contextual questions of values
which affect the current and future practice of evaluative research on the
supervision of offenders. The question 'effective for what?' raises issues
of aims and purpose, which in turn entail some consideration of the values
which lie behind aims and purposes. This is not simply a question about
the values underlying the programmes which researchers evaluate; research itself proceeds from a value-base, whether explicit or covert, and
often has to locate findings in a context of aims and purposes which may
not have been made explicit when the activity under investigation was
begun. The values and purposes of probation services and social work
departments may not coincide with those articulated by Government in
slogans such as 'punishment in the community' or in official documents
such as National Standards, which are themselves often informed more
by considerations of accountability than by information about effectiveness. The development of a range of evaluative research activity in and
around agencies undertaking social work with offenders presents an
opportunity to reclaim some influence on the agenda of the effectiveness
debate and to articulate and clarify beliefs about what counts as effective
practice. This also implies discussion of the values and purposes which
should inform decisions about what counts as effectiveness within a
criminal justice context. What kind of justice, for example, is implied in
probation services' conceptions of effective practice? Answers to such
questions may themselves create new criteria to inform evaluation studies.

To take just one example, Nellis (forthcoming) has recently argued that
the value-base of probation activity could be stated as a commitment to
three main social purposes: anti-custodialism, restorative justice and community safety. He argues that probation services should work in such a
way as to embody these values in their work and to promote their wider
influence within the criminal justice system. Others (such as Raynor
1984b) have argued for broadly similar commitments which integrate
criminal justice policy with wider social policy considerations. Restorative

justice, in particular, aims at constructive rather than punitive responses to the harm caused by offending; this implies the social reintegration of offenders rather than the exclusion, segregation and stigmatisation which seem to underlie much current criminal justice policy, as well as recent political statements on other social policy issues such as single parenthood. If probation and social work services devise ways of making such aims and purposes explicit in their practice, evaluative research will need to consider how far they are achieved, or successfully embodied and communicated. The meaning and purpose of an activity as perceived by relevant social audiences, including offenders, will need to be considered as part of its intended outcome. Evaluation strategies which are both sufficiently broad and sufficiently sensitive to enhance our understanding of such issues can make a major contribution to socially constructive practice. Considered in this context, research on effectiveness should be understood and undertaken not simply as a technical aid to efficient services, but as an active contribution to the improvement and reform of criminal justice.

References

Andrews, D.A., Zinger, I., Hoge, R.D., Bonta, J., Gendreau, P. and Cullen, F.T. (1990) 'Does correctional treatment work? A clinically relevant and psychologically informed meta-analysis.' *Criminology 28*, 3, 369–404.

Bottoms, A.E. and McWilliams, W. (1979) 'A non-treatment paradigm for probation practice.' *British Journal of Social Work 9*, 2, 159–202.

Brewer, C. and Lait, J. (1980) *Can Social Work Survive?* London: Temple Smith.

Brody, S.R. (1976) *The Effectiveness of Sentencing.* London: HMSO.

Clear, T.R., Flynn, S. and Shapiro, C. (1987) 'Intensive supervision in probation: a comparison of three projects.' In B.R. McCarthy (ed) *Intermediate Punishment.* Monsey: Criminal Justice Press.

Copas, J.B. (1992) 'Statistical analysis for a national risk of reconviction predictor' (report to the Home Office). Warwick: University of Warwick.

Fischer, J. (1976) *The Effectiveness of Social Casework.* Springfield: C.C. Thomas.

Folkard, M.S., Smith, D.E. and Smith, D.D. (1976) *IMPACT vol. II: The Results of the Experiment.* London: HMSO.

Gelsthorpe, L. and Raynor, P. (1992) 'The quality of reports prepared in the pilot studies.' In J. Bredar (ed) *Justice Informed, vol. II.* London: Vera Institute of Justice.

Gendreau, P. and Ross, R.R. (1979) 'Effective correctional treatment: bibliography for cynics.' *Crime and Delinquency 25*, 463–489.

Haines, K. (1990) *After-Care for Released Prisoners: A Review of the Literature.* Cambridge: Institute of Criminology.

Hirschi, T. (1969) *Causes of Delinquency.* Berkeley: University of California Press.

Home Office (1984) *Probation Service in England and Wales: Statement of National Objectives and Priorities.* London: Home Office.

Home Office (1988) *Punishment, Custody and the Community.* Cm 424. London: HMSO.

Home Office (1990) *Crime, Justice and Protecting the Public.* Cm 965. London: HMSO.

Keene, J. and Raynor, P. (1993) 'Addiction as a "soul sickness": the influence of client and therapist beliefs.' *Addiction Research 1*, 77–87.

Lipsey, M. (1992) 'Juvenile delinquency treatment: a meta-analytic enquiry into the variability of effects.' In T. Cook, H. Cooper, D.S. Cordray, H. Hartmann L.V. Hedges, R.L. Light, T.A. Louis and F. Mosteller (eds) *Meta-Analysis for Explanation: A Case-Book.* New York: Russell Sage.

Lucas, J., Raynor, P. and Vanstone, M. (1992) *Straight Thinking on Probation One Year On.* Bridgend: Mid Glamorgan Probation Service.

Mair, G. (1991) 'What works: nothing or everything?' *Research Bulletin, Home Office 30*, 3–8.

Martinson, R. (1974) 'What works?' *The Public Interest*, March, 22–54.

McIvor, G. (1990) *Sanctions for Serious or Persistent Offenders.* Stirling: Social Work Research Centre.

Nellis, M. (1995) 'Probation values for the 1990s.' *The Howard Journal of Criminal Justice 34*, 19–44.

Pease, K., Billingham, S. and Earnshaw, I. (1977) *Community Service Assessed in 1976.* London: HMSO.

Petersilia, J. (1990) 'Conditions that permit intensive supervision programs to survive.' *Crime and Delinquency 36*, 126–145.

Raynor, P. (1984a) 'Evaluation with one eye closed: the empiricist agenda in social work research.' *British Journal of Social Work 14*, 1, 1–10.

Raynor, P. (1984b) 'National purpose and objectives: a comment.' *Probation Journal 31*, 2, 43–47.

Raynor, P. (1988) *Probation as an Alternative to Custody.* Aldershot: Avebury.

Raynor, P., Smith, D. and Vanstone, M. (1994) *Effective Probation Practice.* Basingstoke: Macmillan.

Raynor, P. and Vanstone, M. (1994a) *Straight Thinking on Probation: Third Interim Evaluation Report: Reconvictions Within 12 Months.* Bridgend: Mid Glamorgan Probation Service.

Raynor, P. and Vanstone, M. (1994b) 'Probation practice, effectiveness and the non-treatment paradigm.' *British Journal of Social Work 24,* 4, 387–404.

Roberts, C.H. (1989) *Hereford and Worcester Probation Service Young Offender Project: First Evaluation Report.* Oxford: Department of Social and Administrative Studies.

Ross, R.R., Fabiano, E.A. and Elwes, C.D. (1988) 'Reasoning and rehabilitation.' *International Journal of Offender Therapy and Comparative Criminology 32,* 1, 29–35.

Rutherford, A. (1986) *Growing Out of Crime.* Harmondsworth: Penguin.

Sheldon, B. (1984) 'Evaluation with one eye closed: the empiricist agenda in social work research – a reply to Peter Raynor.' *British Journal of Social Work 14,* 6, 635–637.

Smith, D. (1987) 'The limits of positivism in social work research.' *British Journal of Social Work 17,* 4, 401–416.

Smith, G. and Cantley, C. (1984) 'Pluralistic evaluation.' In J. Lishman (ed) *Evaluation.* Aberdeen: University of Aberdeen.

Stewart, G. and Stewart, J. (1993) *Social Circumstances of Younger Offenders Under Supervision.* London: Association of Chief Officers of Probation.

Trotter, C. (1993) *The Supervision of Offenders: What Works?* Melbourne: Monash University and Victoria Department of Justice.

Walker, N., Farrington, D.P. and Tucker, G. (1981) 'Reconviction rates of adult males after different sentences.' *British Journal of Criminology 21,* 4, 357–360.

The Contributors

Gill McIvor   Gill McIvor is a Reader at the Social Work Research
Centre at the University of Stirling and a social
work tutor at the Universities of Edinburgh and
Stirling. Her recent research interests include bail
services, supported accommodation for offenders,
intensive probation and treatment programmes for
sex offenders. She is author of *Sentenced to Serve:
The Operation and Impact of Community Service for
Offenders* (Avebury 1992) and co-author with Juliet
Cheetham, Roger Fuller and Alison Petch of
Evaluating Social Work Effectiveness (Open
University Press 1992).

David Smith   David Smith has been Professor of Social Work at
Lancaster University since 1993. He read Classics
and English at Oriel College, Oxford, and trained
as a social worker at the University of Exeter. He
worked as a probation officer for four years before
moving to Lancaster in 1976. He has researched
and written on a wide range of topics in social
work and criminal justice, and is author of
Criminology for Social work (Macmillan 1995) and
co-author of *Effective Probation Practice* (Macmillan
1994) and *Understanding Offending Behaviour*
(Longman 1994). He is joint editor, with Richard
Hugman, of the *British Journal of Social Work*.

George Mair   George Mair is Professor of Criminal Justice at
Liverpool's John Moore University. He was
previously Principal Research Officer in the Home
Office Research and Planning Unit, where he was
responsible for a programme of research into

community penalties. He is the author of many reports and articles on the work of the probation service, and is currently working on two books (*Evaluating the Effectiveness of Community Penalties*, and *Working with Men*) which will be published later in the year.

Breidge Gadd   Breidge Gadd is the Chief Probation Officer for the Probation Board for Northern Ireland. She undertook her social work training at Queen's University, Belfast and post-graduate qualification at the University of Ulster in Coleraine. She has worked for the Probation Service in Northern Ireland for all of her professional career, undertaking the CCETSW Advanced Diploma in Social Work (management studies) at Queen's University, Belfast in 1983 and the Cabinet Office Top Management Programme in 1991. Mrs Gadd is a visiting lecturer at Queen's University, Belfast and has in the past taught on the Social Work and Youth Work courses at the University of Ulster.

Anne Worrall   Anne Worrall has been a lecturer in Criminology at Keele University since 1993. Prior to that, she was Director of the MA/Diploma in Social Work programme at Keele and had responsibility for the Probation Option. She has been a social work lecturer at Manchester University and a probation officer in Staffordshire. She has researched and published in the area of women and crime, and is the author of *Offending Women* (Routledge 1990) and co-editor with Pat Carlen of *Gender, Crime and Justice* (Open University Press 1987).

Duncan Lawrence   Duncan Lawrence has 15 years experience as a practitioner in the fields of mental health, substance abuse and work with offenders. His teaching interests have focused upon mental health, group work with young offenders, cross-cultural counselling, community work and social work. His current work includes a split role at Goldsmith's College, University of London: lecturing with the Community and Youth Work team, and consultancy work for the Inner London Probation Service in the area of education, training and employment of offenders.

Bryan Williams   Bryan Williams has been Professor of Social Work at Dundee University since 1989. He was educated at the Universities of Hull and Bristol and, following work in the atomic energy industry, as a school-teacher and residential social worker in Chile, he worked as a probation officer in Inner London. He moved to Dundee to become Lecturer in Social Work in 1976. His research interests lie mainly in the field of social work within criminal justice and he has been involved in a number of Government-funded research projects and served on several national commissions and investigative committees. He is immediate past National Chair of SACRO.

Anne Creamer   Anne Creamer is a lecturer in Social Work at the University of Dundee. Her research interests centre around the monitoring and evaluation of social work services to the criminal courts and their impact on sentencing outcomes. She is co-author with Elaine Ennis and Bryan Williams of a risk of custody prediction scale (The DUNSCORE, University of Dundee 1994) for use in the Scottish context. She is currently involved in a research project examining the relationship between the quality of social enquiry practice and court decision-making. She co-ordinates the criminal justice elective for MSW and MA students at Dundee and provides training for qualified social workers in the criminal justice field throughout Scotland. Her practice background includes working in both field and residential settings and for voluntary and statutory agencies.

Mary Barker

Mary Barker is a researcher with the Medical Research Council Environmental Epidemiology Unit at Southampton University. She has degrees in psychology from Southampton University and from Surrey University. Her research experience has been chiefly in the fields of criminal justice and criminology. Before joining the MRC Unit in Southampton, she worked in the Research and Planning Unit at the Home Office, and in the Department of Law at the University of Bristol. Current research interests include the psychological aspects of nutrition and adolescent food choice.

Jean Hine

Jean Hine is Research and Information Officer with Derbyshire Probation Service. She has worked as a researcher within the probation service since 1974, during which time she has regularly undertaken evaluations of community service. She was Senior Research Fellow for the National Study of Community Service (a major Home Office sponsored research project) undertaken by the University of Birmingham in 1988–90.

Neil Thomas

Neil Thomas is Senior Lecturer in Social Policy at the University of Birmingham. He has conducted a wide range of studies into the organisation, delivery and effectiveness of social services. He was Project Director of the National Study of Community Service, sponsored by the Home Office.

Tony Marshall

Tony Marshall is Principal Research Officer in the Research and Planning Unit of the Home Office where he is currently responsible for research on the voluntary sector, refugees, gambling and mediation. He has carried out research on many aspects of criminal justice, community, social policy and voluntary organisations, and was the first Director of MEDIATION UK. His publications include: *Counselling and School Social Work* (Wiley 1975); *Bringing People Together: Mediation and*

Reparation Schemes in Great Britain (Home Office 1985); *Alternatives to Criminal Courts* (Gower 1985); *Crime and Accountability* (HMSO 1990); *Community Disorders and Policing* (Whiting and Birch 1992) and *The Settlement of Refugees in Britain* (HMSO 1995).

Brian Williams   Brian Williams lectures in the department of Applied Social Studies at the University of Keele. He has published widely on prison and probation issues, and is currently researching the uses of counselling in criminal justice settings with both victims and offenders. He is actively involved in the campaign to prevent the Probation Service in England and Wales being deprofessionalised.

Peter Raynor   Peter Raynor is a former probation officer, currently Reader in Applied Social Studies at the University of Wales, Swansea where he has particular responsibility for probation training. He has published extensively on probation issues, including the books *Social Work, Justice and Control* (Blackwell 1985; second edition Whiting and Birch 1993), *Probation as an Alternative to Custody* (Avebury 1988) and with David Smith and Maurice Vanstone, *Effective Probation Practice* (Macmillan 1994).

Research Highlights in
Social Work Series

This topical series of books examines areas currently of particular interest to those in social work and related fields. Each book draws together a collection of articles on different aspects of the subject under discussion – highlighting relevant research and drawing out implications for policy and practice. The project is under the general direction of Professor Joyce Lishman.

No. 4 Social Work Departments as Organisations
Edited by Joyce Lishman
ISBN 1 85302 008 7 Paperback

No. 6 Working With Children
Edited by Joyce Lishman
ISBN 1 85302 007 9 Paperback

No. 8 Evaluation 2nd Edition
Edited by Joyce Lishman
ISBN 1 85302 006 0 Hardback

No. 9 Social Work in Rural and Urban Areas
Edited by Joyce Lishman
ISBN 0 9505999 8 0 Paperback

No. 11 Responding to Mental Illness
Edited by Gordon Horobin
ISBN 1 85091 005 7 Paperback

No. 12 The Family: Context or Client?
Edited by Gordon Horobin
ISBN 1 85091 026 X Paperback

No. 13 New Information Technology in Management and Practice
Edited by Gordon Horobin and Stuart Montgomery
ISBN 1 85091 022 7 Hardback

Jessica Kingsley Publishers
116 Pentonville Road, London N1 9JB

No 14 Why Day Care?
Edited by Gordon Horobin
ISBN 1 85302 000 1 Hardback

**No. 15 Sex, Gender
and Care Work**
Edited by Gordon Horobin
ISBN 1 85302 001 X Hardback

No. 18 Privatisation
Edited by Richard Parry
ISBN 1 85302 015 X Hardback

**No. 19 Social Work
and Health Care**
*Edited by Rex Taylor and Jill
Ford*
ISBN 1 85302 016 8 Hardback

**No. 20 Performance Review
and Quality in Social Care**
*Edited by Anne Connor and
Stewart Black*
ISBN 1 85302 017 6 Hardback

**No. 21 Social Work: Disabled
People and Disabling
Environments**
Edited by Michael Oliver
ISBN 1 85302 042 7 Hardback
ISBN 1 85302 178 X Paperback

**No. 22 Poverty, Deprivation
and Social Work**
*Edited by Ralph Davidson and
Angus Erskine*
ISBN 1 85302 043 5 Hardback

**No. 24 Child Abuse and
Child Abusers: Protection
and Prevention**
Edited by Lorraine Waterhouse
ISBN 1 85302 133 4 Hardback

**No. 25 Developments in
Short-Term Care**
Edited by Kirsten Stalker
ISBN 1 85302 134 2 Paperback

**No. 27 Planning and Costing
Community Care**
*Edited by Chris Clark and Irvine
Lapsley*
ISBN 1 85302 267 5 Paperback

**Jessica Kingsley Publishers
116 Pentonville Road, London N1 9JB**